CONFRONTING PREJUDICE AND RACISM DURING MULTICULTURAL TRAINING

Edited by

Mark S. Kiselica, PhD

AMERICAN
COUNSELING
ASSOCIATION

CONFRONTING PREJUDICE AND RACISM
DURING MULTICULTURAL TRAINING

10 9 8 7 6 5 4 3 2

American Counseling Association
5999 Stevenson Avenue
Alexandria, VA 22304

Director of Publications
Carolyn Baker

Publishing Consultant
Michael Comlish

Copyeditor
Lucy Blanton

Cover design by Spot Color

Library of Congress Cataloging-in-Publication Data

Confronting prejudice and racism during multicultural training / edited by
    Mark S. Kiselica.
        p.   cm.
    Includes bibliographical references and index.
    ISBN 1-55620-206-7 (alk. paper)
    1. Prejudices—Psychological aspects. 2. Racism—Psychological
aspects. 3. Ethnocentrism. 4. Multiculturalism—Study and teaching.
5. Toleration—Study and teaching.   I. Kiselica, Mark S.
    BF575.P9C66   1998
    305.8'0071—dc21   98-30409
                                                              CIP

Dedication

To Sandi . . .

    . . . because you are so much a part of who I am and what I have accomplished in my life.

Contents

Foreword

Writing the foreword to *Confronting Prejudice and Racism During Multicultural Training* is an honor. The topic is one long overdue to be addressed by the counseling profession. Each of us has observed or experienced prejudice and racism being inflicted upon others and, perhaps, on ourselves. Paying homage to generations of individuals who have been oppressed is one way we can acknowledge the historical significance of peacemakers who managed to cope with racism in a manner that allows us even today to live in harmony within and across racial lines. This publication brings prejudice and racism, which continue to be vital concerns as we enter the new millennium, to our attention so that we can better effect positive changes through multicultural training.

Multiculturalism transcends racial and ethnic classifications and encompasses groups of individuals with biologically identifiable (skin color, gender, impairment) and sociologically attributable (race, ethnicity, religion, disability, sexual orientation, age, social class) characteristics. It embodies a recognition of those manifestations of oppression exercised by the dominant culture and a commitment to ensure equity and equality among the many cultures represented in our society.

Multicultural training in the United States emerged from a recognition of the failure to stem overt and covert forms of prejudice and bias toward racial and ethnic groups in our schools and postsecondary institutions in the 1970s. Increased enrollments of racial minorities (African Americans, Hispanic Americans, Asian Americans, and Native Americans) exacerbated latent racial intolerance within the educational system. Affirmative action interventions—cultural studies programs, cultural centers, minority faculty recruitment—further marginalized these minority groups as well as altered the discourse. Subsequently, other groups (disabled, gays, deaf, aged) exercised assertive stances for recognition and acceptance within mainstream society. Regrettably, stigmatizing and scapegoating have yet to be abated.

Multicultural training programs today are both pervasive and fraught with challenges. Generally, program interventions attempt to increase participant awareness of differences between groups and similarities within groups, teach appreciation and respect for diversity, and provide resources for sustaining pedagogy. Program effectiveness measures, however, are as yet inconsistent and inadequate.

This book examines multicultural training program components to assess how trainees adopt, divest, or resist multicultural principles and practices. Of foremost concern are the forms of prejudice—such as racism, sexism, homophobism, and classism—that emerge during program exercises and activities and the strategies effective for divesting culturally encapsulated participants of their dichotomous worldview. To illustrate, willingness of participants to self-disclose and self-assess their level of understanding of the interrelatedness that exists among cultural discrimination (cultural-historical), identity (psychosocial), and cultural relations (scientific-ideological) is a benchmark of multicultural competence. However, determining an appropriate format or strategy for confronting bias without denigrating participants remains elusive for many trainers.

This book also presents heretofore undocumented issues that assail multicultural trainers in a systems approach that draws on the expertise of counselor educators and training practitioners. Steps in this approach include assessing the training participant's covert attachment to the cultural privilege paradigm, examining training intervention constructs, designing strategies to divest structural resistance and transcend cultural disparities, and providing affective experiences for sustaining and enhancing cross-cultural competencies. Major themes embedded within the text include efficacy of confronting racial and cultural prejudice, empowerment and liberation ideology, racial and ethnic identity development models, cultural competencies through counselor education, and multicultural challenges during the 21st century for the counseling profession.

Editor Mark S. Kiselica is acknowledged for envisioning and demonstrating an interest in bringing the topic of prejudice and racism during multicultural training to the attention of readers and instructors. All chapters of this timely book have been thoroughly researched by their authors and are intellectually stimulating and culturally challenging. It is highly recommended as a resource for theory and practice in teaching, research, and consultation as well as for learning and cultural enrichment. Add this excellent volume to your library.

John McFadden, PhD
University of South Carolina
Columbia

Preface: How Can We Help Students Confront and Reduce Their Own Prejudices?

The process of confronting one's own ethnocentrism and prejudices is an essential but potentially unsettling and anxiety-provoking feature of the developmental task of becoming an effective, multicultural counselor (Kiselica, 1991, 1998, in press). Several authorities on the subject of multicultural training have explicitly stated that counselor trainees must examine their cultural heritage, values, and biases in order to become competent at counseling clients from culturally diverse backgrounds (e.g., Arredondo et. al. 1996; Lee, 1997; Locke, 1992; Pedersen, 1994; Sue & Sue, 1990). Important aspects of this training involve helping trainees examine the extent to which they think and behave in ethnocentric and prejudicial ways (Locke, 1992) and, subsequently, engage in an ongoing process of challenging such thoughts and actions and replacing them with attitudes and skills that affirm culturally different clients (Arredondo et al., 1996; Locke, 1992). Because this process requires trainees to discover and confront imperfections about themselves, many react to the training with fear, ambivalence, and varying degrees of resistance (see Reynolds, 1995).

In light of these reactions by trainees, counselor educators and supervisors face a tricky challenge: How can they confront racism, sexism, heterosexism, ageism, ableism, and other forms of prejudice without alienating trainees from the multicultural training process? If the fears and insecurities of trainees are not sensitively addressed, some trainees might shy away from multicultural training and cross-cultural counseling. Others might comply with the training but avoid making any important characterological changes. In either case, the goal of promoting their appreciation for cultural diversity might be undermined.

Addressing this issue is a vital challenge for the counseling profession because training in multicultural counseling has proliferated over the past two decades and, appropriately, will remain important into the 21st century. According to the Council for Accreditation of Counseling and Related Educational Programs (CACREP, 1994), the study of the social and cultural foundations of counseling, including an examination of culturally based attitudes and behavior, is a required core component of CACREP-accredited programs in counseling; consequently, the number of courses on multicultural counseling offered in graduate programs in counseling increased dramatically during the 1980s (Ponterotto & Casas, 1991) and continued to grow during the 1990s (Ponterotto, 1997). The number of continuing education courses and workshops on multicultural awareness and counseling also has been on the rise, in large part because it is now an ethical responsibility of counselors to learn "how the counselor's own cultural/ethnic/racial identity impacts her/his values and beliefs about the counseling process" (American Counseling Association, 1995, p. 2). Clearly, more and more graduate counseling students and professional counselors are engaging in activities designed to confront their ethnocentrism and prejudice.

Although widespread training in multiculturalism is crucial in order for counselors to be competent at serving an increasingly culturally diverse society, the rise in cultural- and self-awareness activities has occurred in the absence of a substantive discussion regarding the educational process of confronting ethnocentrism and prejudice among counseling trainees. Drawing from the writings of Sanford (1963), Reynolds (1995) argued that multicultural education should be designed and conducted with a balance of challenge and support in order to facilitate learning. "Too much challenge causes trainees to withdraw because they feel overwhelmed. Too much support leads to complacency and detachment because there is nothing testing or challenging the trainees" (p. 318). But how do counselor educators and supervisors achieve this balance? What specific conditions facilitate the examination of ethnocentrism and racism? What training techniques and group processes foster the reduction of prejudice while promoting multicultural sensitivity and appreciation for cultural diversity? How should we respond to resistant trainees? How do we confront trainees without alienating them from the training process? What facilitative and supportive measures are necessary for helping students with the painful task of confronting their own isms? What particular issues are likely to emerge as a function of racial identity development? What are the potential classroom dynamics when the students and the instructor are from different racial backgrounds? What models of training can we use to guide us in our work?

The purpose of this book is to address these questions in a series of chapters pertaining to the objective of confronting prejudice during multicultural training in an effective, supportive manner. Fifteen leading scholars of multiculturalism and veteran multicultural educators were invited to share their ideas for achieving this objective.

This book is divided into two parts. Part I consists of nine chapters addressing a variety of theoretical and practical perspectives on confronting prejudice during multicultural training. In chapter 1, Charles Ridley and Chalmer Thompson provide a systems perspective on understanding and responding to resistance to diversity training and offer suggestions for confronting racism in benevolent, nonaggressive ways. In chapter 2, MaryLou Ramsey describes requisite learning conditions for the creation of a climate that promotes cultural appreciation within the classroom. Don Locke and Marie Faubert illustrate in chapter 3 how they utilize Freier's model of critical consciousness raising in multicultural education classes to inspire trainees to embrace the ideals of multiculturalism. Michael D'Andrea and Judy Daniels suggest in chapter 4 how trainers can use a five-stage paradigm of White racism to anticipate and respond effectively to several dispositions about racism expressed by White trainees during multicultural training. In chapter 5, Michael Mobley in collaboration with Harold Cheatham analyzes classroom dynamics related to the racial identity development issues of both counselors in training and their instructors. Next, in chapter 6, Paul Pedersen explains how to use a three-stage training program emphasizing multicultural awareness, knowledge, and skills to reduce ethnocentric, racist, and prejudicial behaviors and attitudes. Mary Swigonski discusses in chapter 7 the application of standpoint theory to provide students with a set of conceptual tools to understand how racism, sexism, and heterosexism constrain our ways of knowing. In chapter 8, I describe the qualities of the empathic-confrontive instructor who joins students in the profoundly human experience of examining their cultural biases and discovering the joys of crossing cultural boundaries. In chapter 9, Saundra Tomlinson-Clarke and Vivian Ota Wang review and critique different approaches to teaching racial-cultural issues to counseling trainees and describe their own model of didactic, experiential, and practical training for racial-cultural sensitivity. In Part II of this book, which consists of three chapters, Harold Cheatham, Amy Reynolds, and I offer our respective reactions to Part I's nine chapters, and we suggest what their content implies for the future of multicultural education.

Although the contributors to this book have developed their chapters separately, we all share a vision that the world will be a better place when all people respect and appreciate their culturally different neighbors. We recognize that promoting human harmony involves the painful, challenging, and imperative task of confronting ethnocentrism and prejudice. Considering the widespread damage caused by prejudice, we believe that counselors have a moral obligation to work to reduce prejudice and its destructive consequences, beginning with the examination and eradication of the harmful biases counselors bring to their professional endeavors. We have committed ourselves to this project with the hope that sharing our ideas can help us and other multicultural educators become more effective in the work we do. Accordingly, this book was designed to fill an important gap in the literature by providing an in-depth analysis of the sensitive issues that emerge during multicultural training and practical recommendations for how to respond to them. Therefore, we believe that this book will be instructive to counselors, psychologists, social workers, physicians, nurses, teachers, ministers, and other professionals who teach courses or conduct workshops on multiculturalism, or provide supervision to individuals in multicultural training programs. In short, this book will be a valuable instructional tool for any educator who deals with issues of prejudice among trainees.

I hope that this book will stimulate focused discussions and empirical research on the subject of confronting ethnocentrism and prejudice during counselor training. Most importantly, it is my sincere wish that this project will result in the increased practice of cultural awareness training activities that help trainees move beyond their fears and prejudices to a greater appreciation for the many beautiful people who comprise the human family.

Mark S. Kiselica

REFERENCES

American Counseling Association (1995). *Code of ethics and standards of practice.* Alexandria, VA: Author.

Arredondo, P., Toporek, R., Brown, S. P., Jones, J., Locke, D. C., Sanchez, J., & Stadler, H. (1996). Operationalization of the multicultural counseling competencies. *Journal of Multicultural Counseling and Development, 24,* 42–78.

Council for Accreditation of Counseling and Related Educational Programs (1994, January). *Accreditation standards and procedures manual.* Alexandria, VA: Author.

Lee, C. C. (1997). Promise and pitfalls of multicultural counseling. In C. C. Lee (Ed.), *Multicultural issues in counseling: New approaches to diversity* (2nd ed., pp. 3–10). Alexandria, VA: American Counseling Association.

Kiselica, M. S. (1991). Reflections on a multicultural internship experience. *Journal of Counseling and Development, 70,* 126–130.

Kiselica, M. S. (1998). Preparing Anglos for the challenges and joys of multiculturalism. *The Counseling Psychologist, 26,* 5–21.

Kiselica, M. S. (in press). Confronting my own ethnocentrism and racism: A process of pain and growth. *Journal of Counseling and Development.*

Locke, D. C. (1992). *Increasing multicultural understanding: A comprehensive model.* Newbury Park, CA: Sage.

Pedersen, P. (1994). *A handbook for developing multicultural awareness* (2nd ed). Alexandria, VA: American Counseling Association.

Ponterotto, J. G. (1997). Multicultural counseling training: A competency model and national survey. In D. B. Pope-Davis & H. L. K. Coleman (Eds.), *Multicultural counseling competencies: Assessment, education and training, and supervision* (pp. 11–130). Thousand Oaks, CA: Sage.

Ponterotto, J. G., & Casas, J. M. (1991). *Handbook of racial/ethnic minority counseling research.* Springfield, IL: Charles C Thomas.

Reynolds, A. L. (1995). Challenges and strategies for teaching multicultural counseling courses. In J. G. Ponterotto, J. M. Casas, L. A. Suzuki, & C. M. Alexander (Eds.), *Handbook of multicultural counseling* (pp. 312–330). Newbury Park, CA: Sage.

Sanford, N. (1963). Factors related to the effectiveness of student interaction with the college social system. In B. Barger & E. E. Hall (Eds.), *Higher education and mental health* (pp. 8–26). Gainesville: University of Florida.

Sue, D. W., & Sue, D. (1990). *Counseling the culturally different: Theory and practice* (2nd ed.). New York: Wiley.

Acknowledgments

First and foremost, I thank my wife, Sandi, and my precious sons, Andrew and Christian, for their love, patience, and understanding regarding the many hours I spent organizing, researching, and writing this book. The ongoing support of my family is one of the principle reasons I count my blessings every day.

Because this book reflects my growing racial awareness, I want to acknowledge several people who have been a substantial influence on my White racial identity development. As a young boy, I read the biographies of two of my sports idols, Jackie Robinson and Bob Gibson. Their life stories opened my eyes for the first time to the inequalities that exist in the United States and helped me begin to understand how my worldview as a White person was different from that of African Americans. Many years later, I explored my worldview in more depth thanks to the presence of Harold Cheatham on the faculty at the Pennsylvania State University, where I completed my doctoral studies in counseling psychology. Although I never enrolled in any classes taught by Harold, his insistence that all students learn about multicultural counseling convinced me to read the classic work of Derald Wing Sue, *Counseling the Culturally Different: Theory and Practice.* Sue's words shook me to my core and inspired me to pursue multicultural training as a predoctoral intern at the University of Medicine and Dentistry of New Jersey (UMDNJ) Community Mental Health Center in Newark. At UMDNJ, I was fortunate to receive excellent training in multicultural counseling from Cheryl Thompson, Frank Dillon, Gloria Steiner, and Nancy Boyd-Franklin, and I encountered dozens of clients who were culturally different from me and who taught me much about the human experience of crossing cultural boundaries. Since that critical year of working as an intern, I have committed my life to studying multicultural counseling and have been mentored in my multicultural journey by the following people: Derald Wing Sue, Don Locke, Larry Gerstein, Joe Ponterotto, Paul Pedersen, Leo Hendricks, Sharon Bowman, Allen Ivey, Lonnie Duncan, Va Lecia Adams, Roger Herring, and MaryLou Ramsey. Because each of these people either inspired or encouraged my desire to be a more culturally sensitive person, I owe each of them many thanks.

I am also indebted to numerous scholars whose work has informed my thinking about multicultural counseling and training. These include many of the people just mentioned as well as Janet Helms, Thomas Parham, Courtland Lee, John Axelson, and Bea Wehrly, whose collective works have impacted me greatly. I thank all of them for enhancing my intellectual and emotional understanding about racial and cultural matters.

I am so very grateful to the fine people who contributed their ideas in this book: Harold Cheatham, Michael D'Andrea, Judy Daniels, Marie Faubert, Don Locke, John McFadden, Michael Mobley, Vivian Ota Wang, Paul Pedersen, Mar Lou Ramsey, Amy Reynolds, Charles Ridley, Mary Swigonski, Saundra Tomlinson-Clarke, and Chalmer Thompson. I am honored by their belief that this book is a worthy outlet for their valuable perspectives on multicultural training. Also, I thank them for sticking with me over the course of the past 2 years as I shepherded this project to its completion.

I benefited greatly from the support of my colleagues at the College of New Jersey while I worked on this project. Suzanne Pasch, our Dean of Education, secured for me release time from teaching so that I could get this project started. Marion Cavallaro, Bill Fassbender, MaryLou Ramsey, and Roland Worthington, my colleagues in the Department of Counseling and Personnel Services, fostered my determination to complete this book, as did Karlene Morrison and Connie Titone, my colleagues from the Department of Educational Administration and Secondary Education. Gloria Valeri, Debra Caroselli, Lynn Powell, Jennifer Schick, Jamie Sandes, and Kim Nash cheerfully assisted with many of the tedious chores associated with preparing this edited book for publication. I am sincerely grateful for these many forms of encouragement and assistance.

Last but not least, I appreciate the support of Carolyn Baker and her colleagues at ACA, including the members of the ACA Media Committee who reviewed my initial proposal for this book and decided that it was a worthwhile project. Carolyn and the staff at ACA Press have been a joy to work with throughout the production of this volume.

About the Editor

Mark S. Kiselica, PhD., NCC, is an associate professor and chair of the Department of Counseling and Personnel Services at the College of New Jersey. He earned his bachelor's degree in psychology from Saint Vincent College, his master's degree in psychology from Bucknell University, and his doctorate in counseling psychology from Pennsylvania State University. He completed his school counseling internship at Tyrone Area High School in Tyrone, PA, and his predoctoral internship in clinical child and adolescent psychology at the University of Medicine and Dentistry of New Jersey Community Mental Health Center in Newark, NJ.

Dr. Kiselica is a National Certified Counselor and a licensed psychologist. He has worked in the following clinical settings: Fair Oaks Hospital in Summit, NJ; Danville State Hospital in Danville, PA; the University of Medicine and Dentistry of New Jersey Community Mental Health Center in Piscataway, NJ; the Albert C. Wagner Youth Correctional Facility in Bordentown, NJ; and the Back Door of Muncie, IN. He also is a former assistant professor and director of the master's program in counseling at Ball State University and a former adjunct assistant professor of psychology at Rider University. Currently, he serves as a consulting psychologist with the Life Development Center of Newtown, PA.

Dr. Kiselica is the author of numerous conference presentations and over 30 juried publications, including *Multicultural Counseling With Teenage Fathers: A Practical Guide*, which was published by Sage. His manuscripts on multicultural counseling and training have appeared as a chapter in the *Handbook of Multicultural Counseling* and as articles in the *Journal of Counseling and Development* and *The Counseling Psychologist*. He has served on the editorial boards of the *Journal of Counseling and Development* and *Journal of Mental Health Counseling* and as the book review editor for *Professional School Counseling*. He is the founder of the American School Counselor Association Professional Interest Network on Teenage Parents, and he is a member of the Teen Pregnancy Task Force of Bucks County, PA. He is president of the Society for the Psychological Study of Men and Masculinity (Division 51 of the American Psychological Association) and serves as a consulting scholar to the Federal Fatherhood Initiative. Dr. Kiselica was named Counselor Educator of the Year (1996–97) by the American Mental Health Counselors Association.

Most importantly, Dr. Kiselica is the husband of Sandi Kiselica and the proud father of two sons, Andrew and Christian, who are nine and five years old, respectively. Dr. Kiselica serves as a volunteer at Saint Andrew School (his sons' school), as a baptism educator for Saint Andrew Parish, and as the coach of his sons' soccer and basketball teams. He and his family reside in Newtown, PA.

About the Contributors

Harold E. Cheatham, PhD, is professor of counseling and educational leadership and dean of the College of Health, Education, and Human Development at Clemson University. He attained professor emeritus status at the Pennsylvania State University and has held faculty positions at Case Western Reserve University, where he also was director of university counseling, and at the United States Coast Guard Academy. Dr. Cheatham was a Senior Fulbright Scholar to India in 1991 and is recipient of the Howard B. Palmer Faculty Mentoring Award at Penn State. In 1993 the American College Personnel Association (ACPA) honored Dr. Cheatham with the Contribution to Knowledge Award and as a Senior Scholar. In 1995–96, he was president of ACPA. Dr. Cheatham is the author of numerous publications and editor or coeditor of two books. He was recognized in the American Psychological Association Division 17 journal, *The Counseling Psychologist*, as a Pioneer in Multicultural Counseling in 1997.

Michael D'Andrea, EdD, is professor of counseling in the Department of Counselor Education at the University of Hawaii. Dr. D'Andrea has been a long-time contributor and activist in the multicultural counseling movement. He has authored and/or coauthored over 100 publications related to multicultural counseling.

Judy Daniels, EdD, is a professor in the Department of Counselor Education at the University of Hawaii. Her research and scholarly interests are in the areas of multicultural counseling and supervision; diversity counseling with a particular focus on homeless children and their families; developmental psychology; and sports psychology. Dr. Daniels cofounded and subsequently became the first state president of both the Hawaii Association for Multicultural Counseling and Development and the Hawaii Association for Counselor Education and Supervision.

Marie Faubert, CSJ, EdD, has been committed to the eradication of racism and the development of cultural competence for 30 years. A member of the Sisters of Saint Joseph, she is presently director of the counselor education program at the University of Saint Thomas in Houston, TX, and president of the Texas Association for Multicultural Counseling and Development. In those capacities, Sister Faubert recruits and retains students committed to becoming culturally competent professional school counselors and licensed professional counselors and facilitates many workshops on the subject of cultural competence and racism, especially as these relate to ethical practice.

Don C. Locke, EdD, is professor of counselor education at North Carolina State University and director of the doctoral program in adult and community college education at the University of North Carolina-Asheville Graduate Center. He has held numerous positions in counseling-related organizations at the state, regional, and national levels. He is the author or coauthor of more than 75 publications that are focused primarily on multiculturalism. He was the recipient of the ACA Professional Development Award in 1996.

John McFadden, PhD, is the Benjamin E. Mays Professor in the Department of Educational Psychology at the University of South Carolina. He is the author of several books, monographs, and journal articles with an emphasis on cultural diversity and multiculturalism. His most recent book, *Transcultural Counseling* (2nd edition), was published by the American Counseling Association. Dr. McFadden has earned an international reputation as an authority in counseling and education, and he travels throughout the world as a consultant on these subjects. He is the founder and director of the Benjamin E. Mays Academy for Leadership Development at the University of South Carolina.

Michael Mobley, PhD, is an assistant professor in the counseling psychology program at the University of Missouri-Columbia. He received his doctorate in counseling psychology from the Pennsylvania State University. His research interests include perfectionism, multicultural counseling and training, and psychosocial and academic enhancement among African American students as well as cultural identity development models in particular racial/ethnic and sexual orientation groups.

Vivian Ota Wang, PhD, is an assistant professor in the counselor education/counseling psychology programs and director of the Asian cultural studies program, both in the Division of Psychology in Education at Arizona State University. Prior to receiving her doctorate in counseling psychology at Columbia University, she was a Board Certified Genetic Counselor at the University of Colorado. She has published and presented in areas related to multicultural counseling program development and evaluation, racial-cultural identity development, and genetics and health psychology in the United States and China. She has also served as the guest editor of the Multicultural Genetic Counseling Special Issue for the *Journal of Genetic Counseling*.

Paul Pedersen, PhD, is a professor in the Department of Human Studies at the University of Alabama at Birmingham. Dr. Pedersen has taught at universities in Indonesia, Malaysia, and Taiwan as well as at the University of Minnesota, University of Hawaii, and Syracuse University. He is a Fellow in Division 17 (Counseling), Division 9 (Society for the Study of Social Issues), and Division 45 (Ethnic and Minority Issues) of the American Psychological Association. He has authored or edited 31 books and written 60 chapters and 84 articles as well as 19 other monographs.

MaryLou Ramsey, EdD, NCC, NCSC, is a professor and coordinator of the school counseling program in the Department of Counselor Education at the College of New Jersey. Dr. Ramsey is a National Train-the-Trainer of the Association for Multicultural Counseling and Development and a member of the curriculum development committee of the Counselors for Social Justice. Her scholarly achievements include 15 state and federal grants, 24 refereed publications, and more than 100 professional conference and workshop presentations, many of which are devoted to issues of diversity and multiculturalism.

Amy L. Reynolds, PhD, is an assistant professor of counseling psychology at Fordham University at Lincoln Center. She is a graduate of the counseling psychology program at Ohio State University. Her research interests and publications include multicultural counseling, training, and supervision; lesbian, gay, and bisexual issues; and feminist psychology.

Charles R. Ridley, PhD, is professor and director of training of the doctoral program in counseling psychology at Indiana University, Bloomington. His primary areas of interest are multicultural assessment, counseling, and training; organizational consultation; integration of psychology and theology; and therapeutic change. Dr. Ridley is a licensed psychologist, a consultant, and the author of *Overcoming Unintentional Racism in Counseling and Therapy: A Practitioner's Guide to Intentional Intervention* (1995).

Mary Swigonski, PhD, LCSW, is an assistant professor of social work at Monmouth University. Dr. Swigonski publishes in the areas of empowerment, cultural diversity, feminist theory, and lesbian and gay issues. She is a member of the Council on Social Work Education's Commission on Gay Men and Lesbian Women as well as the Council's's Task Force on Culturally Competent Social Work Education for the 21st Century. She is also a member of the national coordinating committee of the Association for Women in Social Work, and is adviser to Monmouth University's African American Student Union.

Saundra Tomlinson-Clarke, PhD, is associate professor and director of training of the counseling psychology program in the Department of Educational Psychology, and special adviser for diversity and recruitment for the Office of the Dean at Rutgers, the State University of New Jersey. She received her doctorate from Florida State University. Her research interests focus on multicultural counseling and training and on psychosocial issues affecting student development and learning.

Chalmer E. Thompson, PhD, is an associate professor in the Department of Counseling and Educational Psychology at Indiana University, Bloomington. Dr. Thompson's writings and research interests include the psychology of oppression and the facilitation of change by psychologists and educators in the racial identity of individuals, groups, and organizations.

I | THEORETICAL AND PRACTICAL CONSIDERATIONS

1 | Managing Resistance to Diversity Training: A Social Systems Perspective

Charles R. Ridley and
Chalmer E. Thompson

Without a struggle, there is no progress—Frederick Douglas

In counseling and psychotherapy parlance, psychological resistance refers to those client behaviors that can potentially obstruct the therapeutic process and sabotage positive change. Skilled counselors or therapists not only anticipate client resistance but also accept the challenge of working through it. The challenge for any change agent is similar: those professionals who work to exert positive and constructive changes among individuals and groups need to equip themselves with the tools to overcome resistance to change.

Classroom instructors, group facilitators, and organizational consultants who offer diversity training often encounter resistance in their work. In some cases, certain members of the audience harbor serious doubts about the relevance of diversity to their lives or profession. Still others advocate diversity on one level yet resist making meaningful changes because of what they perceive as the dire cost accompanying change. How well diversity trainers handle the phenomenon of resistance or even recognize it depends largely on their developing expertise in resistance management. Importantly, identifying the various sources of and complexities inherent in resistance is essential to diversity instruction.

In one sense, resistance to diversity training is no different than any type of resistance to positive change and growth; it is an impediment to progress. In another sense, resistance to diversity training is enigmatic. It is a dysfunctional response in an evolving global environment, and it exists in many American organizations (Bradberry & Preston, 1992). Educating people about issues surrounding diversity is difficult, especially when diversity training is geared to examining the sociopolitical status quo critically and, likewise, illuminating the ways in which all people learn to conform to the various systems of unfair social stratifications. By its very nature, diversity training jars the familiarities that people come to know and depend upon. The discomfort that erupts from diversity training is likely to be most threatening to those trainees with a heightened need for safety and security due to personal vulnerability or on occasions of great volatility within the groups, organizations, or institutions with which the trainees are affiliated. In other words, both internal and external factors can influence trainees' susceptibility to resistance and their reticence to change. At all levels within a system, resistance can be nurtured as well as managed.

The purpose of this chapter is to address the problem of resistance to diversity training. We begin by defining resistance, then proceed by discussing the major factors that perpetuate it and therefore serve as impediments to learning. We conclude the chapter by describing methods for addressing resistance, including those strategies for invoking changes at the organizational, institutional, and societal levels.

Four premises serve as the foundation for this chapter. First, resistance to diversity training is a product of social systems. In taking this stance, we assert that the phenomenon is not an accident or chance occurrence. Instead, it is fundamentally systemic in nature, perpetuated and reinforced by the dynamics of social systems in which it exists. Second, effective strategies to militate against resistance are possible. This possibility is the creedal oath to which we cling. The alternative, of course, is to accept that constructive change is impossible. Third, effective resistance management strategies must originate out of an adequate conceptualization of the phenomenon. All too often in the social sciences, symptoms are conceptualized as problems when, in fact, the real problems are undefined. Misconceptions of problems inevitably lead to ineffective interventions. We conceptualize resistance and its diversity training variants in a way that is logical, theoretically consistent, and practical. Fourth, effective resistance management strategies are systemically oriented. Systemic problems suggest systemic solutions. Overall, then, the objectives of this chapter are to assist diversity trainers in (a) conceptualizing resistance to their training endeavors and (b) employing strategies to dismantle this impediment to training.

RESISTANCE DEFINED

Consider the following situations:

- A White male trainee is extremely argumentative in a multicultural training workshop. He claims himself to be free of prejudice but refuses to examine any data that might contradict his claim. He is also angry because the workshop is a continuing education requirement for his counselor certification. He manages to appeal to a small group of workshop attendees to collaborate with him in writing a letter to the accreditation board to request that a course be created to address the concerns of White people whom he and they believe are increasingly beleaguered in contemporary society.

- A White female student does not register for an elective course in diversity issues. Even though the instructor and course have an outstanding reputation, the student insists that the subject matter is not important to her. What she really needs to learn, in her view, are intervention skills that she can apply to any client population.
- An African American employee is highly outspoken and contentious in a corporate-sponsored diversity course. At times, the employee verbally attacks his White colleagues and believes the training should be geared toward White employees only.

Each of these examples illustrates resistance to diversity training. Resistance can occur because of such factors as a student's ill-informed assumptions about the course material, a trainee's unwillingness to learn the material due to his or her biases against diversity training, an instructor's negative feelings about the material and misguided instruction, or a consultee's negative perceptions of the consultant's authority or expertise on the basis of the consultant's race, nationality, gender, and/or ability. All of these factors are influenced by and recursively influence a societal climate that resists pluralism, in part by denying a reality of structural disadvantage. Encircled in a climate of denial, people, either individually or as part of groups or institutions, internalize practices that sidestep or minimize the problems that arise from racism and discrimination (see Jones, 1997; Thompson & Neville, in press). These practices in turn miss the target by focusing on strategies that do not fully address the problems of inequity or unfair treatment. Hence instructors who harbor unresolved anger toward racist and prejudicial acts may be prone to designing learning exercises that leave open rather than help work through the potential wounds of racial self-reflection. Students who experience feelings of rage or guilt about course materials may also be likely to direct hostility toward their instructors. Institutional leaders who are ambivalent about the need for a more racially diverse management team may fail to take the necessary steps to recruit non-White candidates and defend their practices without due consideration of the disparate reality between White and non-White candidates. Like Block (1981) who contended that managing resistance is the most difficult part of the consulting process, we contend that it is also the most difficult part of diversity training.

Features of Resistance

Ridley (1991) defined resistance as counterproductive behavior. "It is behavior directed toward one goal—the indiscriminate avoidance of the threatening demands of constructive change" (p. 47). This is the definition we adopt in this chapter. The definition includes six principles:

1. **The most important thing to say about resistance is that it is reflected in behavior.** Resistance is how people behave—what they actually do.

This behavioral definition places resistance in the category of motor activity. Some authors define resistance in terms of a person's attitude or disposition. Although people may be motivated to resist constructive change, only their actual behavior is resistance. Dismantling resistance typically requires an intervention directed toward the resister's underlying motivation. However, using our definition, this should not be confused with resistant attitudes.

2. **Resistance is counterproductive.** In one way or another, resistance interferes with the change process. It may slow down constructive change. In its extreme form, resistance may undermine an entire change effort. In whatever form resistance manifests itself, the target of change is the real loser. The extent of the loss depends upon the nature of the resistance and how it is managed by the change agent. For example, in the case of the student who mobilized a group of workshop attendees to request that a course be offered dealing with White people, there is evidence that the course material invoked feelings of guilt and anger among some students. If the instructor is given the opportunity to respond to these feelings and can do so appropriately, then resistance may be managed to some degree. However, if the participants fail to voice their feelings for fear of losing credit or appearing politically unenlightened, or if they are persuaded by the charisma of one participant to pursue their "movement," then resistance is fortified and change thwarted.

3. **Resistance is directed toward a goal: the avoidance of the threatening demands of change.** Constructive change, like surgery, is accompanied by costs or losses. If the losses are seen as integral to the person's being or way of relating in the world, then change may not be welcomed. In fact, the resister may perceive that it is more beneficial to pay the cost of not changing than to pay the cost of change. Conversely, if change is seen as involving losses that are necessary, then the individual may be more willing to experience the often painful struggles associated with the change.

4. **Resistance typically involves the indiscriminate avoidance of the demands of change.** For a variety of reasons, resisters may not evaluate the merits of the change effort. Their preoccupation with change's stressful demands typically results in one response: avoidance at any cost. Avoidance could mean staying away from diversity training, as in the case of the White female student just described. It could also mean psychological avoidance by distorting content in reading material or by diminishing the relevance of the instruction because the trainer is perceived as unqualified and the course material seen as unimportant to development or learning. This premature response gives way to uncritical acceptance or rejection of any proposal for change. Unfortunately, the avoidance comes at a high price: forfeiture of the opportunity for personal development and learning.

5. **Resistance may manifest itself in a variety of behaviors.** Some behaviors involve overt rejection of change. Attacking the trainer or putting the trainer on the defensive are examples. Other behaviors involve covert rejection of change. On the surface, the trainee may appear to embrace change, but underneath the person may be ambivalent about or be totally unwilling to change. Agreeing to follow through on an assignment but procrastinating in completing the required preparation between training sessions illustrates covert resistance. In this example, the completion of the assignment may be done for the purpose of doing the tasks necessary to receive a passing grade, whereas procrastinating may be an attempt to avoid exposing oneself to changes that the individual perceives as threatening or unwanted. Regardless of whether the behavior is overt or covert, an examination of the gestalt of behaviors can serve well in locating the resistance (see principle 6). Such an assessment is also integral to identifying the sources of resistance within organizations and institutions.

6. **Resistance is observable, but it may go unnoticed.** By definition, behavior is motor activity and therefore observable. However, the behavior of the resister may not be recognized by the change agent as resistance. The trainee who asks questions to change the topic of conversation subtly may be demonstrating resistance that is public but may not recognized as resistance by the trainer. Or the behavior of the resister trainee may occur in a private setting and be unobserved. In the first scenario, the trainer may be able to develop ways to better detect the resistance; in the second, identification of the resistance is more difficult. Such behavior is not even seen by the trainer, let alone recognized as resistance. Diversity trainers may nevertheless be able to infer that there exists some unobserved resistance by noting the trainees' lack of progress.

Advantageous Uses of Resistance

Although resistance is an impediment to change, diversity trainers can attempt to use it advantageously. They can look at it in much the same manner that Freud regarded the crux of the therapeutic endeavor: working through trainee resistance can help pierce the defenses used to obscure painful aspects of reality. With certainty, confronting resistance is no easy task. Nevertheless, expert trainers should seize every opportunity to explore and interpret the resistance of individuals and client systems. In doing so, they are likely to uncover a host of fears, anxieties, and feelings of vulnerability. They may also encounter ignorance, misinformation, and hostility. Competent trainers use their acquired insights to design resistant management strategies that are person- or system-specific. Therefore, by leveraging resistance, diversity trainers have the dual advantage of having ready access to the resister's underlying motivation and being able to personalize the training intervention.

OVERVIEW OF DIVERSITY TRAINING

The primary goal of *diversity training,* a term used interchangeably here with *multicultural training,* is to assist people in competently and humanistically interacting and working with people who are different from themselves yet share inherent human similarities. Sleeter and Grant (1993), in describing the instructional approaches of teachers in primary and secondary school settings, defined *multicultural education* as those policies and practices that recognize, accept, and affirm human differences and similarities related to gender, race, disability, class, and sexual orientation. These authors also noted that there are many approaches to multicultural education but that most advocates embrace the goals of (a) promoting and strengthening the value of cultural diversity, (b) promoting human rights and respect for those who are different from oneself, (c) promoting alternative life choices for people, (d) promoting social justice and equal opportunity for all people, and (e) promoting equity in the distribution of power among groups.

Trainers may chose one or more aspect of diversity on which to focus their instruction. For example, some trainers may devote their instruction on racial and ethnic diversity, intraracial diversity, or gender. They may also strive to devote equal attention to race, class, gender, and sexual orientation. An important aspect of resistance management is making assessments of the levels of readiness among their learners, then proceeding by taking into account the best way to both meet and challenge these levels. For example, in planning a course that concentrates on racial diversity, instructors of graduate programs in counseling may want to prepare for the course by initially assessing the racial climate in an academic department. This could be achieved by observing the representation of White and non-White students, learning the history of racial integration within the department and institution, and attempting to discern the quality of interracial and intraracial interactions among students and faculty. Although students come to the learning environments with different experiences as racial beings, data on the immediate learning environment can help inform the instructor of the racial dynamics that contribute to students' ongoing socialization. Furthermore, if one multicultural course is offered in the department or university, and if the instructor sees that certain issues falling under the general heading of diversity are relatively untouched in other courses, then he or she may decide to adopt one or more foci that address these unacknowledged or underacknowledged areas, hopefully working in collaboration with other instructors in the department and helping to ensure adequate coverage of diversity issues. In the case of organizational consultants, trainers may conduct assessments of why diversity training may be needed and survey trainee attitudes concerning problems within the setting to tailor their training. Consequently, although diversity or multicultural training has the potential to encompass a host of topics, it seems most appropriate for instructors to determine which topics are covered within the period allotted and the extent of resources available.

Ridley, Mendoza, and Kanitz (1994) proposed that because multicultural training can encompass a range of topics and teaching strategies, diversity educators should develop this training with a considerable degree of thought, planning, and creativity. Ridley and his colleagues conceptualized a process model for developing multicultural training programs that takes into account the needs in the environment and the resources available to the instructor. Fundamental to this model is the *training philosophy* that influences the learning objectives, instructional strategies, program designs, and evaluation of the training. The training philosophy is what drives the instruction and requires, in part, that trainers consider carefully and logically their rationale for teaching the course. When nonconstructive motivations for diversity training are worked through (e.g., guilt, self-righteousness, anger, or paternalism) and when there is a clear articulation of the needs and resources of the community, diversity trainers can begin to develop, implement, and evaluate the training.

FACTORS THAT PERPETUATE RESISTANCE AND IMPEDE LEARNING

The factors that perpetuate resistance to diversity training can be divided into four social system categories or levels: (a) suprasystems (society), (b) organizational systems (educational institutions), (c) small group systems (classrooms, seminars, workshops), and the (d) individual systems (trainees and trainers). Consistent with a systems perspective, these four levels interact and influence each other, thus representing interpenetrating ecological levels. This analysis, which borrows from Szapocznik and Kurtine's (1993) notion of systems embedded in systems, illustrated in Figure 1-1.

Suprasystem Level Factors: Society

In contrast to the pre-1950s era, the past four decades have seen considerable evidence of America's heightened consciousness in issues of diversity. Books about issues of gender, race and ethnicity, the aged, and sexual orientation, which were once difficult to locate or available only in alternative bookstores, can now be found in sections of mainstream bookstores and libraries. Within business and organizational settings the number of people from diverse racial and ethnic backgrounds has increased at all levels of hierarchy, men and women are more diversified into occupations that were formerly primarily divided by gender, and the number of physically challenged persons in work settings has risen. These changes reflect the effects of the social movements of the 1950s and 1960s, of the ensuing delegalization of discriminatory practices, of changing demographics, and of shifts in social attitudes toward greater tolerance and acceptance of diversity. Media images are more representative of the nation's diversity, and the perspectives of those who were once considered outside of society's "moral community" (Opotow,

Figure 1-1 | Levels of Embedded and Interacting Systems as Targets of Diversity Training

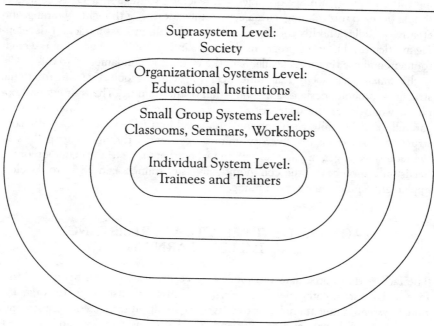

Suprasystem Level:
Society

Organizational Systems Level:
Educational Institutions

Small Group Systems Level:
Classooms, Seminars, Workshops

Individual System Level:
Trainees and Trainers

1990) are included in news, film, and journal productions. To continue the work of promoting fairness and equality among Americans from various walks of life, efforts are being made in all aspects of public life to remedy the problems of America's troubled past. As recently as 1997, the President of the United States, William Clinton, issued an initiative on race and reconciliation to examine continued problems of racism in American society.

What these characterizations tell us is that the past four decades have seen an increased awareness of the need to acknowledge and respect the realities of people of varying races, ethnicities, genders, abilities, and sexual orientations. However, although it is socially desirable to proclaim attitudes favoring fairness and equality, there is ample evidence of society's resistance to practices that meaningfully promote these ideals. People of color are better represented in recent decades in higher ranks within organizations, but their numbers are abysmally low in comparison to Whites (e.g., Pettigrew & Martin, 1987; Sue & Sue, 1990). The gaps between African Americans and Whites in income level and unemployment rates are growing (Dovidio, 1997). After controlling for social class and other relevant variables, racial groups differ in terms of access to nearly every aspect of public life, including housing, occupations, educational attainment, health care, and financial loans (Smith, 1995). Further, despite evidence that affirmative action programs have helped generate more professionals among people of color and

White women over the years, some institutions have dismantled such programs without adequately demonstrating sufficient diversification. Hate crimes have risen over the past two decades, especially with gays and lesbians as targets of victimization (see Garnets & Kimmel, 1988), and recent immigrants are viewed by many Americans as threatening to national identity (Essed & Gircour, 1996). Racism and prejudice have spurred divisive relationships between people of different backgrounds, evidenced both by highly publicized conflicts between people of different races and ethnicities, and (perhaps more subtly) by a flurry of public opinion polls that reveal marked differences in the realities and perspectives of people of different races. Racism and prejudice also have helped spawn problems among people of similar backgrounds, contributing to internalized racism among non-White racial groups, misogyny among women as well as men, and internalized homophobia among gays, lesbians, and bisexuals.

News media have failed to report the pervasiveness of racism or sexism in all facets of American life, and the discomfort and anxiety associated with any discourse on inequality becomes submerged, silenced, or codified (e.g., Fine, 1990; Morrison, 1992; Young-Bruehl, 1996). Denial and distortions of reality have become a means of perpetuating the resistance and keeping alive the phenomena of racism and prejudice. Numerous authors have written about the manner in which structural disadvantage manifests within organizations as inauthenticity in policies and practices (e.g., Nkomo, 1979; Pettigrew & Martin, 1987), within interpersonal relationships by creating deep-seated divisions and misunderstandings (Jones, 1997; Sue & Sue, 1990; Thompson & Carter, 1997), and within individuals by contributing to profound ambivalence, guilt, rage, and depression (Cose, 1993; Helms, 1995; Jack, 1991; Thompson & Carter, 1997).

Organizational Systems Level Factors: Educational Institutions

Resistance pervades organizational and institutional levels. Educational institutions are by no means the exception. Similar to the suprasystem level, the climate relative to diversity can be seen as ambivalent within many organizations. Among the signs of progress are the increased representation of students and faculty at institutions, enhanced mission and policy statements calling for tolerance and acceptance of others, and the presence of course work that incorporates the perspectives and realities of diverse populations. However, from studies that show evidence of racial bias in grading, placement, and behavioral management in grade school settings to the reports of disharmony and violence among students of various races, ethnicities, creeds, and sexual orientation on college campuses, the tenor of educational settings are often beset with problems of marginalization and exclusion. Importantly, even when incidents of discrimination and bias are not publicized, institutional racism and bias can be found. For example, although publicized reports of racism and prejudice were rare on one New England campus, queries of racial attitudes revealed a preponderance of "symbolic" racism as measured by social distance indicators (McClelland & Auster, 1990).

Other indicators of institutional racism and bias can be found in how institutional leaders respond to problems of racism and negative bias. For example, administrators of primarily White institutions of higher learning have implemented policies that reportedly reflect their commitment to increasing racial/ethnic diversity among students and faculty. These policies have, in turn, produced a host of programs geared to enhancing the academic and social integration of diverse groups of students on these campuses. These institutions have also attempted to make strides in creating "warmer" climates for women students of all racial/ethnic backgrounds, seemingly in response to the recent studies showing that instructors call on female college students in class less frequently than they call on their male counterparts, that faculty tend to establish more out-of-class contacts with male than female students, and that female students fear being attacked or raped when walking on campus after dusk. In examining some of the interventions set forth to implement the goal of enhancing diversity, several scholars have criticized these programs for lacking a systemic approach to these problems. Rather than perceiving these problems as being influenced by societal attitudes and therefore structurally embedded into the ethos of institutional conduct, leaders of these institutions have established piecemeal solutions that are often targeted to preparing the student to cope with or manage the environment. As Allen (1992) noted, when interventions stress the responsibility of the student to integrate into the environment rather than the responsibility of both the student and environment to manage changes, the notion conveyed is that the environment is essentially all right and that it is the student who must simply equip or adapt him- or herself in order to be successful.

Within counseling programs, a flurry of mandates and recommendations have been established to ensure that counseling professionals are prepared to work effectively with diverse client populations. One manifestation of resistance to these mandates and recommendations is the failure of institutions to consider their broadstroke implications to the training and competency of their students. Most counseling professionals will probably agree that it is a reflection of a counselor's competency and integrity to provide the best help possible for all of his or her clients. However, because racism and prejudice are often dispensed unintentionally yet with the capacity for creating damage and misunderstanding (e.g., Ridley, 1995), it seems important to require that students undergo some experience that will enable them to overcome racism and prejudice as they approach the counseling endeavor. With foresight and planning, curriculum planners can not only ensure that students receive the instruction they need to achieve these goals but also implement ways to monitor and evaluate their students based on these goals. Ultimately, if counseling professionals are committed to these goals, they have to demonstrate this commitment by setting standards of excellence for their students.

D'Andrea and Daniels (1995) pointed out that the counseling profession falls short of responding to the needs of an increasingly diverse client population. These authors noted, for example, that fewer than 1% of the chairpersons of graduate counseling training programs in the United States come from non-White groups; no Hispanic American, Asian American, or Native American person has ever been elected president of either the American Counseling Association or the American Psychological Association (APA) (with the recent exception of Richard Suinn, 1998 APA president-elect); all the editors, with one exception, of the journals sponsored by ACA and APA are White; and despite the generation of multicultural counseling competencies and standards by experts in the area, the organizational governing bodies of ACA and APA have consistently refused to adopt them formally as guidelines for professional training and development.

By way of a case study, D'Andrea and Daniels described a project in which multicultural counseling activists convened at professional forums to mete out concrete strategies to stimulate changes within the ACA. The model used by these activists consisted of four fundamental strategies: mobilization strategies, which center on the participation of rank-and-file members of ACA to discuss the problems and barriers to achieving the goals of multiculturalism; education strategies, which involve information-sharing, whereby mental health professionals are provided opportunities for learning about issues of racism, multiculturalism, and organizational change processes; organizational strategies, which involve the creation of petitions and demands to ACA to urge the organization to move beyond active neglect and benign accommodation when addressing issues of diversity; and institutionalizing strategies, which focus on submitting petitions, lobbying for their acceptance by the governing body of the organization, and developing a feedback mechanism that includes not only monitoring the action or inaction of governing bodies but also disseminating the status of petitions to the membership. This project, which is ongoing, has resulted in the development of six short-term recommendations, of which three are reported as implemented. Using the four strategies, these activists were instrumental in (a) originating a monthly column in the ACA monthly newspaper, (b) ensuring that governing council members as well as the entire organizational staff were provided training by master multicultural counseling trainers, and (c) securing the approval of a policy change stating that all persons contracted by ACA to provide professional development training services and/or workshops must agree to discuss the ways in which the topics of their training relates to counseling persons from diverse cultural, ethnic, and racial backgrounds.

Small Group Level Factors: Classrooms, Seminars, Workshops

Classroom settings can create intriguing dynamics when issues of diversity are raised. Helms (1990), one of the few scholars who has addressed racial dynamics in small groups, noted that when groups come together to talk about issues of race, the climate of the group is influenced by (a) perceptions of power/level of participant influence, (b) racial identity statuses of participants, and (c) situational factors. When a group of people whose levels of influence are about equal and whose racial identity statuses are similar decide to discuss issues of race or racism, little growth in racial understanding can occur. People generally tend to resonate and fraternize with people who have similar racial perspectives, and in fact, one basis of the relationship is their similarity in racial worldviews. This can occur within race and across racial groups. However, when people engage in meaningful dialogue with people of varying racial identity statuses, several outcomes can occur. Optimal is when people with primarily higher racial identity statuses hold positions of influence or authority and can offer opportunities for learning to individuals with less sophisticated sensibilities.

We believe Helms' formulations on the group process when discussing or learning about race and racism also applies to matters of prejudice. Small group scenarios can include organizational units, such as departments or divisions dealing with the decision to hire an "out" gay candidate for employment, a committee set up by university administration to implement a policy on sexual harassment, school board members deciding whether to offer bilingual education to non-native-English speakers, or a homeowners association attempting to establish how best to deal with the rising presence of African American home buyers in the neighborhood.

Take, for example, the situation within a classroom on diversity. We will assume that the instructor operates primarily at the highest level of racial identity and possesses a level of comfort about him- or herself racially, is aware of the nuances of societal racism, and is committed to the struggle to eradicate racism. The instructor's posture is to make her students aware of racism and, wisely, to anticipate the defenses and resistances that help maintain a racist status quo. Because the instructor assumes a position of power, she has the potential to influence her students positively. Her relative power is attained not only by her ascribed status but also by her ability to model strategies to cope with and address racism and prejudice credibly. The instructor is committed to teaching her students about learning in as effective manner as possible. An even greater degree of learning can occur when other members of the classroom also operate primarily at the highest level of racial development and they too are perceived as credible by their fellow group members.

We emphasize the word *potential* in this example because in the larger scheme of things, resistance may still occur among the group of students. If the students in the department receive instruction in "major" courses where the instructors either summarily dismiss or diminish the salience of race, culture, or gender to case conceptualizations and counseling process, then these students may dismiss the instructor or the instruction in diversity. If the instructor is Latino and certain students believe that Latino women are generally unqualified for academic positions or more subjectively entangled in diversity issues than White instructors, then these students may experience resistance to learning about diversity issues. If the instructor is especially personable or widely known in the field, the perception of influence may be resistance less likely in some cases. Situational factors within or outside the institution such as the airing of the beating of Rodney King by Los Angeles police officers or the rise of David Duke as a candidate for public office in the state of Louisiana may also generally sensitize students' thinking about diversity issues.

Individual Level Factors: Trainees and Trainers

Diversity training can have a powerful, engaging influence on students, and in our experiences, many students use this experience as a springboard for further exploration and learning. They may seek out other learning opportunities through conferences, workshops, and support groups, and encourage other people in their lives to pursue these experiences. At least initially, their quest for further instruction may lead to rewards from others. However, the more deeply an individual probes into the life experiences and perspectives of marginalized people and the vicissitudes of discrimination and inequality across institutions, the more likely the individual is to experience a struggle regarding his or her sense of morality and humanity. These learners may also face ostracism and rejection from family members, friends, and peers and may be reluctant to express their newly enlightened perspectives to authority figures for fear of losing out on opportunities for practicum placements, internships, or employment. In the process of gaining knowledge about diversity, there is also potential for severing relationships. Depending on the relative need for external over internal approval, the individual who undergoes this process may find it difficult to pierce resistance and experience change.

Thompson and Neville (in press) noted that the societal climate is pathological in that it not only fuels the problems that society generally agrees it wants to relinquish but allows people to perpetuate racism and prejudice dysconsciously, that is without their being completely conscious of doing so. One of these strategem involves codification, in which words are recreated to reinvent phenomena according to color-blind perspectives and the vantage points of the dominant culture (e.g., reverse discrimination, political correctness, maintain traditionality). Another strategem involves how language is spoken and written and places distortions on the original issues, as in "Native Americans were killed" versus "White settlers killed Native American people." Many other strategems are also used to deflect the reality of racism and prejudice (Helms, 1995; Sampson, 1993; Skilling & Dobbins, 1991); and because these strategems are part of a process of socialization, they are often taken for granted. Thus one means of piercing the dysconsciousness described earlier is for diversity trainers to point out the strategems that individuals use to perpetuate racism and prejudice. Another is to show how changing, not using the perpetuating strategems, giving up resistance, and looking beyond self-interest will be beneficial to oneself as well as others. When an individual is able to see how his or her ability to change benefits the self as part of a common humanity, and when instruction is pedagogically sound, diversity learning can be successfully accomplished.

RESISTANCE MANAGEMENT STRATEGIES

Seven strategies to manage resistance are described in this section. The first two require the efforts both of diversity trainers and stakeholders in the units or organizations that sponsor or host the training. The remaining five strategies apply primarily to the classroom. We emphasize, however, that success in diversity training depends ultimately on each strand within a system operating conjointly rather than singularly. Hence, each of the seven strategies should be considered combinative in nature.

1. Create an Optimal Environment for Learning and Constructive Change

Although manifestations of resistance are unique to each target of change, the problem can be either exacerbated or minimized depending on the type of process designed to invoke change. Unfortunately, diversity training programs often fail in promoting maximal learning and change. This outcome runs counter to the goals of making diversity appreciation a priority and creating a climate in which various forms of bias are safely examined.

To maximize the learning environment, several critical actions are needed. The first is that diversity trainers should seek to obtain a top-down commitment. Leadership in organizations—whether educational institutions, licensing agencies, professional groups such as APA or ACA, or service delivery systems—must mandate diversity appreciation and responsiveness as a priority. When the leadership commits itself, then organizational members and stakeholders are more likely to make a similar commitment. In our professional experience, bottom-up diversity training rarely succeeds because it is not embraced by the total system. Another benefit of a top-down commitment is that it reflects the interacting nature of open systems. When one system embraces diversity as a priority, other linking systems are influenced to follow suit. For example, when CACREP requires diversity training as one of its criteria for accreditation, graduate programs seeking accreditation fashion their curriculum to comply with this requirement. Diversity trainers should also advocate for the hiring and training of leaders who are capable of establishing policies that reflect diversity appreciation and ensuring that such policies are translated into action. Consultants must elicit participation from higher administrative levels and be prepared to provide training to managerial leaders in order to help establish change within organizational settings. Although the travails of dismantling resistance within these settings can begin with efforts to appeal to those in positions of power, such a strategy should be considered crucial to the overall mission. Indeed, such a strategy should be considered mandatory.

The second critical action is that diversity trainers must project an engaging, nonthreatening posture. Issues of group differences evoke strong emotions such as fear, anxiety, guilt, and apprehension. These feelings can lead to a tendency on the part of trainees to avoid these issues either through not discussing them or through attacking those who broach these topics. The most important thing trainers can do in this these situations is to remain alert to the psychological issues of trainees and open to trainees' need for greater exposure and learning. In addition, they should focus on content issues first, and when focusing on the personal dynamics of the individual, never do so in a demeaning or disrespectful manner. The third critical action is that diversity trainers should make themselves accountable by demonstrating the benefits of diversity training. On the individual level, professionals can attain greater multicultural competence. On the institutional level, organizations can better meet global challenges, improve efficiency and productivity, and creatively solve complex problems (Bradberry & Preston, 1992). The fourth critical action is the diversity trainers should encourage the leadership in organizations to reinforce diversity compliance and sanction non-compliance. The purpose of this action is to develop a system in which diversity appreciation becomes an internalized value.

2. Take a Systems Perspective on Resistance Management

Many times experts who are called upon to introduce changes within an organization have little control over the attitudes and actions of top management. In effect, they are hired to "fix" a situation. They may make the mistake of colluding with the demands of certain factions within an organization by focusing solely on localized change. They may overlook the fact that the whole of a system is greater than the sum of its parts, and all components of a system are interdependent. Consequently, these consultants are unprepared for resistance to change that may emerge from other sectors of the system. As Katz and Kahn (1978) pointed out, social systems tend to be overdetermined; they have many built-in layers that contribute to resistance to change and maintainence of the status quo.

Sue (1995) provided a helpful illustration of resistance based upon overdetermination. Yielding to community pressure initiated by Sue and several colleagues, his former university made concessions to admit large numbers of Latino students under a "special accommodated category." Within 1 year, many of the students failed or voluntarily withdrew from the university. The position of the university was that the students were never really "qualified," and subsequently, the special category provision was dropped. The multiple sources of resistance throughout the university to these students can only be imagined.

Competent diversity trainers and consultants assess and anticipate the impact of training and change on the entire system. They seek resourceful ways to help organizations accommodate change. One of their most important contributions is to help systems recognize that constructive change involves threatening demands. Consider Sue's (1995) heartache over the outcomes of the Latino students admitted to his university. Perhaps the plans for a special accommodation category were doomed to failure from the outset due to a system that probably sabotaged the Latino students and prevented them from succeeding. Providing such a category may not have represented the kind of systemic changes that would facilitate the students' success. The students probably encountered various forms of covert racism (Ridley, 1995) and a lack of salient cultural services on campus. Under such conditions, the students were given a systemic message that they were neither welcomed nor valued. Therefore, plans to effect change must anticipate these large, oppositional forces found in systems.

3. Identify Resistant Behavior

Diversity facilitators and trainers cannot manage resistance unless they first recognize it. To recognize resistance, they need a helpful tool. Figure 1-2 provides a two-dimensional topology for classifying resistant and nonresistant behavior. The two dimensions are trainee responses to training and outcomes of trainee responses. Both dimensions are two-tiered. Trainee responses to training are either change opposing or change promoting. Trainees either cling to established behavioral patterns or seek to adopt new patterns of behavior. The outcomes of trainee responses to training are either constructive or counterproductive.

Combinations of the two tiers of trainee responses to training and the two tiers of effects of trainee responses yield four possible trainee response modes: (a) change-opposing behavior contributing to counterproductive outcomes (overt resistance); (b) change-promoting behavior contributing to counterproductive outcomes (covert resistance); (c) change-opposing behavior contributing to constructive outcomes (protest); and (d) change-promoting behavior contributing to constructive outcomes (compliance). Each of these trainee response modes represents a quadrant of the topology. There are two behavioral manifestations of resistance—overt and covert—and two behavioral manifestations of nonresistance—protest and compliance.

The type of behavior exhibited in quadrant 1 is what is typically thought of as resistance. Trainees here directly and unpretentiously oppose diversity training. They either discount the benefits of training or place priority on other agendas.

Figure 1-2 | Classifying Resistant and Nonresistant Behavior

		Trainee Behavior	
		Change Opposing	Change Promoting
Effects of Trainee Behavior	Counterproductive	Overt Resistance 1	Covert Resistance 2
	Constructive	Protest 3	Compliance 4

Examples of overt resistance are verbally attacking the trainer, antagonizing other trainees, and becoming unnecessarily argumentative.

Covert resistance is found in quadrant 2. On the surface, this type of behavior may appear to be compliance, but in reality, the behavior reflects the trainee's lack of commitment to change and uncritical acceptance of the goals and content of training. When a trainer asks a trainee to comment on the trainer's analysis of racism in the trainee's organization, for example, the trainee might respond in a polite tone, "I have nothing to add to your insights. You have done a good job sizing up the situation." However, the trainee may actually have additional insights but subtly resists contributing to the learning endeavor.

In quadrant 3, the change-opposing behavior is constructive. On the surface, protest may seem to be overt resistance. Unlike overt resistance, protest involves the trainee's basic commitment to constructive change and learning. In fulfilling that commitment, the trainee is constructively critical, even to the point of rejecting proposals of the trainer that seem to have questionable merit. Klein (1985) cautioned change agents about the costs of too easily ignoring, overriding, or dismissing as irrational those individuals who are opponents of change. He recognized the merit of opposition that defends the integrity of a functional system.

In quadrant 4, the change-promoting behavior is also constructive. Compliant trainees actively participate in diversity training, regarding it as an opportunity for constructive individual or institutional change. Even though they may feel uncomfortable with the challenges of learning, they nevertheless cooperate with the constructive proposals of the trainer. Ridley (1991) cited a number of cooperative behaviors, including offering suggestions, providing constructive criticisms, asking clarifying questions, troubleshooting, identifying relevant sources of data, implementing plans for change, and confronting organizational resistance.

Using this topology, diversity trainers and consultants can classify trainee behavior as either resistance or nonresistance. They should carefully examine trainee behavior and match it against the four quadrants in the behavior topology. Competent consultants correctly identify both forms of resistance and both forms of nonresistance. Conversely, they do not incorrectly identify behavior as resistance and nonresistance.

Professionals must rule out the conclusion that overt resistance is actually protest. The best gauge is to reexamine training methods and contents for possible weaknesses. Professionals must also differentiate covert resistance from compliance. Basically, they should try to determine whether or not the trainee has a critical reflection on the training. They should look for signs of this in the form of feedback, constructive criticism, suggestions, or the willingness to offer alternative perspectives and insights. If diversity professionals are uncertain of how to classify behavior, they should directly ask trainees for feedback.

4. Assertively Confront Resistance

Once resistance has been identified, diversity professionals can confront the trainee. Confrontation is not aggression. Instead, it is an assertive strategy to clarify the contradictions, discrepancies, and inconsistencies inherent in the trainee's resistance. For example, a trainee may verbally communicate a content message that is inconsistent with the trainee's relationship message. In the previous illustration, a covertly resisting trainee states, "I have nothing to add to your insights. You have done a good job sizing up the situation." The trainee was, however, also metacommunicating a relationship message, "This subject matter is of no interest to me, and you are wasting my time."

Many trainers are unfortunately oblivious to the contradiction. Trainers who are competent in handling resistance "listen" attentively to the types of messages, ferret out their meanings, attempt to ascertain the inconsistency, and press the trainee to recognize and acknowledge the inconsistency between the two messages. In this case illustration, the trainer might confront the trainee as follows:

> You have stated that you appreciate my insights and have nothing to add to the presentation. This statement implies that I have done such a great job that you could not possibly think of anything else worthwhile contributing. Yet your body language tells a different story. You appeared bored, preoccupied with other matters, and seem anxious to get this session over with. I'm wondering if your politeness is really camouflaged disinterest. Let's talk about this possibility and why this may be so.

5. Clarify the Learning Objectives

One source of frustration among trainees in diversity training programs is the absence of clear, unambiguous learning objectives. This frustration leads to trainee responses that only range from bewilderment to overt resistance. Diversity trainers want to make certain that strong reactions of trainees are not exacerbated by unclear objectives. Ridley, Mendoza, and Kanitz (1994) have proposed 10 learning objectives for multicultural training: displaying culturally responsive behaviors, ethical knowledge and practice pertaining to multicultural issues, cultural empathy, ability to critique existing theories for cultural relevance, development of an individualized theoretical orientation that is culturally relevant, obtaining knowledge of normative characteristics of cultural groups, cultural self-awareness, obtaining knowledge of within-group cultural differences, learning about multicultural concepts and issues, and respecting cultural differences.

Diversity trainers should regard this list as a menu of possible learning objectives. They can select any one of these objectives or combination of objectives as the focus of training. However, the list is not exhaustive, and diversity trainers may identify additional objectives. The most important considerations in selecting learning objectives are that they (a) are congruent with the philosophy of training, (b) clarify for trainees the purpose of the training, and (c) support the mission of the organization. In our experience, we have found that it is better for trainees to challenge the learning objectives than to question the purposes the training serves.

6. Do Not React Defensively to Trainee Resistance

Trainers should remember that the trainer-trainee interaction is the most basic system level and consider how their personal dynamics contribute to the quality of this interaction. Obviously, the contribution should be positive. The most useful personal contribution may be to react nondefensively to a resistant trainee. Defensiveness impairs trainers' objectivity and hinders their ability to problem solve. One recommendation found in the literature is for diversity professionals to develop cultural self-awareness (Bowman, 1996; Richardson & Molinaro, 1996; Sue, Arredondo, & McDavis, 1992). Culturally self-aware professionals know their own assumptions, values, biases, and limitations. They are less likely to be intimidated or coopted by trainees who struggle with their own identity around these issues. The work of Bowman (1996) and Richardson and Molinaro (1996) has provided helpful guidelines to achieve this end.

7. Incorporate Exercises That Help Trainees Identify the Sources of Their Resistance

A powerful strategy for helping students overcome their resistance is to equip them with the tools to identify the sources of the resistance. In a doctoral-level course in diversity, students may be assigned a series of readings that will not only help raise their levels of awareness on issues but also spark Socratic dialogue within the classroom about (a) why the material may be threatening to the status quo, (b) the implications of change to policies and practices in mainstream society, and (c) the irony inherent in how our lack of understanding of certain issues related to inequity and injustice is frustrated by the silencing and codification that surrounds these issues. In classrooms or workshops where trainees can expect to engage in self-reflection and self-exploration, trainers may share samples of transcripts or studies in which codified racism and prejudice is recorded and analyzed. These samples may be useful in serving as an entry into assisting students to do the same in interviews with volunteers. Television or radio news reports, talk shows, or commercial feature-length movies can be excellent sources of material to use in examining how racism and prejudice are perpetuated and conveyed through media. Because such critical examinations can be difficult, we advise trainers to provide investigative tools, such as assigning readings in critical theory, initiating discussions to allow students to share perspectives based on their (ideally) diverse backgrounds, and lectures.

SUMMARY

The development of resistance management can be arduous and frustrating. Societal forces can make the challenges appear complex and insurmountable. For example, how can a trainer change the fact that she may be considered inferior and incompetent by trainees because she is a woman? Diversity trainers may also hold low-status positions within their organizations, which may contribute to the relative lack of impact they have within these settings. Beginning diversity trainers may get easily discouraged when they attempt to do "the right thing," yet their efforts are met with hostility or failure. It may be of some comfort to cite a case described by a well-known psychologist who continues his work in the area of diversity but who experienced difficulty in his handling of resistance early in his career. Derald Wing Sue (1995) described the resistance he encountered in attempting to promote affirmative action at his university—and provided a sobering reflection for every diversity trainer:

> This incident has always haunted me for several reasons. First, my own guilt at having started a movement which suddenly backfired and left all those involved (proponents and opponents alike) with negative feelings toward concepts of affirmative action and diversity. Second, for years after my departure, I could not fully understand what had happened to derail our movement. I was left with a bitter taste in my mouth; I was confused about what had gone wrong; and I was at a loss as to what else we might have done to effect a more positive outcome. (p. 478)

Sue's comments remind us that even when smaller battles are lost in pursuit of the larger goal of striving for equality and justice, it is still imperative to use these experiences for reflection so as to strengthen our efforts in the next round. There is also ample evidence that lost battles have meant a great deal to the overall war on racism and prejudice. For example, the circumstances that surrounded the lynching-murder of Emmett Till, including outcries from the African American community and the ensuing yet unsuccessful pursuit of justice, can be seen as failed attempts. Yet authors of social movements have also argued that these circumstances helped spark the bus boycott in Montgomery, Alabama, the progenitor of the civil rights movement. These circumstances were the seedlings of the struggle, and those who persisted despite the odds were heroic because they did what they believed was right. We strongly encourage diversity trainers to continue their work, learn from their experiences by acquiring a systemic understanding of the resistances to change, and expect failures that might arise from external opposition, limitations in their ability to manage resistance, or a combination of both. Rather than being discouraged by these lost battles, we urge diversity trainers to persist in their efforts and recognize that their short-term failures can still contribute to long-term, constructive change.

REFERENCES

Allen, W. R. (1992). The color of success: African American college student outcomes at predominantly White and historically Black public colleges and universities. *Harvard Educational Review, 62,* 26–44.

Batts, V. A. (1989). Organizational development consultants: Creating a multicultural workforce. *Consulting Psychology Bulletin, 3,* 33–35.

Bell, D. (1994). *Confronting authority: Reflections of an ardent protester.* Boston: Beacon.

Bielby, W. T. (1987). Modern prejudice and institutional barriers to equal employment opportunities for minorities. *Journal of Social Issues, 43,* 79–84.

Block, P. (1981). *Flawless consulting.* San Diego: University Associates.

Bowman, V. E. (1996). Counselor self-awareness and ethnic self-knowledge as a critical component of multicultural training. In J. L. DeLucia-Waack (Ed.), *Multicultural counseling competencies: Implications for training and practice* (pp. 7–30). Alexandria, VA: Association for Counselor Education and Supervision.

Bradberry, J. G., & Preston, J. C. (1992). Cultural diversity and organizational adaptivity in the face of global change. *Organization Development Journal, 10* (3), 67–73.

Brislin, R. W. (1981). *Cross-cultural encounters.* New York: Pergamon Press.

Cose, E. (1993). *The rage of a privileged class.* New York: Harper Collins.

D'Andrea, M., & Daniels, J. (1995). Promoting multiculturalism and organizational change in the counseling profession: A case study. In J. G. Ponterotto, J. M. Casas, L. A. Suzuki, & C. M. Alexander (Eds.), *Handbook of multicultural counseling* (pp. 17–33). Thousand Oaks, CA: Sage.

Dovidio, J. (1997, July 25,). Aversion racism and the need for affirmative action. *Chronicle of Higher Education.*

Essed, P., & Gircour, R. (1996). *Diversity: Gender, color, and culture.* Amherst: University of Massachusetts.

Fine, M. (1990). "The public" in public schools: The social construction/constriction of public schools. *Journal of Social Issues, 46,* 107–120.

Garnets, L., & Kimmel, D. K. (1988). Lesbian and gay male dimensions in the psychological study of human diversity. In J. D. Goodchilds (Ed.), *Psychological perspectives on human diversity in America.* Washington, DC: American Psychological Association.

Helms, J. E. (1990). *Black and White racial identity: Theory, research, and practice.* Westport, CT: Greenwood Press.

Helms, J. E. (1995). An update on Helms' White and people of color racial identity models. In J. G. Ponterotto, J. M. Casas, L. A. Suzuki, & C. M. Alexander (Eds.), *Handbook of multicultural counseling* (pp. 181–198). Thousand Oaks, CA: Sage.

Jack, D.(1991). *Silencing the self: Women and depression.* Cambridge, MA: Harvard University Press.

Jones, J. E. (1997). *Racism and prejudice.* New York: McGraw-Hill.

Katz, D., & Kahn, R. (1978). *The social psychology of organizations* (2nd ed.). New York: Wiley.

Klein, D. (1985). Some notes on the dynamics of resistance to change: The defender role. In W. G. Bennis, K. D.. Benne, & R. Chin (Eds.), *The planning of change* (4th ed., pp. 98–105). New York: Holt, Rinehart, & Winston.

McClelland, K. E., & Auster, C. J. (1990). Public platitudes and hidden tensions: Racial climates at predominantly White liberal arts colleges. *Journal of Higher Education, 61,* 607–642.

Morrison, T. (1992). *Playing in the dark: Whiteness and the literary imagination.* Cambridge, MA: Harvard University Press.

Nkomo, S. (1979). The emperor has no clothes: Rewriting race in organizations. *Academy of Management Review, 17,* 487–513.

Opotow, S. (1990). Moral exclusion and injustice: An introduction. *Journal of Social Issues, 46*, 1–20.

Pettigrew, T., & Martin, J. (1987). Shaping the organizational context for Black American inclusion. *Journal of Social Issues, 43*, 41–78.

Richardson, T. Q., & Molinaro, K. L. (1996). White counselor self-awareness: A prerequisite for developing multicultural competence. *Journal of Counseling and Development, 74*, 238–242.

Ridley, C. R. (1991). Managing resistance in organizational consultation. *Consulting Psychology Bulletin, 5*, 47–54.

Ridley, C. R. (1995). *Overcoming unintentional racism in counseling and therapy: A practitioner's guide to intentional intervention.* Thousand Oaks, CA: Sage.

Ridley, C. R., Mendoza, D.W., & Kanitz, B.E. (1994). Multicultural training: Reexamination, operationalization, and integration. *The Counseling Psychologist, 22*, 227–289.

Sampson, E. E. (1993). Identity politics: Challenges to psychology's understanding. *American Psychologist, 48*, 1219–1230.

Skillings, J. H., & Dobbins, J. E. (1991). Racism as a disease: Etiology and treatment implications. *Journal of Counseling and Development, 70*, 206–212.

Sleeter, C. E., & Grant, C. A. (1993). *Making choices for multicultural education: Five approaches to race, class, and gender* (2nd ed.). New York: Merrill.

Smith, R. C. (1995). *Racism in the post-civil-rights era.* New York: State University of New York Press.

Sue, D. W. (1995). Multicultural organizational development: Implications for the counseling profession. In J. G. Ponterotto, J. M. Casas, L. A. Suzuki, & C. M. Alexander (Eds.), *Handbook of multicultural counseling* (pp. 274–492). Thousand Oaks, CA: Sage.

Sue, D. W., Arredondo, P., & McDavis, R. J. (1992). Multicultural counseling competencies and standards: A call to the profession. *Journal of Counseling and Development, 70*, 477–486.

Sue, D. W., & Sue, D. (1990). *Counseling the culturally different: Theory and practice* (2nd ed.). New York: Wiley.

Szapocznik, J., & Kurtines, W. M. (1993). Family psychology and cultural diversity: Opportunities for theory, research, and application. *American Psychologist, 48* (4), 400–407.

Thompson, C. E., & Carter. R. T. (1997). *Racial identity theory: Applications to individual, group, and organizational interventions.* Hillsdale, NJ: Erlbaum.

Thompson, C. E., & Neville, H. A. (in press). Racism, mental health, and mental health practice. *The Counseling Psychologist.*

Young-Bruehl, E. (1996). *The anatomy of prejudices.* Cambridge, MA: Harvard University Press.

2 | How to Create a Climate for Cultural Diversity Appreciation Within the Classroom

MaryLou Ramsey

For more than a quarter of a century counselor educators have been encouraged to broaden their training programs to prepare counselors more adequately for the increasing cultural pluralism within the United States (Wehrly, 1991). Initially this encouragement came in the form of informal philosophical, ideological, methodological, and empirical recommendations, but now there are formal organizational requirements as well (Ponterotto & Casas, 1991; Ridley, Mendosa, & Kanitz, 1994; Wehrly, 1991). These requirements are reflected in the professional and ethical mandates, standards, and guidelines put forth by the American Counseling Association, the Association for Multicultural Counseling and Development (AMCD), the American Psychological Association, and the Council for Accreditation of Counseling and Related Educational Programs. Representative documents include the *Code of Ethics and Standards of Practice* (ACA, 1995), the *Ethical Principles of Psychologists and Code of Conduct* (APA, 1992), the AMCDs "Operationalization of the Multicultural Counseling Competencies" (Arredondo, et al., 1996), the *CACREP Accreditation Standards and Procedures Manual* (CACREP, 1994), the APA's *Accreditation Handbook* (APA, 1986), and the "Guidelines for Providers of Psychological Services to Ethnic, Linguistic, and Culturally Diverse Populations" (APA, Office of Ethnic Minority Affairs, 1993).

As these documents indicate, training students for multicultural competence is no longer an option in counseling and counseling psychology programs; it is a requirement (Atkinson, 1994). The issue therefore is no longer whether to include some form of multicultural counseling in graduate training programs but rather what kind of training to offer and how best to begin this process.

To date most published accounts of multicultural training programs have been criticized for their overemphasis on cognitive approaches, heavy reliance on the intellectual, or "university," teaching approach (e.g., formal lectures, reading, and writing assignments), and underemphasis on experiential training and affective learning (Merta, Stringham, & Ponterotto, 1988; Pedersen, 1994; Reynolds,

1995; Ridley, Mendoza, & Kanitz, 1994; Wehrly, 1995). Unfortunately, traditional teaching approaches have been remiss in addressing how to change deeply rooted feelings and attitudes (Reynolds, 1995), the interpersonal factors involved in relating across cultures (Gudykunst & Hammer, 1983), and the prospect of students knowing the right response to a multicultural situation but not having the facility or the inclination to use it (Pedersen, 1994).

Cultural self-awareness is prerequisite to the cultural sensitivity required in such instances. Therefore, cultural self-awareness must be the first step in multicultural training programs that address the just-mentioned omissions and develop the multicultural awareness, knowledge, and skills competencies mandated by current professional counselor training standards (Cheatham, 1994; Brown, Parham, & Yonker, 1996; Pedersen, 1994; Reynolds, 1995; Ridley, Mendoza, & Kanitz, 1992; Ridley, Mendoza, Kanitz, Angermeir, & Zenck, 1994). Cultural self-awareness refers to an individual's ability to identify and understand internalized cultural values' assumptions, priorities, and patterns (Cheatham, 1994). Students' effectiveness as multicultural counselors depends upon this ability to be self-analytical (Ridley, Mendoza, & Kanitz, 1994). They have to understand their own cultural values before they can adjust to the values' system of another culture (Pedersen, 1994). Culturally self-aware counselors are also more likely to facilitate client self-exploration as this relates to cultural identity (Ridley, Mendoza, & Kanitz, 1994), and according to the research findings of Brown et al. (1996), cultural self-awareness enhances students' receptivity to multicultural course content.

Knowing how to create a classroom environment, or climate, for cultural diversity appreciation is central to cultural self-awareness training (Reynolds, 1995). This chapter discusses general guidelines for structuring a classroom learning environment to promote cultural self-awareness, how I structure the initial 4 weeks of my multicultural counseling course to begin the cultural self-awareness learning process, and the potential strengths and limitations of this introductory approach.

GENERAL GUIDELINES

The literature on multicultural training, prejudice prevention, and critical thinking offers a number of general guidelines on how to create, or structure, a learning environment to promote cultural self-awareness. For example, Walsh's (1988) work on critical thinking and prejudice prevention indicated that for students to share their personal thoughts and feelings and challenge their own thinking and that of others, a climate of respect and trust must be established. Pedersen (1994) and Reynolds (1995) concurred and added that a multicultural learning climate should be based on openness and provide "enough safety" so students are willing and able to consider changing their prevailing assumptions about other cultures.

One way of promoting this type of safety is to create a highly structured and supportive classroom environment during the initial stages of multicultural counseling training (Carney & Kahn, 1984). According to Carney and Kahn, structure and support provide a predictable learning environment that reduces student anxiety. Wehrly (1995) also suggested that students' anxieties can be reduced by informing them that it is normal, or natural, for them to experience many conflicting emotions as they learn more about multicultural counseling. These reactions are consistent with numerous theories of identity development (e.g., Atkinson, Morten, & Sue, 1993; Cass, 1979; Cross, 1991; Kim, 1981; Ramsey, 1996; Sabnani, Ponterotto, & Borodovsky, 1991) and are important to forewarn students about if they are fully to appreciate and understand their own identity development process as well as develop healthy multicultural counseling competencies (Helms, 1984). Helms believed that as students gain more information about themselves and the world in which they live they actually experience a sense of healthy cognitive dissonance that helps them to broaden their worldviews. Pedersen (1994) expressed a similar belief when he stressed that the learning climate has to provide enough "challenge" so that students will accept the necessity to learn new cultural assumptions.

To facilitate the development of an atmosphere of safety, trust, and support, Tatum (1992) and Walsh (1988) suggested establishing several ground rules at the onset of a multicultural counseling course. These include requiring students to respect others' opinions and confidences during classroom disclosures, permitting others to finish their statements before responding, avoiding personal criticism and put-downs of peer reactions or positions they do not share, and committing to understanding the latter from the contextual framework of these peers. In addition to these basic ground rules, Walsh felt that a community of inquiry is best created by helping students recognize that there are multiple answers to any question, not just one correct one. In effect, students have to be encouraged to develop a flexible and open-minded approach, or what Sfeir-Younis (1995) called a multicultural vision, in which they are able to consider a variety of beliefs and views as equally legitimate although different.

According to Reynolds (1995), the first rule of multicultural course design is to focus on the person rather than on the subject matter. To succeed in this focusing effort, all students must perceive themselves to be multicultural beings (Arredondo, 1994; Ramsey, 1996). For this to occur, the scope of multicultural counseling training should be broadened and reframed to include multiple cultural identifications, not just those of a racial-ethnic origin. Cultural identifications pertaining to gender, sexual orientation, disability, spirituality, class, race, and ethnicity must be viewed as equivalent in importance with no assumption of an identification hierarchy wherein one must take precedence over another (Ramsey, 1996). When students see themselves as cultural beings, they are less isolated in the multicultural counseling classroom. They are also less apt to resist multicultural training and more receptive to shifting their thinking because they see their own niche in multiculturalism (Arredondo, 1994).

Another related and widely debated issue pertaining to instructional scope and focus is whether to address cultural similarities or differences in multicultural counseling training. Ponterotto and Casas (1991) noted that there are actually advantages to both and recommend a balanced focus. By studying similarities, students see that people are more alike than different, and a shared, collaborative climate for learning is created. Differences also need to be identified, acknowledged, and affirmed. Otherwise students may view cultural differences as disadvantages and assume a culturally deficient perspective of other cultures.

In the literature on multicultural counseling there is considerable convergence on the merits of experiential, or hands-on activities, as the most effective instructional strategies for promoting a climate for cultural self-awareness and diversity appreciation. This is not to say that didactic, lecture-based classroom instruction is not valuable. It is; but for persons who are unfamiliar with culture, experiential instructional methods have worked more efficiently (Harrison & Hopkins, 1967). Operant learning activities are a means of increasing interpersonal contact with people of diverse cultures, dispelling cultural stereotypes, and fostering multicultural appreciation (Ponterotto & Pedersen, 1993). Corey, Corey, and Callahan (1998) suggested self-exploratory exercises to help students identify their cultural blind spots, and Reynolds (1995) indicated that such experiential exercises are key to encouraging the emotional, or affective, learning required in cultural self-awareness training. Through experiential learning methods and cultural simulations, students can experience the effects of cultural similarities and differences akin to those felt by culturally diverse people. According to Pedersen (1994), the experience of becoming someone from another culture that occurs during these cultural simulations can change a student's level of awareness and ability to see a situation accurately from another person's cultural perspective. Brown et al. (1996) also added that cultural self-awareness is enhanced when students participate in exercises that promote identification, analysis, and emotional and cognitive processing of their personal and collective experiences in oppressive situations.

Thus cultural self-awareness is best initiated and advanced in a classroom environment that exposes students to experiential activities that (a) promote a nurturing and challenging learning environment, (b) encourage group bonding, (c) raise their consciousness of personal biases and oppressive behaviors, and (d) promote their relating knowledge of the personal self to knowledge of the professional self in working with culturally diverse clients (Brown et al., 1996).

THE INITIAL 4 WEEKS

During the initial 4 weeks of my multicultural counseling course, I employ a series of structured experiential exercises and developmental tasks to create a nonpartisan learning environment, or constructed world, in which students can feel safe and secure in exploring and reflecting upon the unfamiliar. This is a world in which there are no familiar cultural norms and in which comparisons with the familiar are secondary to the learning tasks at hand. This is also a world in which all are encouraged to participate, all cultural identifications are affirmed and viewed as equivalent in importance, everyone engages in and candidly reacts to fictitious cultural experiences, and no one is more informed than another. In effect, all students are united in their shared journey through an ambiguous new world, and a sense of collective trust and safety is derived from this group experience and concomitant bonding.

Within this world I stress the importance of learning from one another, and I urge students to have the courage to share with their classmates their personal reactions to, and experiences with, cultural issues within and beyond the classroom. When prejudicial views are expressed in this learning environment, I support the honesty and the risk taking inherent in these self-disclosures as well as the pain that is incurred by others who are offended by them. I then ask students to explore the content of these prejudicial views, their possible origins, their impact on others within and beyond the classroom, and what information is available to rebut these prejudicial views. In this way I both explicitly and implicitly establish classroom norms of collaboration, mutual support, and caring confrontation that reinforce and encourage student risk taking and interactive learning. By not presuming to be an authority on all cultures, telling students that I am not, and trusting them to assume responsibility for their own learning during these and subsequent classroom activities and assignments, I also deemphasize the teacher-student instructional hierarchy and establish norms of mutual power sharing and cultural debate between students and instructor.

In this constructed world mistakes are also normative, and everyone is expected to make them, so there is less tendency to feel embarrassed or ashamed when they occur. Instead, mistakes in unfamiliar circumstances are embraced and reframed as intrapersonal and interpersonal learning opportunities. In this world students are challenged to seek out the unfamiliar and to modify their own communication style to understand, appreciate, interact with, and negotiate unfamiliar situations successfully. In this new learning environment, differences become a challenging puzzle that all are engaged in and in which all have a personal interest in solving. Students are taught there are many means of communication available to them and that they are capable of learning or developing these in greater depth. They are also encouraged to pursue this learning process actively, to further expand and enrich their counseling skills repertoire.

Entry into this constructed world is through the affective arena, and the cognitive follows. Intuition, trial-and-error learning, self-reflection, and process observation are the principal learning tools in this world. These tools reinforce the importance of contextual learning and help students understand another person's world through that person's eyes. From this perspective a classroom atmosphere of curiosity, interest, and, at times, even intrigue is created as both students and instructor individually and collaboratively try to demystify, understand, and celebrate cultural differences instead of denigrating, judging, or attempting to discredit them. Within this learning climate, behavior and affective reactions are viewed as contextually meaningful, and students seek to understand and appreciate, not criticize, whatever they observe or encounter.

In this constructed world students are involved in a simulated microaccul-turation experience that encourages their movement through the first three stages of a four-stage Diversity Identity Development (DID) training model that I have proposed for multicultural training (Ramsey, 1996). The stages of this DID training model are consistent with four transcendent racial-ethnic devel-opment themes found in Arce (1981), Atkinson et al. (1993), Cross (1991), Kim (1981), and Phinney (1993) as well as those themes found common to gay and lesbian identity development (Cass, 1979) and the White racial identity development theories of Hardiman (1982), Helms (1984, 1990), Ponterotto (1988), and Sabnani et al. (1991). In order of their progression, these stages and corresponding themes include (a) Fascination (dominant culture preference-minimal awareness), (b) Differentiation (multicultural contact-increased awareness), (c) Confrontation (ethnocentric preferences and hostilities), and (d) Application (reevaluation and appreciation of multiple cultures) (Ramsey, 1996). In the week-by-week discussion that follows, I describe how my multi-cultural counseling course is structured to enhance students' cultural self-awareness and facilitate their movement from the first, or Fascination, stage through the third, or Confrontation, stage of the Diversity Identity Develop-ment training model.

Week 1: Fascination (Minimal Awareness)

At the onset of the multicultural counseling course, I typically encounter a class-room of students who are excited but somewhat anxious about being perceived as prejudiced or making cultural mistakes; who never thought of themselves as cul-tural beings; who are culturally unaware or misinformed, ethnocentric thinkers, ethnically homogeneous; or who are resentful that this is a required departmen-tal course (Ramsey, 1996). During the first class I therefore attempt to minimize students' anxieties; engage them in the learning process through the creation of a nonjudgmental, warm, and accepting learning environment; and stimulate their interest in their own cultural identity as well as the broader concept of cultural identity. In order to do this, I use a variety of nonthreatening, self-reflective, intro-ductory experiential exercises. Sometimes, I ask students to introduce themselves to one another by their name, their cultural identity, what they like or admire most about their cultural identity, and/or what strengths they draw from their cul-tural identity. At other times I use an exercise developed by Swigonski (1993) in which I distribute index cards describing persons with multiple cultural identifi-cations (e.g., lesbian African American or blind Latino who has multiple sclero-sis) and ask students to share how their lives would be different if this were their cultural identity. At still other times I ask students to circulate around the room, form partnerships, and introduce themselves via a series of questions (e.g., what were some of your initial experiences with sexism, racism, heterosexism, or homo-phobia?) pertaining to their early experiences with, outstanding recollections about, and/or current reactions to issues of gender, racial-ethnic identity, sexual orientation, or persons with disabilities.

As I process these exercises with students, I explore whether they considered such identifications as gender, sexual orientation, social class, age, and spirituality as well as racial-ethnic identifications in their self-defined cultural identity introductions. From this processing I move to a discussion of key multicultural terms and concepts (e.g., race, ethnicity, culture, minority, cross-cultural versus multicultural counseling), various definitions of culture, and my preference for the broader, or universal, definition of culture as expounded by Fukuyama (1990), Locke (1992), Pedersen (1994), and Sue, Arredondo, and McDavis (1992).

Throughout this class I affirm the various and multiple cultural identifications students share and encourage them to consider why they may identify with the ethnic heritage of one side of their family more than the other, why some identities seem more salient than others, and why still others may seem lost or unknown. During this exploration I find it helpful to show students how such things as sociopolitical events, gender, family or other significant support systems, and geographical relocation may disproportionately influence cultural identity. For example, many German Americans who immigrated to the United States after World War II sought to distance themselves from events in their country of origin. As a result, their ethnic identification is less salient than their other cultural identifications. Often I add a discussion of statistical trends and projections to this experiential orientation to illustrate how cultural identifications may change and become increasingly more complex in the future.

As this class progresses and students are affirmed for their multiple cultural identifications and shown that no identification is necessarily more important than another, an open, supportive learning climate begins to form. Students start to view their cultural identifications from a positive perspective that Ponterotto and Pedersen (1993) and Wehrly (1995) observed as providing a strong basis for understanding and respecting the worldviews and cultural identifications of others. Concurrently, students feel acknowledged, not overlooked or discounted because they cannot relate to a unidimensional (e.g., White versus Black or minority versus majority) cultural discourse. They become curious to explore why some of their cultural identifications are more salient than others, and in this exploration, students find additional opportunities to identify with each other and bond together as a group. This group bonding is important in multicultural training because it supports greater risk taking and affords students the chance to learn from one another as well as from the course instructor and content.

In addition to introductory chapter readings about racial-ethnic and diverse populations (e.g., gay men, lesbians, women, persons with disabilities, and the aged) from course texts by Locke (1992) and Atkinson and Hackett (1995), respectively, I require students to read supplementary articles on internalized culture (Ho, 1995) and multiculturalism (Pedersen, 1991) for this first class session.

Week 2: Differentiation (Increased Awareness)

During the second week of the multicultural counseling course, I strive to demystify the concept of culture by showing students what variables constitute cultural identity and how individuals' responses to these variables differ across cultures. To do this I use a revised version of the Personal Cultural Perspective Profile (PCPP), a 14-item cultural continua educational tool that I developed to facilitate cultural self-awareness training (Ramsey, 1994). The revised PCPP breaks the concept of culture down into 13 concrete, yet comprehensive, cultural continua that enable students to grasp the complexity of culture. These continua show students where cultural variations may arise in individuals, within the same culture, and/or among different cultures and suggest how students may need to adjust their counseling approaches to communicate more effectively across cultures. The cultural continua in the revised PCPP include time (two types), age, sex roles, family structure, thinking/reasoning style, verbal and nonverbal communication patterns (three types), interpersonal distance, power/control, sexual orientation, spirituality, and the mind-body paradigm in mental health.

As I explain and illustrate differences that can occur along all of these cultural continua, I ask students to indicate with an X their personal orientation on each. After this self-reflective charting, I ask students to form small groups and explore their collective commonalties and differences on a few (four to six) low-risk, readily discernible cultural continua (e.g., time, age, verbal and nonverbal communication). In their exploration I ask students to discuss how these differences may enhance and/or impede interpersonal relations and communications within their small group and how they may need to adjust their interactions to overcome any perceived obstacles.

Following this exercise, I identify the Personal Cultural Perspective Profile cultural continua positions that underscore traditional counseling and psychotherapy in the United States, and I discuss how Sue and Sue (1990) and Wehrly (1991) have found these positions to mirror White Western European values and beliefs (e.g., verbal emotional expressiveness, openness and intimacy, linear thinking). As this connection is made, I attempt to help students appreciate the importance of understanding and incorporating non-Western, or what I term *culture-specific*, therapeutic beliefs and practices in multicultural counseling. The first step in this appreciation process is again an experiential one. Through small group processing of McGrath and Axelson's (1993, pp. 211–216) Non-Western Therapeutic Beliefs and Practices Survey, which students complete prior to class, students explore their personal degree of comfort with numerous non-Western healing practices. This self-examination exercise then serves as a pathway to our discussion of how cultural values influence various healing practices, the ethical implications for counseling clients whose cultural values are different than our own, the monocultural nature of counseling in the United States, and why students must understand the importance of and include non-Western healing practices and practitioners in multicultural counseling.

As this class draws to a close, I encourage students to consider how age, ethnicity, gender, sexual orientation, social class, geography, spirituality, family and/or significant community groups, and historical events/eras affect their current PCPP cultural continua positions and how these positions may change over time (e.g., if they chose a life partner from a different ethnic background). I also ask them to look at the commonalties and differences they found within their classroom groups as not unlike those they will encounter and need to negotiate effectively when counseling across cultures. To encourage students to see cultural differences as a challenging puzzle to be solved, I suggest unsettling multicultural experiences are often the result of individual differences on the PCPP cultural continua. In contrast, variable commonalties can become communication bridges that promote interpersonal understanding and enable individuals to identify with one another. In this way, the Personal Cultural Perspective Profile becomes a professional learning tool as well a personal one. By using the PCPP to conceptualize and explore cultural differences and commonalties, I am able to create an atmosphere of mutual discovery and collaboration, instead of evaluation, and my classroom learning environment continues to grow more open, honest, and safe as a result.

Alternate worldview and cultural conceptualization models that may be introduced during this class include those developed by Arredondo and Glauner (1992), Gudyhunst (1994), Ibrahim and Kahn (1987), and Sue (1978). Required readings for this week include articles pertaining to traditional healing practices and methods used in Native American (Hennick, Corbine, & Thomas, 1990), Japanese (Ishiyama, 1990), Chinese (Knoblauch, 1985), and African (Vontress, 1991) cultures.

Week 3: Differentiation (Continued)

As a result of students' participation in 2 weeks of engaging, nonthreatening, cooperative experiential multicultural exercises, a classroom environment embodied by mutual respect, trust, and interpersonal safety forms by the third week of the course. Within this learning climate students now possess the personal courage and collective support necessary to move forward and experientially explore how individuals react when they encounter other cultures.

At this stage in their self-awareness training, I involve students in cultural simulations such as BaFa BaFa (Shirts, 1977) or Pedersen's (1994) Outside Experts to afford them the opportunity to interact with, and react to, the attitudinal and behavioral differences of fictitious cultures representing an amalgamation of several cultures and identification experiences (Ramsey, 1996). Through these simulations I try to place students in a state of dissonance regarding what Ponterotto and Pedersen (1993) referred to as positive prejudices toward their own group and negative prejudices toward other groups. As a result, real-life acculturation experience parallels emerge subtly, yet powerfully, and the protective defenses that both majority and minority group members use to justify ethnocentric thinking are replicated.

During these simulations, students personally explore how they cope with the stress of entering a different culture (i.e., culture shock), feel and react as a minority within a majority culture, and often perceive and evaluate other cultures from their own cultural values' systems (i.e., ethnocentrism). In these fictitious cultures, students are fully absorbed in trying to negotiate successfully an ambiguous new living experience and are therefore unencumbered by fears of appearing prejudiced toward real-life cultures. Within this type of learning environment, they feel safe to ask questions, freely express their thoughts and feelings, and spontaneously react to and explore their own group interaction dynamics. As a result, students discover and candidly explore their feelings toward themselves as cultural beings, members of their own culture, and members of other external cultures over time. In these explorations they also encounter and better understand the underpinnings of cultural stereotyping, indifference, intolerance, and/or defensiveness. They see and begin to appreciate how individuals are prone to view their own culture as superior to other cultures and therefore feel justified in imposing their group normative standards on these culturally different groups. Through these fictitious cultural experiences, students become more conscious of how susceptible they are to ethnocentric thinking and the ramifications of this type of thinking on themselves and others. By examining students' personal attitudes and behaviors over the course of these simulations, I am also able to introduce and facilitate students' understanding of theories of unidimensional identity development (e.g., racial-ethnic, gay and lesbian, and White), multidimensional (or diversity) identity development, cultural worldviews, and multicultural socialization.

Supportive lecture materials and required readings for this week may include worldview conceptualization works by Sue (1978), Ibrahim (1991), and Ibrahim and Kahn (1987) as well as works on the complexities of diversity (e.g., Reynolds & Pope, 1991) and culture-specific identity development models (e.g., Cross, 1991, on African Americans; Kim, 1981, on Japanese Americans; and Arce, 1981, on Mexican Americans). Other recommended identity development readings include those on minority identity development (e.g., Atkinson et al., 1993); White racial identity development (e.g., Hardiman, 1982; Helms, 1990; Ponterotto, 1988, 1993; Sabnani, et al., 1991); gay and lesbian identity development (e.g., Cass, 1979); and diversity identity development (e.g., Ramsey, 1996).

Week 4: Confrontation (Ethnocentric Preferences and Hostilities)

Following personal exploration of their ethnocentric thinking and its ramifications during week 3, students enter week 4 with a clearer appreciation of how cultural differences are readily misperceived and adversely evaluated. But they have yet to experience the impact of these cultural judgments, or prejudices, when someone possesses the power to impose them on others. In other words, students have yet personally to experience and confront the issue of cultural oppression within this constructed learning environment.

During this stage in their cultural self-awareness training, students often feel they are incapable of, or can rise above, oppressive actions. Essentially they believe this to be true because they are now more attuned to cultural differences, seriously committed to social justice and equality, and/or intent on becoming humanistic helping professionals. To "affectively" confront these mistaken beliefs, I conclude the climate setting phase of the multicultural counseling course with power/powerlessness simulations such as Starpower (Shirts, 1971) or Powerlab (DICEL, 1980). In these power simulations, which bear minimal resemblance to specific cultures, I challenge students to examine their own reactions to issues of power and oppression by placing them in ambiguous social living situations in which different strata groups with unequal power gradually evolve (Ramsey, 1997).

During these simulations students participate in what they perceive to be, or intend to construct as, a socially level playing field. But with prolonged playing time, they gradually see how power is central to, as well as exercised in, culturally stratified groups. They become more attuned to their own feelings, experiences, and behaviors related to having or lacking power. While involved in these simulations, students have an opportunity directly to observe and explore Pinderhughes' (1989) three levels of power (i.e., individual, interactive, and societal) as well as the relationship between power and various forms of oppression such as sexism, racism, heterosexism, and ageism (Ramsey, 1997). In addition, they personally witness and feel the effects of the types of power (i.e., wealth/resources, knowledge/information, and force/violence) described by Naisbitt and Aburdene (1990), intentional and unintentional racism or cultural oppression (Ridley, 1989), overt and covert oppression, and dominant culture privilege (i.e., White privilege).

As students react to these power/powerlessness simulations, they do so on two different levels of consciousness. The first level is immediate and specific to the exercise at hand. This level includes reactions such as confusion, frustration, anger, disappointment, or hurt over being misunderstood, rejected, or maligned by their classroom peers. The second level is more concealed and hydraulic in nature because it pertains to students' feelings and recollections about current external, or historical, real-world experiences. The second level frequently breaks down along racial-ethnic or other cultural identity lines. For example, students who are or have been victims of cultural oppression (e.g., ethnic minorities; women; gay, lesbian, and bisexual individuals; persons with disabilities) recall these oppressive experiences and the role Whites (especially White, heterosexual, able-bodied males) play in such oppression. When students recall these experiences, they also tend to view themselves as unidimensional cultural beings; gravitate towards singular, not multiple group identifications; focus on differences, not commonalties; and dichotomize their experiences into an "us versus everyone else" scenario (Ramsey, 1996).

During these simulations, culturally oppressed students may become more vocal in their anger toward Whites as well as in their rejection of dominant culture norms and oppression (Ramsey, 1996). Whites (especially White heterosexual, able-bodied males), in turn, sense this anger and get more in touch with their feelings about Whiteness, the privileges it carries, and being members of the oppressive dominant culture. As this occurs, Whites often experience many conflicting feelings. For example, some may feel guilty, confused, or depressed about the role they have played in perpetuating cultural isms and want to make amends. Others may feel angry and defensive about being held accountable for the sins of their forefathers. If they have been advocates for social justice and equality, some Whites may feel hurt, angry, or frustrated that their efforts are being rejected. As culturally oppressed students continue to express their anger and hostility towards Whites, still other White students may want to retreat into the comfort and safety of their own, more culturally compatible, world.

To help all students personally understand and appreciate such complex feelings, it is necessary to give full breadth to their expression. In order to encourage this expressiveness, I carefully adhere to initial ground rules regarding cultural confrontation, and I draw heavily on the group cohesiveness and the caring confrontation skills that students have developed during the initial 3 weeks. I also try to conceptualize and carefully explore interstudent conflicts, challenges directed toward me as the leader, and students' discomfort or frustration with classroom learning activities from the perspective of cultural continua differences and commonalties such as those represented on the Personal Cultural Perspective Profile.

As students are encouraged to discuss their feelings in this fashion, they experience a healthy emotional catharsis because they are permitted to express previously bottled up, repressed, culturally restricted, and/or unresolved life experiences. In addition, students gain greater insight into, and understanding of, one another's life experiences and cultural identifications as well as the depth of oppressed groups' frustration and anger with the dominant culture. Through these shared self-disclosures, students also become a more united and mutually supportive learning group.

To help students personally own and openly share their reactions to these power/powerlessness simulations, I precede this debriefing with a discussion of Ponterotto's (1991) Flight or Fight Response Theory of Racial Stress as well as the four cultural interaction response styles (i.e., anger, placate, withdrawal, or move toward) that I identify during the Confrontation Stage of the Diversity Identity Development training model (Ramsey, 1996). In this way, I proactively recognize and affirm various response styles people may evidence in multicultural encounters. As a result, students feel less fearful and defensive about, as well as more willing to discuss, their own interpersonal reactions.

Other issues that I explore during the debriefing of these power/powerlessness simulations include the parallels between students' reactions and various identity development models discussed the week before; the developmental nature of racism as described by D'Andrea and Daniels (1994); how those in power protect, preserve, and perpetuate their power or privilege; how the powerless attempt to neutralize their alienation and pain and reclaim a sense of personal power; and the cyclical nature of power (Pinderhughes, 1989). As the systemic nature of cultural oppression is exposed, I also challenge students to consider the various proactive roles that counselors must assume to prevent prejudice and effect change at the individual, interactive, and societal levels of power (Atkinson et al., 1993; Ponterotto & Pedersen, 1993; Ramsey, 1997). To strengthen and support these discussions of power and cultural oppression I refer to, and may require students to read, selected sections of *Counseling for Empowerment* (McWhirter, 1994) and *Understanding Race, Ethnicity, and Power: The Key to Efficacy in Clinical Practice* (Pinderhughes, 1989).

To conclude this debriefing, I ask students what parallels they perceive between this simulation and the real world and what they have learned, personally and professionally, that may help them in future real-world situations. In this way, I bring students to a more cognitive level of discussion that serves as a closing summary for this introductory climate-setting experience as well as an entree to the study of other cultures and multicultural counseling skills (i.e., the Application stage of the Diversity Identity Development training model) that comprises the remaining 11 weeks of the multicultural counseling course.

At this juncture in their multicultural counseling training, students are more sensitive to themselves and others as multicultural human beings. They know how and where to search for cultural commonalties and differences that impact cross-cultural communications. They know how easily they can become part of the problem (i.e., oppressors) if they ignore, abuse, or misuse their power as counselors. Lastly, students are now interested in, intrigued by, and eager to know more about other cultures as well as their own, and they see the importance of and want to know how to become competent multicultural counselors.

POTENTIAL STRENGTHS AND LIMITATIONS OF THIS INTRODUCTORY APPROACH

According to Pedersen (1994) and Sue et al. (1992), the first level of developing multiculturally skilled counselors requires that students become more aware of their own cultural heritage, respectful of the cultures of others, and able to identify the many salient but complex and dynamic cultural identities within an individual. Culturally competent counselors are expected to have specific knowledge about their own cultural heritage and its cultural values' underpinnings as well as values' commonalties and differences that may exist between themselves and clients from other cultures. They must know how cultural values' preferences (i.e., ethnocentrism) coupled with power may impact others and lead to cultural oppression, discrimination, and stereotyping. Culturally competent counselors are also expected to know how their cultural worldviews affect their definitions of normality and abnormality as well as the counseling process itself.

The self-awareness exercises and simulations used in this introductory approach address these competencies. Through these experiential learning methods, students see themselves as multidimensional, not unidimensional, cultural beings. During introductory icebreaker and Personal Cultural Perspective Profile exercises, students learn what variables constitute cultural identity and where cultural variations may occur. In these exercises they have an opportunity to discover, explore the origins of, and retrieve what is lost or silenced in their own cultural heritages. In their reactions to initial diversity icebreaker exercises, students report, "I learned that although I'm not closely associated with one ethnicity, I still have my own sense of culture because I am a woman"; "I learned that I knew very little about my cultural heritage . . . it raised my interest in wanting to find out more"; and "I've realized there is so much to one's culture."

Through the PCPP cultural continua and cultural simulations such as BaFa BaFa or Outside Experts, students recognize how the social world may be experienced differently by various cultural groups as well as the importance of knowing how to negotiate overlapping or contrasting cultures. Students state "I liked this activity [PCPP] because it gave me answers to why I do what I do"; and "It helped me grasp the basic concept of differences between cultures." When the PCPP is followed by McGrath and Axelson's (1993) non-Western Healing Practices Survey, students say it is "interesting to explore others' beliefs and rituals as well some from my own culture and then compare [them] to see how they are alike and different"; and "[The survey] told me what areas I might need to be a little more open-minded about."

During cultural simulations such as BaFa BaFa, students confront their own ethnocentrism, monocultural assumptions that often emanate from a dominant culture, and how these assumptions can affect their personal as well as their professional lives. In response to cultural simulations such as BaFa BaFa, students indicate "it really opened my eyes to the difficulties of immigration"; "[It was] a good opportunity to incorporate what we learned and give us a chance to experience cultural differences"; and "It's probably the closest one can come to experiencing culture shock without actually entering a different culture."

In the power/powerlessness simulations, students explore how they respond to having or lacking power and the relationship between power and cultural oppression as well as how racism, sexism, and other isms are used to silence and subordinate various cultural groups. When talking about their involvement in these simulations, students state "this exercise really brought the feelings of covert cultural racism/prejudice to life"; "It felt terrible to be oppressed"; "[This is a] good way to really make students feel what racism feels like and what it does to self-esteem"; "I was amazed at how many parallels emerged in the short time we were involved in the activity"; and "[This was] a good opportunity for [the] class to experience racism/power and privilege. Many of us never had to deal with this, but this brings it into the classroom and we can understand how it feels."

In addition to these advantages, there are several limitations to be aware of in this introductory approach. First and foremost, this approach is based upon a universal, or broad, definition of culture that is not shared by all counselors. When students proceed through this structured training process, their personal learning experiences are subject to individual variations in initial self-awareness, depth of understanding, progression pace, and stage of personal identity development. Experiential exercises require substantial debriefing time during the class in which they are used as well as in subsequent class sessions because students often feel the need to revisit and/or further discuss their reactions. Some students may be reluctant or unable to participate in experiential exercises because of individual, cultural, and/or physical differences. Experiential exercises also pose additional ethical, emotional, and physical injury risks for participants and leaders; therefore facilitators should be multiculturally competent counselors as well as highly skilled group leaders to conduct and process these exercises properly. Because students' ability to identify with the leader promotes greater self-disclosure, training facilitators should subscribe to and personally represent multiple cultural identifications as well as carefully weigh the potential benefits and risks to themselves and their students of self-disclosing invisible or hidden identifications (e.g., coming out as gay in a military setting).

SUMMARY

Experiential activities can transform a multicultural counseling course classroom into an educational laboratory in which students learn directly from their own affective reactions, observations of group process dynamics, and interactive questioning. These learning methods increase students' level of cultural self-awareness and ability to see a situation accurately from another person's cultural perspective (Pedersen, 1994). When sequenced according to the DID training model (Ramsey, 1996), these experiential activities create a nurturing, supportive learning environment. They encourage learner group bonding and inspire students to want to know more about their own and other cultures. They also raise students' consciousness of personal biases and oppressive behaviors and promote students' relating knowledge of self (the person) to knowledge of self (the professional) in multicultural counseling.

REFERENCES

American Counseling Association. (1995). *Code of ethics and standards of practice.* Alexandria, VA: Author.

American Psychological Association. (1986). *Accreditation handbook.* Washington, DC: Author.

American Psychological Association. (1992). *Ethical principles of psychologists and code of conduct.* Washinton, DC: Author.

American Psychological Association, Office of Ethnic Minority Affairs. (1993). Guidelines for providers of psychological services to ethnic, linguistic, and culturally diverse populations. *American Psychologist, 48,* 45–48.

Arce, C. A. (1981). A reconsideration of Chicano culture and identity. *Daedalus, 110*, 177–192.

Arredondo, P. (1994). Multicultural training: A response. *The Counseling Psychologist, 22*, 308–314.

Arredondo, P., & Glauner, T. (1992). *Personal dimensions of identity development model.* Boston, MA: Empowerment Workshops.

Arredondo, P., Toporek, R., Brown, S. P., Jones, J., Locke, D. C., Sanchez, J., & Stadler, H. (1996). Operationalization of the multicultural counseling competencies. *Journal of Multicultural Counseling and Development, 24*, 42–78.

Atkinson, D. R. (1994). Multicultural training: A call for standards. *The Counseling Psychologist, 22*, 300–307.

Atkinson, D. R., & Hackett, G. (1995). *Counseling diverse populations.* Dubuque, IA: Brown & Benchmark.

Atkinson, D. R., Morten, G., & Sue, D. W. (Eds.). (1993). *Counseling American minorities: A cross-cultural perspective* (4th ed.). Dubuque, IA: Brown & Benchmark.

Brown, S. P., Parham, T. A., & Yonker, R. (1996). Influence of a cross-cultural training course on racial identity attitudes of White women and men: Preliminary perspectives. *Journal of Counseling and Development, 74*, 510–516.

Carney, C. G., & Kahn, K. B. (1984). Building competencies for effective cross-cultural counseling: A developmental view. *The Counseling Psychologist, 12*, 111–119.

Cass, V. C. (1979). Homosexuality identity formation: A theoretical model. *Journal of Homosexuality, 4*, 219–235.

Cheatham, H. E. (1994). A response. *The Counseling Psychologist, 22*, 290–295.

Corey, G., Corey, M. S., & Callanan, P. (1998). *Issues and ethics in the helping professions* (5th ed.). Pacific Grove, CA: Brooks/Cole.

Council for Accreditation of Counseling and Related Educational Programs. (1994, January). *CACREP accreditation standards and procedures manual.* Alexandria, VA: Author.

Cross, W. E. (1991). *Shades of Black: Diversity in African-American identity.* Philadelphia: Temple University Press.

D'Andrea, M., & Daniels, J. (1994). The different faces of racism in higher education. *Thought and Action: The NEA Higher Education Journal, 10*, 73–89.

Developing Interpersonal Competencies in Educational Leadership (DICEL). (1980, May). Powerlab simulation, Women in Leadership training program. Boston, MA: Author.

Fukuyama, M. A. (1990). Taking a universal approach to multicultural counseling. *Counselor Education and Supervision, 30*, 6–17.

Gudykunst, W. B. (1994). *Bridging differences: Effective intergroup communication* (2nd ed.). Thousand Oaks, CA: Sage.

Gudykunst, W. B., & Hammer, M. R. (1983). Basic training design: Approaches to intercultural training. In D. Landis & R. Brislin (Eds.), *Handbook of intercultural training: Vol. I. Issues in theory and design.* New York: Pergamon Press.

Hardiman, R. (1982). *White identity development: A process-oriented model for describing the racial consciousness of White Americans.* Unpublished doctoral dissertation, University of Massachusetts, Amherst.

Harrison, R., & Hopkins, R. (1967). The design of cross-cultural training: An alternative to the university model. *The Journal of Applied Behavioral Science, 3*, 431–460.

Helms, J. E. (1984). Toward a theoretical explanation of the effects of race on counseling: A Black and White model. *The Counseling Psychologist, 12*(4), 153–165.

Helms, J. E. (Ed.). (1990). *Black and White racial identity: Theory, research, and practice*. New York: Greenwood Press.

Hennick, R. K., Corbine, J. L., & Thomas, K. R. (1990). Counseling Native Americans. *Journal of Counseling and Development, 69,* 128–133.

Ho, D. Y. F. (1995). Internalized culture, culturocentrism, and transcendence. *The Counseling Psychologist, 23,* 4–24.

Ibrahim, F. A. (1991). Contribution of cultural worldview to generic counseling and development. *Journal of Counseling and Development, 70,* 13–19.

Ibrahim, F. A., & Kahn, H. (1987). Assessment of worldviews. *Psychological Reports, 60,* 163–176.

Ishiyama, F. I. (1990). A Japanese perspective on client inaction: Removing attitudinal blocks through Morita therapy. *Journal of Counseling and Development, 68,* 566–570.

Kim, J. (1981). *Process of Asian American identity development: A study of Japanese American women's perceptions of their struggle to achieve positive identities as Americans of Asian ancestry.* Unpublished doctoral dissertation, University of Massachusetts, Amherst.

Knoblauch, D. L. (1985). Applying Taoist thought to counseling and psychotherapy. *American Mental Health Counselors Association Journal, 7,* 52–63.

Locke, D. C. (1992). *Increasing multicultural understanding: A comprehensive model.* Newbury Park, CA: Sage.

McGrath, P., & Axelson, J. A. (1993). *Accessing awareness and developing knowledge: Foundations for skill in a multicultural society.* Pacific Grove, CA: Brooks/Cole.

McWhirter, E. H. (1994). *Counseling for empowerment.* Alexandria, VA: American Counseling Association.

Merta, R. J., Stringham, E. M., & Ponterotto, J. G. (1988). Simulating culture shock in counselor trainees: An experiential exercise for cross-cultural training. *Journal of Counseling and Development, 66,* 242–245.

Naisbitt, J., & Aburdene, P. (1990). *Megatrends 2000: Ten new directions for the 1990s.* New York: Morrow.

Pedersen, P. (1991). Multiculturalism as a generic approach to counseling. *Journal of Counseling and Development, 70,* 6–11.

Pedersen, P. (1994). *A handbook for developing multicultural awareness* (2nd ed.). Alexandria, VA: American Counseling Association.

Phinney, J. S. (1993). A three-stage model of ethnic identity in adolescence. In M. E. Bernal & G. Knight (Eds.), *Ethnic identity: Formation and transmission among Hispanics and other minorities* (pp. 61–79). Albany: State University of New York Press.

Pinderhughes, E. (1989). *Understanding race, ethnicity, and power: The key to efficacy in clinical practice.* New York: Free Press.

Ponterotto, J. G. (1988). Racial consciousness development among White counselor trainees: A stage model. *Journal of Multicultural Counseling and Development, 16,* 146–156.

Ponterotto, J. G. (1991). The nature of prejudice revisited: Implications for counseling intervention. *Journal of Counseling and Development, 70,* 216–224.

Ponterotto, J. G. (1993). White racial identity development and the counseling profession. *The Counseling Psychologist, 21,* 213–217.

Ponterotto, J. G., & Casas, J. M. (1991). *Handbook of racial/ethnic minority counseling research.* Springfield, IL: Charles C Thomas.

Ponterotto, J. G., & Pedersen, P. B. (1993). *Preventing prejudice: A guide for counselors and educators.* Newbury Park, CA: Sage.

Ramsey, M. (1994). Use of a personal cultural perspective profile (PCPP) in developing counsellor multicultural competence. *International Journal for the Advancement of Counselling, 17*, 283–290.

Ramsey, M. (1996). Diversity identity development training: Theory informs practice. *Journal of Multicultural Counseling and Development, 24*, 229–240.

Ramsey, M. (1997). Exploring power in multicultural counselling encounters. *International Journal for the Advancement of Counselling, 19*, 277–291.

Reynolds, A. L. (1995). Challenges and strategies for teaching multicultural counseling courses. In J. G. Ponterotto, J. M. Casas, L. A. Suzuki, & C. M. Alexander (Eds.)., *Handbook of multicultural counseling* (pp. 312–330). Thousand Oaks, CA: Sage.

Reynolds, A. L., & Pope, R. E. (1991). The complexities of diversity: Exploring multiple oppression. *Journal of Counseling and Development, 70*, 174–180.

Ridley, C. R. (1989). Racism in counseling as an adverse behavioral process. In P. B. Pedersen, J. G. Draguns, W. J. Lonner, & J. E. Trimble (Eds.), *Counseling across cultures* (3rd ed., pp. 55–77). Honolulu: University of Hawaii Press.

Ridley, C. R., Mendoza, D. W., & Kanitz, B. E. (1992). Program designs for multicultural training. *Journal of Psychology and Christianity, 11*, 326–336.

Ridley, C. R., Mendoza, D. W., & Kanitz, B. E. (1994). Multicultural training: Reexamination, operationalization, and integration. *The Counseling Psychologist, 22*, 227–289.

Ridley, C. R., Mendoza, D. W., & Kanitz, B. E., Angermeier, L., & Zenck, R. (1994). Cultural sensitivity in multicultural counseling: A perceptual schema model. *Journal of Counseling Psychology, 41*, 125–136.

Sabnani, H. B., Ponterotto, J. G., & Borodovsky, L. G. (1991). White racial identity development and cross-cultural training: A stage model. *The Counseling Psychologist, 19*, 76–102.

Sfeir-Younis, L. F. (1995). Reflections on the teaching of multicultural courses. In D. Schoem, L. Frankel, X. Zuniga, & E. A. Lewis (Eds.), *Multicultural teaching in the university* (pp. 61–75). Westport, CT: Praeger.

Shirts, R. G. (1977). *Starpower.* Del Mar, CA: Simile Training Systems.

Sue, D. W. (1978). Worldviews and counseling. *Personnel and Guidance Journal, 56*, 458–462.

Sue, D. W., Arredondo, P., & McDavis, R. J. (1992). Multicultural counseling competencies and standards: A call to the profession. *Journal of Counseling and Development, 70*, 477–486.

Sue, D.W., & Sue, D. (1990). *Counseling the culturally different: Theory informs practice* (2nd ed.). New York: Wiley.

Swigonski, M.E. (1993). Feminist standpoint theory and the questions of social work research. *Affilia: Journal of Women and Social Work, 8*, 171–183.

Tatum, B. D. (1992). Talking about race, learning about racism: The application of racial identity development theory in the classroom. *Harvard Educational Review, 62*(1), 1–24.

Vontress, C. (1991). Traditional healing in Africa: Implications for cross-cultural training. *Journal of Counseling and Development, 70*, 242–249.

Walsh, D. (1988). Critical thinking to reduce prejudice. *Social Education, 52*, 280–282.

Wehrly, B. (1991). Preparing multicultural counselors. *Counseling and Human Development, 24*(3), 1–24.

Wehrly, B. (1995). Pathways to multicultural counseling competence: A developmental journey. Pacific Grove, CA: Brooks/Cole.

3 | INNOVATIVE PEDAGOGY FOR CRITICAL CONSCIOUSNESS IN COUNSELOR EDUCATION

Don C. Locke and Marie Faubert

Why have several professionals been asked to write about teaching multicultural counseling to individuals from the dominant mainstream culture? Why is this question limited to teaching members of the dominant mainstream culture? Why do we not get asked a similar question about courses we teach in counseling theories, individual counseling, group counseling, or guidance? Framing the question more broadly might be more helpful: How do we prepare culturally competent counselors of all races to deal forthrightly with issues of race and other multicultural issues in all counselor education courses?

Although these questions are not addressed directly in this chapter, they frame descriptions of the methods and approaches we use in our classroom instruction across the counselor education curriculum as well as discussions of the personal issues that students bring to the multicultural class. This chapter presents a theoretical paradigm based on a model developed by Paulo Freire, the renowned Brazilian educator (Freire, 1973, 1985, 1993, 1994; Gadotti, 1994; Shor & Freire, 1987). The chapter then describes innovative teaching techniques that use Freire's paradigm and provide our students opportunity to share individual cultural realities, and discusses the essential components for implementing Freire's paradigm.

FREIRE'S PARADIGM

Freire's theoretical framework is chosen for three reasons:

- His general critique of education presents an analysis that challenges the neutrality of the models dominant in U.S. schools. Freire argued that any curriculum that ignores racism, sexism, the exploitation of workers, and other forms of oppression is one that sanctions, sustains, and even promotes continuing dehumanization of the oppressor and the oppressed. Culturally competent counselors have the responsibility to recognize and challenge the neutrality of the traditional psychology and counseling theories and models (Ivey, 1993).

- In Freire's framework, oppression is described as *cultural invasion*, a tool of oppression in which members of the dominant culture impose not only their values on the oppressed but also the very definition of self that the oppressor holds of the oppressed.* The oppressed begin to define themselves as the oppressor defines them. Enhancing self-definition is the essence of culturally competent counseling.

- Freire's critical, mutual pedagogy provides concrete methods for implementing *conscientizacao*, the development or awakening of critical awareness, a primary goal of counseling (Freire, 1993). Freire's processes of awareness raising, encouragement to action, and vigorous reflection are essential to the preparation of culturally competent counselors.

Freire proposed a cultural action for freedom, describing it as *cultural synthesis*, in which the dominant group enters into a true partnership with the dominated group and promotes developing its own means for attaining authentic education. Education is to be the path to permanent liberation and involves two phases. In the first, people become aware ("conscientized") of their oppression; the second (praxis) is a lifelong process of liberating cultural action and reflection.

Effective teaching for the purpose of preparing culturally competent counselors involves both "conscientization" and praxis phases and includes raising awareness, encouragement to action, and vigorous reflection. In raising awareness, Freire described four stages: intransitive, semi-intransitive, naive transitive, and critically transitive. Moving from semi-intransitive awareness to naive transitive awareness might happen without the help of educational intervention because of the "strength of infrastructural transformations;" but choosing critical transitivity rather than naive transitivity is a transformation that requires "serious educational effort" (Freire, 1994, p. 102). Thus the Freirian stages of consciousness/awareness require comprehensive, integrative effort across the counselor education curriculum and in all aspects of the counselor education program.

---

*There is no question that the history of psychology and counseling has been that of cultural invasion. Historical evidence abounds. An example is Carl Jung's statement to the second Psychoanalytic Congress in 1910—which provoked neither outrage nor challenge:

> The cause of repression can be found in the specific American Complex, namely, to the living together with lower races, especially with Negroes. Living together with barbaric races exerts a suggestive effect on the laboriously tamed instinct of the White race and tends to pull it down. (Thomas & Sillen, 1991, p. 14)

Intransitive

Freire's first stage is intransitive. Verbs that do not act upon an object are intransitive. Intransitive individuals do not influence their environment. They are not even conscious that they can influence their environment. They are frozen in such a way that they have lost a sense of their humanity and of their culture.

Awareness of and action upon reality are two constituents of a critical relationship with the world. Awareness or consciousness that does not challenge the world is uncritical and intransitive; object self is acted upon by the world. Thus the first phase in the emergence of consciousness, in raising awareness, is to develop an awareness of subject self, that is, of one who acts on the world.

Surprisingly, some students who come to a counselor education program manifest some signs of this stage. One student shared a personal journey through a class that used the Freirian model to prepare culturally competent counselors:

> The class gave me the strength to accept who I am as being Hispanic. Because for a while there I didn't want to accept it because according to my bringing up, my background, whatever, it was saying White is superior and you should look up to White. You have to follow the White person's ways. So at the same time it [the class] released me—I was kind of stuck in the middle. I really didn't want to be White and I didn't want to be Hispanic. So now I'm where I accept the Whites as being who they are, and I accept who I am and—for me—I need to work on who I am.

By means of raised awareness and encouragement to action, this student moved from being object (acted upon by the environment) to being subject (acting upon the environment). This student is moving toward critical consciousness, toward a lifelong journey of liberating cultural action and reflection.

Semi-Intransitive

The second stage, semi-intransitive, is the state of those whose sphere of perception is limited by the needs of basic survival. Because they focus on the immediate essentials of food, clothing, and shelter, they are impervious to challenges situated outside the demands of biological necessity.

Freire observed that persons in this stage can amplify their power to perceive and respond to suggestions and questions arising in their context, and can increase their capacity to enter into dialogue not only with others but also with their own world. Where before they reacted only to particulars, now they are empowered to react to the general scope of a particular issue. Their consciousness becomes transitive.

In a counselor education program, students often manifest concerns related to survival that may be indirectly physical; these apprehensions are directly related to their personal survival in the program:

> I started this program with I'm going to be in this program for *me*. It's whatever it takes for *me* to get to the top. I don't care who I have to run over. I admit I felt like

that. We just all look out for number one. But after reading this book [Freire, 1993], to me, several of us have formed such close bonds and friendships because we've knocked down the barriers and the walls. [long pause]

I don't want to be oppressed by my classmates, and I don't want to oppress them. [long pause]

I think that we all respect that from each other. [long pause]

What does *oppressed* mean in that context [counselor education program]? Getting to the top and *squishing* whomever. [long pause]

Respect, helping . . . we're on a team now. We don't compete with each other. Competing to me was a really big issue when I first joined this [counselor education] program. I felt like, "I don't know if I can compete on this level." I felt like we were all in this huge race, and it depended upon who got to the finish line first won. Now after reading this [Freire, 1993], we're all just kind of arm-in-arm going together. It's like a group effort and we're all going together. It's not just a *me* thing. It's a *we* thing now. [long pause]

I don't believe this book [Freire, 1993] formed the bonds that many of us have with one another, but I believe it laid the groundwork for us to break down our walls and really get to know each other [African American, Hispanic American, European American] on an equal level.

This student is discovering and responding to suggestions and questions arising in the context of the counselor education program and is increasing the capacity to enter into dialogue not only with the other members of the program but also with personal experience in the environment. Previously this student reacted only to the particulars of personal success; now the student is empowered to succeed in the context of shared achievement with others who are now seen as friends rather than competitors. The journey is toward transitive consciousness.

Naive Transitive

The beginning of self-directed consciousness is the third stage, naive transitive. Naive transitive individuals oversimplify a problem, have nostalgia for the past, underestimate ordinary people, and have strong tendencies to gregariousness. They are disinterested in investigation, have a fascination with fanciful explanations of reality, and are romantic in the way they view the world. They are quick to accept common myths and slogans; they are easily manipulated; they have the tendency to blame the victim; and they practice polemics rather than dialogue.

Freire observed that this stage is never totally and irrevocably surpassed. For all who enter the learning process, the journey from naive transitive remains a lifelong task. Students of counselor education often think, feel, and behave in this stage, especially when dealing with issues of cultural diversity. Students will feel some pain as they walk through the journey of a Freirian-based educational experience.

Some White students shared that they were not taught prejudice in their families and that they became conscious of their own prejudices only after their participation in education for critical consciousness/awareness in the counselor education program. Other White students shared that they feel angry when their motives for friendship with people of color are challenged. Students have said that they have told clients that it is easy to meet their goals when they know how; these counselors in training believe that if they tell a client who has suffered oppression that it is easy to achieve his or her goals and even tell him or her how to achieve the goals, the client will understand and act. A classic example of naive transitive is a student who says, when speaking of feelings about clients of color, "I see a blank slate." Or as another student stated,

> I am so tired of all the attention to race. When I look at you [African American counselor educator] I don't see color. When I look at you I see you first as a person and later as Black. I think it would be prejudiced to see you as Black first. And I believe that your focus on color hurts you more than if you saw yourself as a person first.

This student was expressing a prevalent view among dominant culture European Americans. When the student was asked to explore how people come to be defined, the importance of people defining themselves, and the place of power in the defining process, he seemed to have valued the dialogue and later expressed to the class his own definitions of himself and how race was a part of his self-definition.

Human interaction in general is complex; when culture or race are included in the context, the interaction becomes more complicated and even enigmatic. A naive transitive understanding of relationships will not suffice for a culturally competent counselor. The counselor education program that uses the Freirian model continually challenges the students to think critically, act dialogically, and reflect on their thoughts, feelings, and behaviors.

Critically Transitive

The journey of counselor education students toward cultural competence includes struggle with becoming critically transitive, Freire's fourth stage. In this stage, which is characterized by depth and clarity, problems can be posed, interpreted, and solved; observations can be tested; and reflection is expanded to allow for revision and reconstruction.

One student with an undergraduate degree in philosophy had completed more than half the counselor education courses in a Freirian-based program. In reflecting on the personal journey toward critical consciousness, he told this story:

> I think this book [Freire, 1993] affected me really personally because to me it was like my putting the words to a journey that I took. All my life I felt that I was oppressed. . . . When I was in high school, I didn't know who I wanted to be or what I wanted to be . . . . I had an ontological problem because I didn't know how to be. . . . I thought, "Oh, this is what I did, these are the steps that I took to become the person that I am—to become free and to be. . . ."

Critical consciousness is distinguished by an openness to new knowledge and insight that leads to action. Passivity is rejected. Relationships become dialogical rather than polemic. Action is based on critical reflection. Critical consciousness is a goal of counselor education.

Using the Freirian model, students become "protagonists of their own stories" (H. Torres Karna, personal communication, April 2, 1996). For example, as one student shared,

> Some of us are bilingual. We spoke Spanish at home. When we went to school, we had to speak English. What would that tell us? That would tell me, "Look I'm not worthy; being Hispanic must be bad because when I go to school I have to hide it."

Another counselor education student presents workshops on special education to the students in a school of education in a local university. When this student changed the format of the presentation from lecture to dialogue, the activity was described as electrifying, invigorating, and energizing. Dialogue resulted in participants describing the presenter as genuine. This student was practicing what she learned in the counselor education program. An effective way to prepare counselor education students to listen effectively to the stories of their clients, and to apply what they learned to the dialogical education they will be doing in schools and agencies, is to listen to their stories in the counselor education program.

INNOVATIVE PEDAGOGY USING FREIRE'S PARADIGM

How can the Freirian model be implemented in counselor education? This section considers innovative pedagogy using Freire's paradigm first by reflecting upon aspects of students' cultural reality, looking behind immediate cultural situations to determine their root sources, and examining the implications and consequences of the issues. In each of these areas, reflections on being raised in an environment of bigotry, reflections on others defining the self, and reflections on rejection serve as illustrations. The section then further considers innovative pedagogy through helping students become aware of the need for action focused on the cultural issues identified by the Freirian process.

Reflecting Upon Aspects of Students' Cultural Reality

When the Freirian model is used in counselor education, there is substantial opportunity to share individual cultural reality. As Freire (1993) used the cultural reality of the Brazilian peasants to teach them to read and change their environment, authentic reflection on lived experience can be used to help counselor trainees become critically conscious and engage in praxis. Three examples follow.

Reflection on being raised in an environment of bigotry. A student shared the struggle of being raised in an environment of prejudice:

- I have hope. I was raised in a prejudiced environment, and everything that I know about multiculturalism and allowing people of different cultures than myself to be in my life I had to learn, and it's been an experience for me. It's something I consciously had to work at. I'm on the right track, and maybe I can make a difference.

Reflections on others defining me. Some students have experienced having others tell them who they are and have had to grapple with the consequent feelings:

- *Student One:* My mother is Spanish. Clerks continuously tell me that I am Hispanic. They tell me I am Hispanic because I have a Spanish surname. No amount of explaining can change their minds.
- *Student Two:* When I went to pick up my birth certificate in the process of finding information about my birth mother, a clerk told me I was not adopted. I've been told that I was adopted for 44 years. I could not convince the clerk that I was adopted.

Reflection on rejection. This student shared a painful experience in a counselor education program:

- After one class in which I was rejected by some of the other students, I felt maybe I did not belong in the program. I would have quit except for the support of the professor and of other students who came to me personally and on the telephone with encouraging words. I had been thinking, "Maybe I don't belong in this program. Maybe I'm saying something wrong; maybe I'm not supposed to be so vocal." With the professor talking to me and having other students in the class back me up, that really kept me. It made me feel I'm OK. Some people may not agree with my views. I remember thinking whether to call the professor and let the professor know what's going on because I felt real bad and I didn't like feeling that way. If I did not get this support, I would have quit. Clients do the same thing; they quit coming to counseling when they are treated like I was treated.

Looking Behind Immediate Cultural Situations to Determine Their Root Sources

Illustrations of looking behind immediate cultural situations to determine root sources based on student testimonials are helpful in understanding how the Freirian model can be implemented in counselor education.

Reflection on being raised in an environment of bigotry.   Students obtain historical information and reflect on the antecedents of present family bigotry and attitudes and behaviors toward diversity. This can include any of the content included in the Locke paradigm, for example, personal and global issues, acculturation, sociopolitical factors, and family structure (Locke, 1998). The words of one student are illustrative:

- Sometimes I wonder if I'm really changing anything. My family is somewhat bigoted, and there are certain words my family won't say in front of me any more. I'm trying so hard, and I'm still from this White suppressive family that believes everyone else is . . . all these things . . . out of ignorance. Maybe I am making a little bit of difference; maybe I can change things.

Reflection on others defining me.
Students investigate the distorted perceptions that others have of them and the reasons that others try to define them. The following dialogue is growth producing and illustrative of what happens in a supportive, challenging, counselor education class based on the Freirian paradigm:

- *Student One:* The other students in the class were not used to my interpretation; they didn't know who I was, and they weren't used to a person of color who was very vocal; they did not expect me to know what I was talking about. I have extensive experiences working as a case worker. Going into that classroom where I thought everybody already banded together, I felt that I was an intruder. "We'll have to check this one out, too vocal; we're not going to accept. . . ."
- *Student Two:* Not only were you an intruder, you were an intruder of color. They stereotyped you immediately as being militant.
- *Student Three:* Maybe it scared some people in there. They felt they needed to protect what they saw as their own territory.
- *Student One:* Instead of telling me, "I really don't agree with your views; I feel really offended," they attacked me. I think a similar thing can happen in counseling.

Reflection on rejection.   When racism surfaces in class in the way students treat one another, and value or devalue the contributions of one another, an opportunity for growth exists. Counselor educators have an ethical responsibility to address the situation by examining the source of the behavior, changing behavior and attitudes inappropriate for a culturally competent counselor, and developing communication skills. It must be made clear to the perpetrators that their behavior is not tolerated in the program, and they must be encouraged to tell the "devalued student" or the "student with devalued views" how they feel about these expressed perspectives, in an appropriate manner. Students must be taught to disagree without attacking others. In addition, they must be told that the counselor educator will not support unacceptable behavior and that the counselor educator will support the person under attack by facilitating dialogue. Furthermore, it must be made very clear to students who may feel devalued by fellow students that the counselor educator values them and supports them, and that the counselor educator will facilitate disagreements in a dialogical manner equitably.

Examining the Implications and Consequences of the Issues

In a Freirian-based class, counselor trainees discuss the implications and consequences of the issues raised as they share their stories. The counselor educator paraphrases their reality and uses dialogue to teach necessary content. Students have testified that dialogue among students and counselor educator is one of the most meaningful learning experiences.

Reflection on being raised in an environment of bigotry.   As students learn that they have come out of an experience of prejudice and rejection of diversity, they examine the implications and consequences with specific activities. For example, they may engage in the White Privilege Activity (McIntosh, 1988), which provides an opportunity through discussion of privilege for dialogue in a multicultural counseling class. Reflecting on culturally accepted behaviors that are defined by privilege provides opportunity for development of understanding that the oppressed are victimized not only by the isms and all they represent but also by the arrogance of the privileged.

In the activity, McIntosh (1988) has provided counselor education students from traditionally privileged groups with the opportunity to challenge their use of power and privilege and to examine and redefine the terms upon which culturally different individuals respond to them. She has also provided an opportunity for counselor education students from traditionally devalued groups the opportunity to challenge their reactions to feeling powerless and without privilege in specific situations. Using her framework, students may examine and redefine the terms upon which they might have given individuals from the dominant culture the license to dominate them. Thus the use of this source as a means for Freirian dialogue can move counselor education students toward critical consciousness.

Reflection on others defining me.   Students from devalued groups have had many experiences of others defining them. Professors have the responsibility to provide a supportive environment in which students will feel comfortable being assertive:

- *Student One:* Where do you come from?
- *Student Two:* I was born in Texas.
- *Student One:* Where did your parents come from?
- *Student Two:* My parents were born in Texas. If you want me to tell you, my grandparents were born in Texas when Texas was part of Mexico. My ances-

tors were here before any of your ancestors. You would not ask that question of another White person; you ask me that question because you think I was born in Mexico and because I am a person of color.

The above dialogue is not unusual in Texas. Brown-skinned people are frequently suspected of being illegal immigrants even when they are TexMex, that is, members of families whose ancestors can be traced to the original people of the territory. To help counselors in training think about how people of color are judged irrationally, introduce Carter's (1976) book *The Education of Little Tree*, and this quotation: "Grandpa said ye had to understand. But most people didn't want to—it was too much trouble—so they used words to cover their own laziness and called other folks 'shiftless' " (p. 85). Then ask, "Is there a time when you were judged on something other than your merit? Can you describe how it felt?" Our experiences reveal that almost all students respond to this question in the affirmative. Their feelings help them move to an empathic and understanding view of how culturally different individuals feel when they are similarly judged.

Reflection on rejection. The concept of culture by itself is not enough to describe how people get along and live their lives. This concept, in the hands of students who lack an understanding of the integrity and autonomy of communities whose cultural identities are different from their own, can be dangerous, reinforcing and perpetuating stereotypes leading to further rejection. Even when students begin to understand the multicultural counseling complex, they must experience various cultures as nearly as possible as those who live the culture on a daily basis. Reading about different cultures is not sufficient; reading by different cultures is more helpful. Obviously, we are convinced that a didactic course is not sufficient. A student may be able to learn the whats and hows of culturally different groups in a didactic class, but not the whys. The salient questions can only be answered within a dialogical model such as the one provided by Freire (1985, 1993):

- Why do those who do not belong to the dominant mainstream culture resist efforts of that mainstream society to assimilate them?
- Why do so many from traditionally devalued groups remain marginalized despite the best efforts of the dominant mainstream society to help them?
- Why do so many individuals from traditionally devalued groups continue to have problems with their education despite enormous resources being expended by well-meaning people and programs?

Persons from traditionally privileged groups and persons from traditionally devalued groups can best be in counselor education programs in which the pedagogy is Freirian. Counselor training approaches or methods that target only the mainstream dominant culture, no matter how well meaning, will not succeed. They are inherently Eurocentric and racist. They exclude the very people the program is trying to teach the counselors in training to counsel. Our approach is to foster an environment of rational dialogue in an atmosphere of mutual support and challenge.

Related to the issue of rejection is the issue of qualification. Some clients come to counseling thinking that they have been discriminated against just because a person of color was promoted to a position they think they should have had. Many European American men are socialized to compete with other European American men but not with women or men of color. European American men and women need help in restructuring their cognitions on the matter of merit. For example, men and women of color who have consistently seen European Americans promoted when it was they who had earned the position know what it feels like to be judged by their color and not their achievement.

Helping Students Become Aware of the Need for Action

In counselor education, students reflect on the rationale and the manner in which interventions in schools and agencies consciously plan to develop all clients from the youngest ages. Counselor education students are aware that the answer to the question, "How am I to be?" is an ongoing one answered iteratively and in successively complex ways again and again over their professional life span. Culturally competent counselors name, reflect, and act on their *being* journey knowing that they are influenced by many cultures in the process. There is no room in a Freirian model for a them-and-us posture; only for us thinking, feeling, and acting together dialogically. Thus the cultural issues that have been collectively identified by culturally diverse students participating in the Freirian process need action.

An activity that can help counselor education students become operationally aware of a need for action in providing inclusive opportunities for their clients, especially in school settings, is to ask the students to identify 10 great people in history and follow this up by asking these students to identify 10 great people in the history of counseling or psychology. Often the results are 10 DWEMs (dead white European or European American males) in answer to both questions. It is rare to have a single student identify a female or a person of color in either list. Then have students explore the reasons that they listed people as they did. They sometimes conclude that women and men of color have contributed to history in general and to the history of psychology and counseling in particular. The next step is for students to consider how their answering these questions the way they did is salient to their preparation as culturally competent counselors. Counselor educators may provide students with an opportunity to reflect on the reasons that considerations of race, gender, and culture should be topics to be discussed, not only in counselor education but also in counseling with clients: If not, why not? If so, when and how?

This activity provides a teachable moment to point out that representatives of diverse racial and cultural groups and of both sexes, including those who have been erased from history by reductionism, have shaped civilizations and the profession of counseling. The conceptual framework out of which each counselor works indicates whether or not he or she is inclusive or exclusive of broad contributions to history and to counseling.

If in this activity students of color mention women or men of color in their answers, the difference between the responses of the White students and the students of color provides another opportunity to develop critical consciousness. Counselor educators may explore the reasons that women and students of color found significant contributions among people with whom they personally identify.

An experience in which anger and fear are felt and analyzed in a supportive classroom can be a tool for developing critical awareness/consciousness as well as for helping students become aware of the need for action. Myrdal (1944) found in his germinal study that European Americans feared African Americans' anger. In a climate that fosters growth, African American students can be encouraged to express their anger, European American students to express their fear. For example, one of the authors described his fruitful use of anger and how it helps to develop critical consciousness in the counselor education students as follows:

> I let students know that I am not only tired of the oppression to which I and other groups are subjected, but that I am tired of my fellow men dropping dead 8 years earlier than women from stress; I am tired of my fellow African Americans dropping dead 12 years earlier than European Americans from the stresses of being oppressed.
>
> I let students know it is not my anger that pushes students out of educational institutions; nor does my anger hire people and then bulldoze them out of the system. My anger does not cause women and students of color to feel crushed and oppressed by their environments; my anger does not cause gay men and lesbian women to hide their identities for fear of their lives; my anger does not prevent people with disabilities from attempting many routine tasks in educational and employment arenas.
>
> I let students know that my anger is an honest response to a dishonest situation. My anger is creative in that it is turned into energy to acknowledge racism and to eradicate racism. All of my students can grow as a result of my sharing my anger with them in creative ways.

ESSENTIAL COMPONENTS FOR IMPLEMENTING FREIRE'S PARADIGM

Freire's theoretical framework provides counselor educators with a paradigm in which to think of the development of culturally competent counselors, but there are additional requirements if his pedagogy is to be authentically operative. These include recruiting and retaining faculty and students from traditionally devalued populations, modeling process and content, creating dialogue, and tapping the lived experiences of students.

1. Recruit and Retain Faculty and Students From Traditionally Devalued Populations

Recruiting and retaining faculty and students from historically devalued populations are essential to the development of culturally competent counselors. The more diverse the faculty and student body, the more effectively culturally competent counselors can be prepared. Cultural competence cannot be lectured; it has to be demonstrated and experienced. It can only be practiced in a culturally diverse program that implements education for liberation. Furthermore, students of the dominant mainstream culture can not adequately be taught about racism unless the faculty and student members of the counselor education program represent the cultural mix of the clients that the students are being prepared to serve.

- *Student One:* What brought me to this point . . . other people were reacting . . . and were sharing. . . . I was thinking, if for me to say "I've been oppressed" feels comfortable in here, I can also transfer it somewhere outside the classroom. If you're not going to judge me or say something bad and walk out of the room and never talk to me—if I had not had this freedom in the classroom, then I would not have applied it outside the classroom.

2. Model Process and Content

Modeling process and content is essential for counselor educators. For example, chairs can be placed in a circle so that students can dialogue facing one another, and so that when professors sit, they are on the same level and in the same type of chair as students.

- *Student One:* When you look at the very way the class was conducted, we were all equal participants. There was no oppression in the classroom, and I think being able to participate in that kind of a society—granted a very small society—was a living example of how you don't have to have oppression inflicted on you.
- *Student Two:* During class we all brought certain things about ourselves to class . . . and these different aspects contributed to make one large picture of diversity. Diversity was respected.

3. Create Dialogue

The necessary content in counselor education can be taught in a context of dialogue. Assigned readings provide the salient issues that are essential components to the dialogue. Counselor educators using the Freirian model encourage students to make the commitment to complete assigned readings carefully by the time they come to class.

- *Student One:* I'm beginning to see the cycle in the community. The women in my community need education. Education will cause a whole lot of turmoil in their lives. Often, our women only know how to be one way.
- *Student Two:* This is an ontological problem; they don't know how to be. Maybe White United States Americans have had this knowledge of self from the beginning, whereas I don't think I did.
- *Student Three:* It's amazing how this model makes me feel so much more competent. It makes me feel so much more knowledgeable. It makes me want to go on. I am more confident. I am encouraged to do more. I feel better. Really, I'm smart.
- *Student Two:* One consequence of oppression is that one doesn't have the awareness of possibilities. I had a lot of awareness and no opportunity.
- *Student Four:* The class allowed us to see how different people in the class experienced oppression. Hispanic, adopted, African American. It could not have happened in every class. The people in our class were very open. If I had not felt that openness, I would not have been quite as sharing.

Counselor educators have the responsibility to model dialogue that enhances the degree of openness and sharing just illustrated. Authentic, productive, worthwhile sharing takes place maximally in a classroom distinguished by diversity.

4. Tap the Lived Experience of Students

By using the lived experiences of the students, counselor trainees in a Freirian-based counselor education program are given the opportunity to strengthen their own critical consciousness.

- *Student One:* It's not that I'm always suspicious. I'm not, but if I get a certain feeling about a person, I'm going to pay attention to it. It's almost always in the back of my mind.
- *Student Two:* I use the Freirian model with my five kids. The modeling of sharing in class has changed me as a parent and as a future counselor.
- *Student Three:* Previously, I felt comfortable with people infringing on and belittling my reality. When I realized that my reality really matters, then I could be open and willing to allow the reality of others into mine. OK, this is what I see and believe, but what do you see and believe? Freire changed my relationship with others personally and professionally.

If students are going to respect the testimonies of their classmates, they must be given the opportunity to reflect on the issue of objectivity. Counselor educators must confirm that the notion of objectivity is a romantic fantasy, that simply does not exist. The important factor is to know one's own biases and not let them interfere with the ability to hear others whether in the counselor education program or in the counseling setting. The pseudostance of objectivity must be undermined. The falsehood of the objective voice, heralded for so long as the only appropriate voice in academia, is no voice at all because it is inauthentic. It only serves the status quo.

SUMMARY

Counselor educators cannot claim to be the spokespersons for devalued groups or privileged groups, either marginalized or mainstream, but rather the voices of the facilitators of liberation. Teaching is much more than "it looks that way to me." The Freirian paradigm provides a framework for what education must be: a process of reflective, integrative, and participative thought, feeling, and practice. The methods described in this chapter include examining the origins, influences, and directions of social issues from the point of view of all who participate in the action and from the points of view of the diverse students in the classroom who reflect on the action. A truly integrative, exciting, and effective teaching method must critically analyze a system of interactions and institutions in which cultural problems or social issues arise. In addition to employing teaching methodologies that illustrate several differing forms of knowledge, effective counselor educators of multicultural counseling integrate their own and their students' experiences. This can be accomplished maximally only in a setting that is itself diverse, and in which students and counselor educators represent the populations to be served by the counselor trainees.

Interactive techniques are designed to create dialogue with the intent of making students think about the course content and talk to one another about their experiences and how they are related to the course content. Teachers must give fully of themselves while teaching, must go beyond the mere transmission of information by lecture. In doing so, counselor educators will provide their students an opportunity to move toward the lifelong journey of critical consciousness in order to be culturally competent counselors.

REFERENCES

Carter, F. (1976). *The education of Little Tree.* Albuquerque: University of New Mexico.

Freire, P. (1973). *Education for critical consciousness.* New York: Continuum.

Freire, P. (1985). *The politics of education: Culture, power, and liberation* (D. Macedo, Trans.). South Hadley, MA: Bergin & Garvey.

Freire, P. (1993). *Pedagogy of the oppressed* (Rev. 20th anniversary ed., M. B. Ramos, Trans.). New York: Continuum.

Freire, P. (1994). *Pedagogy of hope: Reliving pedagogy of the oppressed* (R. R. Barr, Trans.). New York: Continuum.

Gadotti, M. (1994). Reading Paulo Freire: His life and work (J. Milton, Trans.). Albany: State University of New York Press.

Ivey, A. E. (1993, February). *Psychotherapy as liberation: Multicultural counseling and therapy at the center of our practice.* Paper presented at the Annual Columbia University Teachers College Winter Roundtable on Cross-Cultural Counseling and Psychotherapy, New York.

Locke, D. C. (1998). *Increasing multicultural understanding: A comprehensive model.* Newbury Park, CA: Sage.

McIntosh, P. (1988). *White privilege and male privilege: A personal account of coming to see correspondence through work in women's studies* (Working Paper 189). Wellesley, MA: Wellesley College Center for Research on Women.

Myrdal, G. (1944). *An American dilemma.* New York: Harper.

Shor, I., & Freire, P. (1987). *A pedagogy for liberation: Dialogues on transforming education.* South Hadley, MA: Bergin & Garvey.

Thomas, A., & Sillen, S. (1991). *Racism and psychiatry.* New York: Carol.

4 Understanding the Different Psychological Dispositions of White Racism: A Comprehensive Model for Counselor Educators and Practitioners

Michael D'Andrea and Judy Daniels

One of the most serious tragedies that continues to scar our nation involves the various ways in which White racism is perpetuated in our modern society. Although many White Americans think this problem was largely taken care of during the civil rights movement (D'Andrea, 1996), there is an abundance of evidence that points to the fact that White racism continues to have a serious toxic effect on the lives of millions of persons in the United States.

Examples of how White racism continues to be perpetuated in our society include the frequent reports of individual acts of racial violence and harassment that occur on many school and university campuses (Feagin & Vera, 1995; Harvey, 1991; Magner, 1989) as well as numerous acts of racial discrimination and intolerance that continue to be manifested in many businesses and communities across the nation (Cose, 1993; Feagin & Vera, 1995; Southern Poverty Law Center, 1997). Beyond these individual acts of racism, more insidious and impactful forms of institutionalized racism continue to impact large numbers of non-White persons negatively. Examples of institutional racism include the disproportionate number of African American, Hispanic American, and Native American persons who are currently unemployed, undereducated, in prisons, and living in poverty in this country (D'Andrea, 1992). Other indicators of this ongoing national dilemma include both the apathetic and increasingly hostile reactions many White persons have to the various forms of racism just listed (D'Andrea & Daniels, 1994).

Denying the Pervasive Nature of the Problem

Given the numerous ways in which White racism continues to affect a large segment of our citizenry adversely, why are not more time, energy, and resources used to address this social pathology? Major factors that contribute to the lack of attention and resources directed at ameliorating racism in our society include the widespread sense of denial that many Whites exhibit in responding to this issue. There are several reasons why many White persons tend to deny that this problem continues to exist in our nation. One is that the perpetuation of racism represents a serious moral contradiction for those persons who genuinely support the democratic principles upon which our nation is based. This moral contradiction is reflected in the fact that although the United States is based on principles promoting the notion of "justice for all," millions of non-White persons continue routinely to experience various forms of racial discrimination that negatively impact the opportunities they have for personal, educational, and career advancement (Bowser & Hunt, 1996; Cose, 1993; Jones, 1997). Thus, given the complex and negative nature of this contradiction, many White persons avoid dealing with the moral underpinnings of this dilemma by believing instead that racial discrimination simply does not exist in the United States, or at least not to the degree that many scholars report.

Another reason is that many White people feel personally helpless in terms of being able to address this complex problem effectively. As a result, many White persons are likely to cope with this serious problem by denying that it exists. Counseling practitioners are well aware of the common use of denial as a coping mechanism when individuals are confronted with problems they feel relatively helpless to do much about.

Yet another reason is that confronting the problem of racism necessitates addressing the various ways in which individuals benefit from White privilege in our modern society (McIntosh, 1989). However, because many White persons react defensively to the notion that their racial background provides them with various privileges in our society, they tend to downplay the existence of racism and the negative impact that it has on large numbers of people in our nation. It has been hypothesized that much of the apathy that White persons (including many well-meaning counselor educators, practitioners, and students) demonstrate toward the problem of racism represents a defense mechanism that effectively distances them from the responsibility of dealing with the uncomfortable issue of White privilege (D'Andrea, Locke, & Daniels, 1997).

Although these reasons help explain why many White persons operate from a state of apathy and denial when it comes to dealing with racism, much more research is needed to expand our understanding of the different types of reactions these individuals have to this broad-based social pathology.

Investigating the Psychology of White Racism

To gain a better understanding of the psychology of White racism, we have been involved in an ongoing exploratory research project that has extended over the past 15 years. Our approach to researching White racism is different from many of the other studies that have been done in this area in the past. Rather than focusing on the ways in which White racism impacts people of color (as has been the case in most of the studies done in this area), we intentionally directed our attention to the persons who are fundamentally responsible for perpetuating this problem in our society. For this reason, we primarily focused on the reactions that White persons have toward racism and the current state of race relations in the United States.

To date, this exploratory study has involved more than 1,200 White persons who reside in the northeastern, southeastern, midwestern, southwestern, and far western parts of the United States. These persons come from a broad range of socioeconomic backgrounds and include unemployed White persons, doctors, lawyers, state legislators, law enforcement personnel, ministers, business persons, teachers, psychologists, social workers, university professors, undergraduate and graduate students at public and private universities, professional counselors, and counselor educators. Although we intentionally studied the ways in which these persons responded to issues related to racism and the state of race relations in our nation, much of our research involved assessing the reactions counselor educators, practitioners, and graduate students had to these issues.

There were two primary reasons for directing attention to these persons. First, as members of the counseling profession, we were particularly interested in assessing how counselor educators, practitioners, and graduate students think, feel, and behaviorally respond to the various forms of racism that exist in the United States. To our knowledge, no research has been conducted to examine the ways in which counselor educators, practitioners, and graduate students react to the problem of racism in these ways. Second, we hoped that our findings would help generate new ideas about the types of interventions counselor educators and practitioners could use to deal more effectively with the complex problem of White racism in our society.

By using a variety of research approaches (i.e., naturalistic research techniques, semistructured interviews, participant-observation, and field studies), we were able to record a broad range of cognitive, affective, and behavioral reactions that White persons exhibited when discussing issues related to racism and race relations in the United States. A synthesis of these reactions led to the identification of five distinct "psychological dispositions" of White racism. These psychological dispositions are characterized by qualitatively different cognitive, affective, and behavioral reactions individuals have to the problem of racism. (A more detailed description of our research methods and findings is available in D'Andrea and Daniels, 1998.)

The findings that were generated from this exploratory study have important implications for the work of counselor educators and practitioners. Given the different cognitive, affective, and behavioral reactions individuals have to racism, it is important that counselor educators and practitioners determine which dispositions are dominant among the persons with whom they are working. By doing so, they are better positioned intentionally to select interventions that will (1) foster more complex ways of thinking about racism, (2) stimulate more passionate emotional and empathic responses toward those persons who are victimized by the perpetuation of racism, and (3) promote the development of various skills that White persons can use to address the problem of racism in our society effectively.

With this in mind, this chapter is designed to serve two purposes. One is to provide descriptions of the different cognitive, affective, and behavioral characteristics that are associated with the five psychological dispositions of White racism that emerged from our research (Affective-Impulsive Rational, Liberal, Principled, and Principled Activistic). The other purpose is to present intervention strategies that counselor educators and practitioners may find useful in fostering healthier and more effective ways of dealing with the problem of White racism among students and clients who exhibit characteristics associated the different dispositions in our model.

AFFECTIVE-IMPULSIVE DISPOSITION OF WHITE RACISM

Characteristics

Cognitive characteristics.   Persons manifesting this disposition are characterized by a cognitive style that reflects simple, hostile, and oftentimes illogical ways of thinking about individuals from different racial groups. Statements reflecting this sort of racist cognitive perspective include such base remarks as, "Niggers are lazy good for nothings," and "I don't like those Asian gooks because they're only trying to take over America by buying all kinds of land and stuff" (D'Andrea & Daniels, 1994, p. 77).

These reactions reflect a delay in the development of an individual's ability accurately to conceptualize similarities and differences among persons from different racial and ethnic groups. This developmental delay helps explain many of the inaccurate cognitions and stereotypes that are associated with this psychological disposition. Feagin and Vera (1995) provided a good description of the type of thinking that characterizes this disposition:

> The cognitive notions and stereotypes of contemporary racism, which include myths of the dangerous Black man, the lazy Black person, the Black woman's fondness for welfare, and Black inferiority and incompetence, makes as little empirical sense as the hostile fictions that underlay the Nazi Holocaust. However, such anti-Black fictions are sincerely held by many Whites. (p. 12)

Affective characteristics.   This psychological disposition is also marked by heightened feelings of hostility and aggressiveness toward persons from non-White racial groups. Persons manifesting this psychological disposition do not appear to be ashamed or embarrassed by openly and publicly expressing the negative feelings they have toward non-White persons. Although the affective hostility associated with this disposition is reinforced by the inaccurate and stereotypic thinking just described, it is often fueled by what appears to be a deep-seated anger and hatred toward non-White persons in general.

Behavioral characteristics.   Persons who manifest an Affective-Impulsive Disposition frequently demonstrate marginal impulse control when reacting to non-White persons. This results in a variety of behaviors that range from physical violence (e.g., participating in beatings of non-White persons) to destroying or defacing property (e.g., burning African American churches, painting obscene racial graffiti on buildings, participating in cross burnings) to making openly hostile and demeaning comments about non-White persons. Locke's (1992) discussion of "overt-intentional forms of racism" accurately described the types of behavioral reactions commonly associated with persons who operate from this disposition.

As might be expected, none of the counselor educators, practitioners, or graduate students included in our study of White racism manifested characteristics associated with this psychological disposition. We did encounter a number of persons (e.g., clients with whom we worked, individuals who identified themselves as members of hate groups, and some students who were enrolled in public universities) who manifested many of the cognitive, affective, and behavioral characteristics of this psychological disposition. However, it is possible that such individuals might enroll in multicultural training classes as a part of their requirements for some degree. It is also possible that a rare counseling student or candidate for a graduate degree in education who is highly racist may slip through the admissions screening process and be accepted for training. For this reason, counselor educators need to be prepared to deal with these individuals should they appear in the classroom.

The descriptions of the cognitive, affective, and behavioral characteristics associated with the Affective-Impulsive Disposition are likely to conjure images of persons who are affiliated with the Ku Klux Klan, Skinheads, and other hate groups, but it is a mistake to limit thinking in this way. In fact, history has shown that even well-respected leaders in business and government have demonstrated characteristics that are linked to the Affective-Impulsive Disposition. This includes insensitive and obscene comments made by the President of the United States and some of his advisers during the 1980s. As Feagin and Vera (1995) reported,

> During the 1980s then president Ronald Reagan spoke of "welfare queens." Reagan cabinet member Terrell Bell, a moderate Republican, complained that middle level White aides in the Reagan White House told racist jokes, referred to Dr. Martin Luther King as "Martin Lucifer Coon," spoke of Arabs as "sand niggers," and called Title IX the "lesbians' bill of rights." (p. 25)

Recommendations for Affective-Impulsive Disposition Intervention Strategies

Our research findings suggested that there continues to be a substantial number of persons in the United States whose cognitive, affective, and behavioral reactions to persons of color correspond to the characteristics associated with the Affective-Impulsive Disposition. Thus counselor educators and practitioners need to be prepared to address this form of racism. Counseling practitioners may be called upon to work directly with individuals who have been identified as having problems because of their racist attitudes, beliefs, and behaviors. This sort of referral is likely to be made by court and law enforcement officials, school principals, university administrators, and organizational/business managers. Usually such a referral occurs because an individual has been accused of some criminal activity (e.g., involvement in a hate crime), demonstrated some form of racial harassment (e.g., calling non-White persons derogatory names, sending obscene e-mail messages to persons of color), or behaved in a way that reflects a heightened level of disrespect for non-White persons.

Further, given the number of racially based incidents that continue to occur on high school and university campuses, in various workplaces, and in communities across the United States, many administrators and policy makers are interested in knowing what can be done to prevent such incidents from occurring in the future. Often these administrators and policy makers are particularly concerned about preventing the sort of incidents that are catalyzed by individuals who manifest behaviors associated with the Affective-Impulsive Disposition of White racism. Given their training and expertise in human development and interpersonal communication, counselor educators and practitioners are likely to be called upon to consult with these persons regarding the types of preventive intervention strategies that could be instituted to reduce the problems that persons operating from an Affective-Impulsive Disposition might cause.

Unfortunately, most counselor educators and practitioners are ill-prepared to deal effectively with these sorts of clinical and consultation challenges. Their ineffectiveness in dealing with these challenges can be traced to the fact that these issues are not adequately addressed in counselor education programs. Despite their lack of training in this area, it is nevertheless important for counselor educators and practitioners to be knowledgeable of the types of strategies that might be employed to deal effectively with the challenges manifested in this disposition.

Given the description of the psychological characteristics associated with the Affective-Impulsive Disposition and based upon experiences working with persons assessed to be operating from this disposition, we have found that direct counseling services are often less effective than other types of interventions intentionally designed to stimulate behavior control among these persons. These interventions include advocating for the development and implementation of antiracist policies in schools, universities, businesses, and communities; providing antiracist training and education services; and encouraging the use of individual consultation services.

Many counselor educators and practitioners may find it odd that we do not recommend the use of direct counseling services with persons who manifest the characteristics associated with the Affective-Impulsive Disposition of White racism. However, we have noted that the use of traditional counseling services with individuals who manifest this disposition are not only ineffective but also counterproductive in many instances. (For a more detailed discussion of the general inappropriateness of direct counseling services with persons who are operating from the Affective-Impulsive Disposition, see Individual consultation services later in this section.)

Advocating for the development of antiracist policies. To help prevent the types of problems easily catalyzed by persons who exhibit this disposition, counselor educators and practitioners can work with administrators and policy makers in developing antiracist policies to be institutionalized in schools and universities, workplaces, and communities. Such policies need to be explicitly stated and made readily available to all persons in these settings. Punitive consequences for violating these policies also need to be clearly and explicitly stated in order to deter individuals from exhibiting the sort of behaviors commonly associated with the Affective-Impulsive Disposition.

Training and education services. To strengthen the potential impact of these antiracist policies, counselor educators and practitioners should urge administrators and policy makers to support the ongoing implementation of antiracist training and education services. The sexual harassment training and education programs successfully used to combat sexism in a variety of settings are good models to follow.

In addition to providing information to increase individuals' understanding of the different ways that racism may be manifested in these settings, antiracist training and education services should clarify the types of punitive actions that will be taken if the institution's standards and policies regarding respect for racial differences are violated. This sort of clarification is important for persons operating from an Affective-Impulsive Disposition because they are more inclined to control their racist impulses when they know what punitive actions are likely to be taken against them for intentionally violating antiracist policies.

Individual consultation services. Individuals operating from an Affective-Impulsive Disposition are unlikely to seek individual counseling voluntarily for issues related to racism. In fact, the only clients assessed to be operating from this disposition to whom we have provided individual counseling services were either required to participate in counseling as a part of a court order or referred by a school administrator for exhibiting inappropriate and racist behaviors. When working with these persons, we found that the positive, accepting, and respectful manner used by counselors to approach their clients frequently produced further articulations of racist views and beliefs. These sorts of counterproductive behaviors frequently continued even after confrontive and cognitive restructuring techniques were introduced in the counseling sessions with these persons.

Thus rather than using traditional counseling services with clients who are operating from this disposition, we advocate the use of individual consultation, remedial exercises, and racial awareness enhancement activities services designed to (1) educate these individuals about the negative (legal and organizational) consequences for exhibiting racist attitudes and behaviors, (2) help reduce any confusion as to why their behaviors are perceived by others to be racist, (3) provide suggestions regarding ways in which they might work to change some of their racist attitudes and beliefs, and (4) make appropriate referrals to other school- or community-based organizations that might help these individuals develop a more accurate, sensitive, and respectful perspective on racial differences.

Because it is possible that a student demonstrating characteristics associated with the Affective-Impulsive Disposition may slip through the admissions process and be admitted to a graduate counseling program, counselor educators should be prepared to deal with this sort of situation should it arise. It is not appropriate for an individual who manifest characteristics associated with the Affective-Impulsive Disposition to become a member of the counseling profession because this person's attitudes clearly conflict with the ethical code of our profession. However, when confronted with a situation in which such a person is identified as a student in a counselor education program, it is recommended that (1) the student be required to take a leave of absence from the program, (2) the student be encouraged to participate in remedial exercises or enhancement activities specifically designed to address the individual's rigid and prejudicial attitudes, and (3) the student be required to provide evidence of his or her progress as a result of participating in these services/activities before the individual is considered for readmission to the counseling program.

RATIONAL DISPOSITION OF WHITE RACISM

Characteristics

Cognitive characteristics.   The cognitive style of persons manifesting this disposition is typically marked by what William Perry (1970) called *dualistic thinking*. That is, life experiences are generally characterized in either-or terms in which interpersonal conflicts are rigidly analyzed from a "someone is right and someone is wrong" perspective. Persons manifesting a Rational Disposition are cognitively distinguished from those individuals exhibiting an Affective-Impulsive Disposition in that they are generally more knowledgeable about racial differences, aware of some of the historical forms of oppression that have negatively impacted persons of color in the United States, and more cognizant of some of the ways in which racial discrimination has been a central part of this country's legacy.

However, they are similar to individuals who manifest an Affective-Impulsive Disposition in that they adhere to numerous racial stereotypes. These cognitive notions are commonly used to rationalize justification for certain separatist beliefs frequently manifested by persons who operate from this disposition. For example, numerous persons manifesting a Rational Disposition of racism indicated they would not buy a home in a racially integrated neighborhood out of fear that their land value would deteriorate. Others express opposition to interracial dating and marriages because they think these relationships are likely to fail as a result of the negative social pressures and stigmatization believed to be associated with them.

Affective characteristics. Beyond the stereotypic thinking manifested by persons operating from the Rational Disposition, several affective characteristics differentiate this psychological disposition. One is that these persons typically demonstrate "a superficial niceness" when it comes to discussing issues related to racism (D'Andrea & Daniels, 1994). However, this affective superficiality is commonly replaced with expressions of hostile emotionality when these individuals are confronted with stressful situations that involve racial issues. Feagin and Vera (1995) have provided a good description of this sort of affective characteristic by reporting on the ways in which many of the citizens in Dubuque, Iowa, shifted from a seemingly positive emotional disposition to one that was characterized by heightening anger and hostility when they thought that a local initiative to recruit African American families to their community might result in a loss of jobs for Whites during the mid-1990s.

Behavioral characteristics. Individuals manifesting this disposition generally exhibit greater impulse control in terms of expressing negative views and beliefs about persons of color in comparison to those individuals who operate from an Affective-Impulsive Disposition. This is not to suggest that individuals with a Rational Disposition do not exhibit strong negative reactions toward persons of non-White groups. In this regard, these individuals are frequently noted to exhibit behaviors that clearly indicate their lack of support for those groups of persons who have historically suffered from discriminatory racist practices in the United States. This is particularly apparent when these individuals are engaged in discussions about racial quotas and affirmative action policies and practices. However, although persons with an Affective-Impulsive Disposition are likely to exhibit their hatred of non-White persons in more overt and violent ways, individuals exhibiting a Rational Disposition are more likely to participate in other forms of racist behaviors, such as taking part in petition drives that support the elimination of affirmative action practices in their local communities (Feagin & Vera, 1995).

Another behavioral characteristic noted among individuals who manifest the Rational Disposition involves the manner in which they commonly speak about racism and persons of non-White backgrounds, including their frequent use of phrases such as, "I think there is only one race—the human race," and "when I am working with Black persons, I don't think of their color, I only think of them as people." These comments reflect both a cognitive naivete about the ways in which race impacts non-White persons' lives and the superficial affective niceness that typically characterizes many persons operating from this disposition.

Recommendations for Rational Disposition Intervention Strategies

In conducting our exploratory research on the psychology of White racism, we encountered many persons who manifested cognitive, affective, and behavioral characteristics that fit this psychological disposition. This included numerous graduate students in counseling programs as well as experienced counselor educators and practitioners in the field. The types of intervention strategies thought to be developmentally appropriate for persons who operate from the Rational Disposition include those designed to promote their cognitive development in this area. Typically this involves services that encourage individuals to reformulate the way they think about racism and race relations in the United States. Many of the cognitive restructuring techniques commonly used by counseling practitioners are useful in working to achieve this goal. Counselor educators may also find that classroom interventions, such as remedial exercises and multicultural enhancement activities specifically designed to promote graduate students' cognitive understanding of racism, are useful in stimulating students' thinking in this area.

Cognitive restructuring. Persons, who are operating from a Rational Disposition of racism tend to be better prepared psychologically to benefit from individual counseling services and classroom interventions designed to enhance their cultural and racial sensitivity in comparison to persons who are operating from the Affective-Impulsive Disposition. Counseling approaches and classroom interventions designed to expand individuals' cognitive structures by focusing on the unexamined racial myths and stereotypes associated with the Rational Disposition are particularly useful in this regard. However, it is important to keep in mind that these unexamined myths and stereotypes are often embedded in a highly self-protective attitude (Loevinger, 1976) that characterizes the way many persons with a Rational Disposition respond to discussions about White racism in counseling and/or classroom settings.

This self-protective attitude is often linked to what Feagin and Vera (1995) called *zero-sum thinking* about racism and race relations in the United States. In short, zero-sum thinking reflects the belief that any gains achieved by non-White persons in this country (e.g., gains in the number of non-White persons who get jobs) automatically result in losses for White people (e.g., job losses for White persons). Feagin and Vera (1995) pointed out that the numerous unexamined myths and stereotypes associated with this sort of zero-sum thinking help "to keep America balkanized along racial lines" (p. 3).

Given that a self-protective attitude and zero-sum thinking characterizes the psychology of persons operating from the Rational Disposition, counselor educators and practitioners need to help these individuals discover the benefits they are likely to derive from thinking about and responding to non-White persons in more positive, respectful, and effective ways. This can be done, in part, by (a) discussing the ways in which our society is being affected by the rapid cultural-racial changes that are occurring in this nation's demography (Atkinson, Morten, & Sue, 1993) and (b) emphasizing the importance of developing the types of multicultural competencies necessary to work effectively and ethically in a culturally and racially diverse society. When using cognitive restructuring techniques with persons operating from the Rational Disposition of White racism, it is particularly important to emphasize the social and economic benefits White persons are likely to experience as a result of becoming more culturally competent.

Training and educational services. Helping individuals learn about the benefits of living in a multicultural, multiracial society is also a useful approach to take when working with counseling students who are operating from the Rational Disposition of racism. In this regard we have noted that White graduate students who are operating from this disposition frequently exhibit negative reactions and overt resistance to learning about the pervasive nature of White racism in multicultural counseling courses. Even using the term, *White racism* causes many of these students to react in negative and resistant ways.

However, this sort of negativity and resistance can be overcome when counselor educators use instructional approaches that effectively address the dualistic and zero-sum thinking associated with the Rational Disposition of racism. Thus, to be effective with these students, it is useful to provide information that helps them (a) learn about the types of challenges mental health professionals will face in the future as the United States continues to undergo significant cultural-racial changes in its demography (Atkinson, Morten, & Sue, 1993; Sue & Sue, 1990) and (b) understand that their overall effectiveness as professional counselors will largely depend on their willingness to develop a host of counseling competencies that reflect an increased level of awareness, knowledge, and skills when working with persons from diverse racial and cultural backgrounds (Sue, Arredondo, & McDavis, 1992). By pointing to the types of benefits they are likely to derive from expanding their own levels of multicultural awareness, knowledge, and skills, counselor educators provide the sort of incentive that is likely to motivate many students operating from this disposition to learn more about racism and the ways in which it is manifested in counseling.

Peer consultation and development activities. Although some of the counseling students included in our research manifested characteristics associated with the Rational Disposition, the majority demonstrated more mature cognitive, affective, and behavioral reactions to racism. Because students have numerous opportunities to learn from one another during graduate school, counselor educators should intentionally match individuals who exhibit characteristics associated with the Rational Disposition with other students who are operating from a more mature racial disposition. Particularly useful could be intentionally making these dispositional matchings when assigning course work that requires students to discuss ways in which White racism continues to be manifested both in society and in the counseling profession (D'Andrea, 1992; Sue & Sue, 1990). By consulting with other students who think in more expansive and complex ways about this serious problem, students who are operating from the Rational Disposition are often encouraged to reassess and reformulate some of their own thinking about White racism and its continuing impact on non-White persons in our country.

Community service projects.   Another way that counselor educators and practitioners can assist individuals to move beyond the stereotypic thinking that characterizes the Rational Disposition is to have them work in settings comprised of persons routinely subjected to various forms of racism. The use of community service projects is particularly useful in this regard. We have noted specifically that White students and clients who exhibit characteristics associated with the Rational Disposition begin to manifest more complex and accurate ways of thinking about the problem of White racism as a result of taking part in the various community service projects we have helped coordinate. These projects have included participating in a Christmas time community celebration that involved providing free meals to poor African American youths and their families; doing volunteer work in a voter registration campaign that targeted African American persons who resided in economically depressed urban areas; and working in a project that provided mental health and social support services to non-White homeless children and their mothers in Hawaii.

Because persons operating from the Rational Disposition typically have limited contact with persons of color, community service projects provide excellent opportunities for them to learn first hand about many of the day-to-day difficulties that persons from non-White groups experience. One of the important roles counselor educators and practitioners can play in these community service projects is to take time to discuss what White graduate students and clients learn about themselves and persons of color as a result of participating in these activities. By taking time to process their reactions to these community service projects, White persons operating from the Rational Disposition frequently report that they have experienced cognitive dissonance regarding their thinking about non-White persons. This is manifested in such statements as, "I never realized the types of difficulties these people experience every day of their lives," and "I used to think that people are just people and that if you have problems it is up to you to take care of them. But by taking part in this project, I am beginning to think differently about things. I mean I can see where being poor and Black adds a lot of pressure to a person's life that I didn't think of before."

LIBERAL DISPOSITION OF WHITE RACISM

Characteristics

Cognitive characteristics. The Liberal Disposition of White racism is marked by more complex and abstract ways of thinking about racism and human rights, such as:

- a more in-depth understanding of the various ways in which White racism is manifested in our society (e.g., individual, institutional, cultural forms of racism);
- a recognition of the universality and respect for a set of basic human rights including the right to life, liberty, and pursuit of happiness; and
- an increased awareness and respect for the different values, attitudes, behaviors, and worldviews that are exhibited by persons from diverse racial-cultural backgrounds.

The increased awareness and respect for racial-cultural differences commonly manifested among persons operating from this disposition are complemented by the emergence of a new cognitive ability that enables them to understand more accurately the perspectives of others. Perry (1970) referred to this intellectual ability as *multiplistic thinking*.

Multiplistic thinking represents an advancement in individuals' cognitive maturity. It does not, however, free these persons from the tendency to think in ethnocentric terms about issues related to racism and race relations in the United States. This sort of ethnocentricity is commonly manifested by persons operating from the Liberal Disposition because it appears to give more legitimacy to the values, attitudes, and behaviors endorsed by a White, Eurocentric worldview (Carter, 1995) than to those expressed by non-White persons from diverse cultural backgrounds. Comments that reflect this sort of unintentionally racist and ethnocentric thinking include the following statements made by individuals included in our study:

- While I respect the differences that exist between White and non-White people, I don't think these bilingual programs are a good idea because, ultimately, the Mexican American children who are in them will have to learn to speak English if they are going to be successful in this country.
- I really learned a lot about racial and cultural differences in my cross-cultural counseling class and am glad I took it. But I was kind of confused and frustrated because the instructor kept emphasizing the differences between Whites and non-White people. It seems to me that too much time was placed on the differences rather than looking at what we have in common. I mean we are all Americans and, like it or not, have to learn how to act and dress and talk a certain way to make it in this society.

Noteworthy is that most of the White counselor educators, practitioners, and students included in our study can be identified as operating from the Liberal Disposition. These persons typically express an interest in learning about multicultural and diversity counseling issues. However, even though they express interest in increasing their understanding of a variety of issues related to the mental health needs of persons from diverse groups (e.g., gays and lesbians, women, and persons with disabilities), they generally exhibit less motivation to learn about the ways in which White racism has impacted the mental health and personal well-being of non-White persons in this country. Most of these counselor educators, practitioners, and students also indicate that they do not see themselves as being particularly motivated to take action to address this issue in their personal or professional lives.

Affective characteristics. Although the counselor educators, practitioners, and students in our study were willing to talk about the problem of racism when asked about it, their overall affective reaction to this social pathology can be typically characterized by a general sense of apathy. This apathy is reflected in a number of ways including a lack of any anger concerning the numerous ways in which non-White persons continue to be impacted negatively by the various forms of racism perpetuated in the United States, a lack of statements indicating a sense of sadness or concern about the types of injustice and discrimination that non-White persons routinely experience in their lives, and the absence of any sense of urgency about the need to address this problem in the future.

One of the factors that may contribute to the apathy manifested by persons operating from the Liberal Disposition is the lack of empathy that White persons commonly demonstrate when it comes to accurately understanding the ways in which non-White persons are impacted by racism in the United States (Feagin & Vera, 1995). In writing about the pervasive sense of apathy that characterizes the psychological disposition of many White persons in higher education settings, we pointed out that

> It is difficult to explain exactly why people with this disposition exhibit an intellectual interest to learn about different cultural, ethnic, or racial groups and yet consistently demonstrate little emotional or behavioral responsiveness to the numerous acts of racial injustice and violence that occur in society. A partial explanation may be that since the negative and violent aspects of racism have little direct impact on the daily lives of most White administrators, faculty, and students, there is no immediate impetus to act on the behalf of those persons experiencing the ramifications of racism. (D'Andrea & Daniels, 1994, p. 80)

Behavioral characteristics. In addition to the apathy and lack of empathy just mentioned, the Liberal Disposition is also marked by inaction when it comes to dealing with the problem of racism. There are numerous reasons why most White persons (including the majority of White counselor educators, practitioners, and graduate students included in our research) are reluctant to deal with the problem of racism. Factors likely to contribute to this inaction include the apathy and low level of empathy that characterize persons who operate from the Liberal Disposition (D'Andrea, Locke, & Daniels, 1997).

The desire to avoid negative reactions from others is another factor that contributes to the unwillingness of many White persons to deal with the problem of racism. The importance of avoiding negative reactions from others was raised in our research by numerous counselor educators, practitioners, and students identified as operating from the Liberal Disposition. In explaining why they thought they were not very active in dealing with this problem, several counseling students stated that they refrained from initiating discussions about racism because they felt they would not be taken very seriously or would be met with defensive reactions by many White persons they knew. A number of counseling practitioners reported they did not care for the "negative emotionality" and "argumentative attitude" that often occurred in discussions with other White persons about issues related to multiculturalism and racism.

Several counselor educators also talked about the negative reactions some of their colleagues had toward White persons noted to be strong antiracist advocates in the counseling profession. These reactions to the White counselor educators and practitioners who strongly supported the multicultural counseling movement and articulated antiracist views included comments that reflected suspicions about the motivations (e.g., "I am not sure what his agenda is for constantly raising that [racism] issue"), negative reactions about the manner in which White antiracist advocates presented their views (e.g., "I don't like her style when she talks about the problem of White racism"), and even questions about the mental health of those persons who raise critical and controversial questions about the ways in which White racism continues to be manifested in the counseling profession (e.g., "I heard a colleague say that he thought the comments that [a White anti-racist advocate] made were bizarre and that he was acting like he was psychotic when he confronted other mental health professionals about the ways in which racism is manifested in the profession").

It is important to point out that these sort of comments serve two purposes. First, they can be used to discredit those White counselor educators, practitioners, and students willing to articulate openly their concerns about the perpetuation of racism in society in general and in the counseling profession in particular. Second, they reinforce the tendency of persons operating from a Liberal Disposition to refrain from taking action to address the problem of White racism out of fear of being stigmatized by other White counselor educators, practitioners, or students in the field.

Another factor likely to contribute to the lack of antiracist action associated with the Liberal Disposition involves the types of issues White persons often have to face when they begin actively to confront the problem of racism in our society. Several persons have noted that the process of developing an antiracist disposition inevitably requires individuals to acknowledge the ways in which various forms of White privilege (McIntosh, 1989) and superiority (D'Andrea, in press) help to perpetuate this problem. Because acknowledging these issues causes much discomfort for White persons operating from the Liberal Disposition, it is easier (and certainly less challenging) to avoid situations that might force them to confront the ways in which they personally benefit from perpetuation of racism. As one professional counselor who participated in our study stated, "I have been around people who have talked about the privileges White people have in society, and it really turns me off. I don't participate in conversations like that because I don't feel privileged. I have worked very hard to be successful."

Recommendations for Liberal Disposition Intervention Strategies

Given the psychological profile that characterizes persons operating from the Liberal Disposition, counselor educators and practitioners need to use intervention strategies designed to enhance students' and clients' emotional responsiveness to the problem of racism. By first working to increase emotional responsivity to this problem, counselor educators and practitioners are better positioned to help these persons consider ways in which they might act to address the problem of racism in the future.

Individual and group strategies that foster affective development. When working to stimulate the affective development of White persons operating at the Liberal Disposition, it is useful to begin by encouraging them to think about feelings they have had as a result of being discriminated against, stereotyped, and/or oppressed in their own lives. Such discussions can be done in individual or small group counseling sessions as well as in larger consultation, training, and classroom settings. However, because of the sensitivity and personal nature of these sorts of discussions, some individuals may feel apprehensive talking about these personal experiences in these settings. Thus counselor educators and practitioners may want to begin the process of stimulating students' and clients' affective development in this area by asking them to write narratives or personal essays that describe times they have been discriminated against, stereotyped, or oppressed in their own lives and to describe the feelings that resulted from these experiences.

This activity is particularly useful when working with White persons who manifest the sort of affective characteristics associated with the Liberal Disposition of racism because it encourages them to get more in touch with and articulate the emotional reactions experienced in their own lives when they felt they were unfairly treated by others. This process may involve as few as two or three individual or group counseling/classroom meetings or include several meetings in which individuals have more time to explore their reactions to these experiences in greater depth.

When initiating this activity, counselor educators and practitioners may want to be specific in their instructions by requesting individuals to take time to think about those instances in their own lives when they felt that they had been unfairly treated because of their gender, sexual preference, religious beliefs, economic class background, or physical appearance. After they have had time to reflect on their experiences, individuals can then be asked to write a narrative or personal essay that describes their feelings about these experiences. They should be encouraged to discuss what they have written in the next individual or group counseling session or classroom meeting. This discussion should also be aimed at getting them to see how their own experiences of oppression and discrimination are similar to and different from those that people of color experience on a daily basis.

This activity can be particularly effective when working with White women and gay and lesbian persons as it provides an opportunity for them to express their feelings about some of the difficulties they have had in their own lives as a result of experiencing sexist and homophobic reactions. However, this activity is also useful in encouraging White males to discuss their feelings about being unfairly discriminated against and stereotyped by others. In fact, many White men we have worked with have stated that they are not often provided an opportunity to share their feelings about these issues with others.

Using the expression of these feelings to stimulate emotional and empathic development. By providing White persons operating from the Liberal Disposition with opportunities in which they are able to talk about some of the feelings they have experienced as a result of being unfairly treated by others, counselor educators and practitioners are able intentionally to help them focus on the affective reactions they have to these situations. However, the next step in attempting to foster greater emotional and empathic responsiveness among these persons involves helping them make a connection between the types of anger, frustration, and pain experienced and similar feelings that non-White persons routinely experience as a result of being routinely subjected to various forms of racism in their daily lives.

To do this, counselor educators and practitioners are encouraged to invite non-White persons to serve as consultants who can work directly with students and clients in group counseling and classroom settings. The selection of these consultants should be based upon the composition of the group and the specific issues that the participants discussed in the group setting. For example, if the group is primarily comprised of White women, many of whom revealed their feelings about being subjected to various forms of sexism, it will be important to invite a woman of color to serve as a consultant for the group. For another example, if some of the group members talked about the pain and negative feelings they experienced as a result of being unfairly treated because of their gay or lesbian lifestyle, it will be useful to recruit a non-White consultant who has shared a similar affectional disposition to help expand the group's thinking about White racism.

There are two reasons for recruiting non-White persons to serve as consultants in these group settings. First, they can talk about their understanding of the types of feelings that the group members have expressed because, like many of the group members, they have experienced similar forms of discrimination and stereotyping (e.g., as a woman, as a gay or lesbian person). Second, they can play an important role in promoting development by discussing the similarities that exist between the feelings the White group members have experienced as a result of being victimized by various forms of discrimination and stereotyping and the feelings non-White persons experience as a result of being subjected to various forms of racism in their daily lives. Thus by helping White persons make the connection between the feelings they have experienced as a result of being unfairly discriminated against in the past with feelings that non-White persons experience by being routinely subjected to various forms of racism, counselor educators and practitioners can stimulate greater emotional and empathic responsivity among those persons who are operating from the Liberal Disposition.

Stimulating behavioral responsivity to racism. When working with students and clients who are operating from the Liberal Disposition, it is important for counselor educators and practitioners to focus initially on increasing their affective responsivity to racism before trying to stimulate new behavioral responses to this social pathology. By taking the time to foster greater emotional receptivity and empathy for the pain, anger, and frustrations that people of color commonly experience as a result of being subjected to racism, White persons are more likely to be genuinely committed to initiate new ways of dealing with the problem of White racism. By using the interventions described in the preceding section to increase individuals' emotional and empathic responsivity to racism, counselor educators and practitioners can help Whites develop the affective strength and conviction necessary to try out new behaviors aimed at dealing with this problem.

In conducting numerous antiracism workshops and teaching multicultural counseling courses that included White persons who manifested many of the characteristics associated with the Liberal Disposition, we have used a simple technique that has proven to be effective in stimulating an increase in the participants' and students' behavioral responsivity to racism. This technique is used to bring closure to workshops/multicultural counseling courses and is intentionally designed to encourage workshop participants and counseling students to consider actions they might be willing to take to help ameliorate the problem of racism in the future. To accomplish this, in the final 30 minutes of the workshop or course participants/students are first asked to take a couple of minutes to reflect on the various issues discussed during the day/semester. Then they are asked to think of one thing they might be willing to do to help deal with the problem of racism. We emphasize that it does not matter how large or small their proposed actions may be. Rather, it is their willingness to articulate and undertake some specific action in the future that really counts. Finally, we ask those individuals who are willing to do so to share their action plans with the rest of the participants/students in the workshop/class.

We have been impressed with the different strategies and goals that workshop participants and graduate counseling students personally committed themselves to in an effort to combat racism in the future. Actions they have agreed to take include initiating discussions about racism with friends or colleagues at work, incorporating the topic of racism in other counseling courses that the students were required to attend, writing a letter to the editor of a local newspaper that discusses the importance of dealing with the problem of racism in the community in which the workshop participant lived expressing displeasure when someone tells a racist joke in the future, setting time aside to talk to family members about the frustration and sadness a counseling student experienced each time one of them made racist comments, and agreeing to implement a racism prevention project for elementary school students that the participant had developed but not found time to initiate.

PRINCIPLED DISPOSITION OF WHITE RACISM

Characteristics

Cognitive characteristics.   Major cognitive advancements are noted at the Principled Disposition in the way individuals' think about White racism. More specifically, these persons demonstrate a unique understanding of the ways in which beliefs about White superiority and privilege help fuel the problem of racism in the United States. In this way, they are able to discuss the complex interrelationship between various forms of White privilege, White superiority, and White racism (D'Andrea, Locke, & Daniels, 1997). As a result of acquiring this understanding, persons operating from the Principled Disposition are able to explain how the various forms of racism that continue to exist in the United States are largely perpetuated by consciously and/or unconsciously held beliefs about the superiority of a worldview and lifestyle that emerges from a White, Eurocentric perspective.

Persons operating from this disposition are very knowledgeable about the historical and social-political underpinnings of White racism. Jones and Carter (1996) more clearly described this cognitive dimension by pointing out that "the unpleasant and uncomfortable histories and perspectives of peoples who have been oppressed by Whites can be comprehended and understood, as well as the present consequences of long-term racial inequities" (p. 7).

In addition to understanding the historical, institutional, cultural, and social-political underpinnings of racism and being knowledgable of the ways in which these factors contribute to the widespread perpetuation of racism, individuals operating from this disposition are relativistic thinkers (D'Andrea & Daniels, 1994). A relativistic thinking individual understands that the different behaviors, values and worldviews manifested by persons in a diverse society typically emerge from the different historical-cultural-racial-socioeconomic contexts in which they have developed. Unlike the multiplistic thinking person, relativistic thinkers recognize the legitimacy and value of the diverse perspectives and behaviors that emerge from the different human contexts (Perry, 1970). Besides thinking in more relativistic and abstract ways about the problem of racism than persons operating from the other dispositions described in this chapter, Principled Disposition persons incorporate what Kohlberg (1978) and Gilligan (1982) referred to as a justice and caring perspective in the way they think about and act on the problem of White racism.

The advancements noted in their cognitive capacities also allow individuals operating from the Principled Disposition to make criticisms of the counseling profession rarely raised by persons exhibiting Affective-Impulsive, Rational, or Liberal Disposition characteristics. These include a recognition that the counseling profession continues to operate generally from a racially biased epistemology (Scheurich & Young, 1997). Several White persons operating from the Principled Disposition have explained that, despite the positive impact that the multicultural movement has had on the counseling profession, a racially biased epistemology continues to be perpetuated in the profession as a result of the large number of counselor educators and practitioners who insist on using counseling theories and approaches that are rooted in a White, Eurocentric worldview (Carter, 1995; Sue, Ivey, & Pedersen, 1996). The perpetuation of this sort of racially biased epistemology represents an ethical problem for many of the counselor educators, practitioners, and students who operate from the Principled Disposition because they recognize that it promotes ethnocentric ways of thinking about human development and mental health that often conflict with the way persons from non-White racial-cultural groups conceptualize the notion of healthy psychological development.

Affective characteristics. The cognitive abilities just described complement a host of emotional characteristics commonly manifested by persons operating from the Principled Disposition. These include a heightened passion and sense of excitement about the possibility of ameliorating racism in society. Persons operating from the Principled Disposition are also consistently noted to demonstrate a heightened sense of idealism that fuels their optimism and hopefulness about the possibility of reducing the level of racism that exists in society, an idealism not evident in persons operating from the other dispositions in this model.

Paradoxically, however, a number of White persons who exhibit many of the cognitive characteristics associated with the Principled Disposition express cynicism and dejection regarding the state of race relations in this nation. Because the emergence of cynicism has been associated with the frustration of idealism, it is possible that individuals who operate from the Principled Disposition experience this negative reaction as a result of being frustrated by the lack of progress that has been made in the United States regarding the problem of White racism. This tentative explanation is offered because, in talking with individuals who exhibited this sort of cynicism, many state that they are disappointed and frustrated with the inability and/or unwillingness of many Whites to recognize and help address the numerous ways in which racism is manifested in the United States. In talking about these issues in greater depth with these persons, they also commonly express sadness and frustration about the level of hostility and distrust that exists between White and non-White persons in this country, stating that they feel these negative interracial factors represent serious barriers that prevent the realization of social justice in our society.

Behavioral characteristics. An integration of the cognitive and affective characteristics associated with persons operating from the Principled Disposition support the emergence of different types of behavioral reactions to racism not commonly manifested by individuals operating from the other dispositions. From our research observations we noted that individuals operating from the Principled Disposition not only exhibit overt disgust for all forms of racism but often feel compelled to address this social pathology in personal and professional ways. Consequently, these persons are much more likely to express concern about the state of race relations in the United States and initiate discussions about racism with their friends, colleagues, and students than are individuals who operate from the other dispositions.

Counselor educators and practitioners operating from this psychological disposition indicate that they occasionally infuse discussions about racism in working with graduate students and clients. However, these discussions are typically not part of a planned or intentional educational or clinical strategy. Rather, they commonly emerge as a result of comments made by students or clients that invite counselor educators and/or practitioners to address this issue in a classroom or clinical setting.

Many counselor educators and practitioners operating from this disposition acknowledge that progress has been made in terms of the counseling profession's commitment to multicultural counseling issues. Most of these persons also agree, however, that the profession could do a much better job at dealing with the various forms of racism that exist in the United States. However, the majority of these persons fall short in acknowledging the numerous ways in which counselor educators and/or practitioners unintentionally contribute to the problem of racism by failing consistently, intentionally, and systematically to address this problem in their work with students and clients. Further, a few counselor educators and practitioners operating from this disposition state that they have occasionally raised questions with other colleagues or supervisors about the ways in which various types of unintentional and covert forms of racism (Locke, 1992) might be played out in the organizations, schools, universities, business, or communities in which they work. Most persons manifesting this disposition indicate reservations about taking this sort of courageous action and acknowledge that they personally do not know how they might go about creating systemic changes to address the types of unintentional and covert forms of racism that continue to be embedded into many of our social, educational, professional, business, and community organizations.

On a more personal level, several White counselor educators, practitioners, and graduate students identified as operating from this disposition have indicated that they do not receive much support from their family, friends, and/or colleagues when they express their antiracist views or take action to address this social pathology. In fact, in several cases, family members and colleagues have encouraged them to reduce their level of involvement in these activities out of fear that it may have a detrimental impact on their careers. Others talk about the suspicious and negative reactions they receive from persons of color who question their motivation for being actively involved in anti-racist actions.

Little has been written about the sense of isolation and suspicion many White persons experience as a result of making an effort to address the problem of White racism in their personal and professional lives. However, we have noted that these factors play an important role in promoting a sense of cynicism, reducing individuals' sense of hopefulness, and undermining their motivation to continue to demonstrate the courage and commitment needed to address the problem of White racism effectively.

Recommendations for Principled Disposition Intervention Strategies

In designing interventions for persons operating from the Principled Disposition, attention should primarily be directed to strategies that foster the development of a more expansive set of behaviors and skills that can be used to help ameliorate the problem of racism. These interventions should secondarily focus on ways of addressing the affective needs often manifested by individuals manifesting this disposition.

Antiracist consultation and training services. Antiracist consultation and training services are excellent ways to promote the development of persons operating from the Principled Disposition. In providing these services, antiracist consultants and trainers should outline some of the ways in which other White persons have worked to address issues of racism successfully in school, university, business, and/or community settings. These services should direct particular attention to

- examining the types of barriers, problems, and challenges other White antiracist activists have encountered in working to address this social pathology;
- identifying the personal and professional qualities that characterize White persons who have been successful in dealing with the problem of racism in various settings;
- learning how to assess which disposition of racism individuals may be operating from and implementing strategies that are intentionally designed to address the unique cognitive, affective, and behavioral characteristics associated with the different dispositions outlined in this chapter;
- fostering the development of assessment skills that can be used to evaluate the ways in which individual, institutional, and/or cultural forms of racism impact schools, universities, businesses, and/or communities; and

- exploring those interventions that have been used and found to be effective in addressing the negative impact that individual, institutional, and cultural racism have on persons from various educational, business, and/or community settings.

Individual and group support services. As mentioned earlier, White persons who operate from the Principled Disposition and are genuinely committed to addressing the problem of White racism put themselves in a precarious position in terms of the ways other White persons and people of color relate to them. They often experience a general sense of isolation from family members, friends, and colleagues because of the stands they take in confronting the problem of White racism. In our research several persons also stated that they frequently encounter suspicion from persons of color who ask what their real agenda is for working to reduce the level of racism that exists in our society.

Over time these reactions can foster a sense of cynicism and reduce the level of motivation that White persons operating from the Principled Disposition exhibit in terms of dealing with this complex problem. Consequently, it is important that they receive ongoing support and encouragement from other persons. White counselor educators and practitioners should to provide this sort of support and encouragement in their individual interactions with students and clients operating from this disposition. However, a more efficient and potentially powerful way to help address their affective needs involves developing support groups for White persons interested in making personal connections with other antiracist activists.

Some White counselors and counselor educators operating from the Principled Disposition also report that they greatly value the support received from the non-White persons with whom they interact. Given the lack of support often encountered within their own White communities when making a stand against White racism, it is important that non-White counselor educators and practitioners continue to articulate their support for the efforts of White persons operating from the Principled Disposition.

PRINCIPLED ACTIVISTIC DISPOSITION OF WHITE RACISM

Characteristics

Cognitive characteristics. Less than 1% of White persons who were studied in our research operate from the Principled Activistic Disposition. These persons demonstrate cognitive competencies similar to those of individuals operating from a Principled Disposition, especially regarding their ability to think from a relativistic perspective. However, we noted that persons operating from the Principled

Activistic Disposition are distinguished by more abstract, comprehensive, systemic thinking abilities, and that the sort of systemic thinking that characterizes these persons reflects a more in-depth understanding of the various ways that White racism continues to be embedded in our educational, economic, media, political, and social institutions. As a result of acquiring the ability to conceptualize the problem of White racism from this sort of systemic perspective, these persons manifest a much greater understanding of the types of individual, institutional, and cultural changes that need to occur to ameliorate this form of social pathology successfully. This understanding is clearly apparent in the way these persons are able to articulate clearly the specific types of changes that our societal institutions need to undergo to foster a more genuine and greater sense racial justice.

Affective characteristics. Although persons operating from the Principled Activistic Disposition are more knowledgeable about the intricacies and complexity of the problem of White racism, they appear neither overwhelmed with the magnitude of the problem nor made cynical by the time and resources they think are required to deal with this social pathology effectively. Unlike the cynical attitude commonly reflected in the affective reactions of many persons operating from the Principled Disposition, White persons functioning at the Principled Activistic Disposition consistently demonstrate a greater sense of hopefulness and optimism in terms of dealing with the problem of racism in our society. It is important to emphasize that the positive and hopeful affective reactions these persons have to this problem are not based upon a naive or oversimplified understanding of this social pathology. On the contrary, these persons have acquired a complex and objective understanding of the various ways in which individual, institutional, and cultural factors help perpetuate White racism in the United States, and they also share a deeply held belief and faith in the unrealized nature of human potential.

Interesting to note is that when Principled Activistic Disposition individuals discuss their beliefs and faith in the unrealized nature of human potential and how it contributes to the perpetuation of racism, they frequently refer to the lack of spiritual connection and moral empathy commonly manifested among many persons in our society. In talking about the lack of spiritual connection and moral empathy they believe underlies much of the problem of racism in our society, these persons are not advocating for a particular religion with which they may be affiliated. Rather, individuals operating from the Principled Activistic Disposition commonly indicate that White persons would demonstrate a greater motivation to work toward creating more caring, responsive, and just communities in our country if they developed a greater sense of spiritual connection and moral empathy with persons routinely subjected to racism in our society. These comments mirror many of the ideas that Dr. Martin Luther King talked about when he emphasized the importance of building "beloved communities" as a way to address effectively the complex problem of White racism in our nation (Washington, 1986).

Persons manifesting a Principled Activistic Disposition agree that most if not every human being possesses the potential to live a life guided by the sort of spiritual values and moral empathy that would lead to the elimination of racism in our society. However, they also readily acknowledge that the vast majority of persons in our country have not realized their own potential in these areas. Furthermore, persons operating from the Principled Activistic Disposition indicate that White persons' unrealized potentials to develop a heightened spiritual understanding and an increased level of moral empathy for persons from diverse racial-cultural backgrounds represent two of the most significant barriers impeding our ability to overcome the problem of White racism as a nation. Although they consistently acknowledge that the task of fostering an increased level of spiritual connection and moral empathy among White and non-White persons in our country represents a formidable task that will require a major transformation in our community, educational, economic, media, political, and religious institutions, it is an end to which many persons operating from the Principled Activistic Disposition have committed themselves.

Behavioral characteristics. Although many persons operating from the Rational, Liberal, and Principled Dispositions talk about the need to deal with the problem of racism and make an effort to address this problem in their personal or professional lives, individuals operating from the Principled Activistic Disposition are clearly distinguished by their level of commitment to combat this social pathology. These persons are commonly viewed as being social-political activists who consciously and consistently work to foster the empowerment of individuals associated with groups traditionally devalued and oppressed by the dominant cultural group in our society. This includes but is not limited to addressing the types of racism that African Americans, Asian Americans, Hispanic Americans, and Native Americans routinely experience in their lives as well as striving to overcome the types of stereotyping and discrimination that physically challenged persons, poor people, women, and gays and lesbians continue to experience in the United States.

Individuals operating from the Principled Activistic Disposition are also distinguished from those individuals who manifest characteristics associated with the other dispositions by the degree to which they strive to live an integrated and congruent life. That is, they exhibit concern about how their personal and professional lives reflect an integration and actualization of principled, moral thinking when it comes to addressing the issues of White racism. In doing so, these individuals live a more fully examined life by trying to act consistently in ways congruent with a set of values that reflect the importance of developing a greater sense of spiritual connection and moral empathy with others while striving actively to promote racial justice in our nation.

Few of the counselor educators, practitioners, and graduate students included in our research demonstrate the characteristics associated with the Principled Activistic Disposition. Those persons identified as operating from this disposition are all involved in working to create a greater sense of awareness about the problem of White racism in society in general and in the counseling profession in particular, but their progress is often limited by the lack of support they receive from leaders within the counseling profession, from administrators and policy makers at the institutions where they work, and from other colleagues in the field.

Recommendations for Principled Activistic Disposition Intervention Strategies

Providing leadership training and consultation services. Given the level of commitment and understanding these persons have regarding the problem of White racism in our society, they appear to be personally and professionally invigorated by participating in activities in which they can use their knowledge, enthusiasm, and skills to combat this social pathology. Counseling researchers have noted that persons often benefit personally and professionally from situations in which they are required to help others realize their own developmental potential (Lewis, Lewis, Daniels, & D'Andrea, 1998). Thus counselor educators and practitioners identified as operating from the Principled Activistic Disposition should be given opportunities to provide leadership training workshops and offer consultation services for other members of the counseling profession interested in learning how to deal more effectively with coworkers. These opportunities can not only increase awareness among those persons receiving the leadership training and consultation services but also energize the Principled Activistic Disposition individuals who provide such services.

Participating in a supportive community. Because individuals operating from the Principled Activistic Disposition are commonly viewed as controversial figures as a result of consistently making strong antiracist stands in their work, they are often misunderstood, criticized, subjected to hate mail, and in some cases verbally and even physically attacked by White persons functioning from the other dispositions described earlier in this chapter. Such criticisms and attacks can tax the personal and psychological resources of persons operating from the Principled Activistic Disposition. It is important, therefore, that Principled Activistic Disposition persons work toward building a supportive community for themselves in order to share experiences, thoughts, and questions concerning ways to address the problem of White racism in society in general and in the counseling profession in particular.

It is also important that these individuals find creative ways to have regular contact with one another in order to receive support and encouragement from others experiencing similar challenges and frustrations. By building and maintaining their own "beloved community" of like-minded colleagues, persons operating from the Principled Activistic Disposition can avoid burn-out as they undertake the difficult task of effectively dealing with the problem of White racism in isolation. A description of the evolution of the National Multicultural Ad Hoc Committee in D'Andrea and Daniels, 1995, provides a good example of the ways in which individuals operating from the Principled Activistic Disposition are able to build such a supportive community.

SUMMARY

This chapter describes five different psychological dispositions that White persons demonstrate in regard to the problem of White racism in the United States. The dispositions reflect the different cognitive, affective, and behavioral reactions that White persons have manifested in a study we have been conducting for the past 15 years. Our findings have led us to the following conclusions:

- In gaining an understanding of the various ways that White racism is perpetuated in our modern society, it is important to learn about the different psychological dispositions Whites exhibit when reacting to this social pathology. We hope that the descriptions of the five dispositions presented in this chapter help to illuminate the psychological complexity of this problem.
- In order for counselor educators and practitioners to address the problem of racism with other White students and clients effectively, it is important to (a) assess accurately which disposition they and their students/clients are likely to be operating from and (b) select an intervention strategy that complements the different cognitive, affective, and behavioral components of the disposition(s) manifested by their students/clients. The interventions outlined in this chapter reflect some of the strategies counselor educators and practitioners can consider in working with individuals operating from the different dispositions of our model.
- Numerous scholars and researchers have begun to examine more closely the types of individual and systemic factors that contribute to the perpetuation of racism in the United States, but much more research is needed to increase our understanding of this complex problem and help inform us of the strategies that can be used effectively to ameliorate this problem in the future. We hope that our model of White racism stimulates greater interest in this area among counselor educators, practitioners, researchers, and students; but our greatest hope is that our work encourages colleagues in the field to make a greater effort to address the problem of racism effectively in their personal and professional lives.

REFERENCES

Atkinson, D. R., Morten, G., & Sue, D. W. (1993). *Counseling American minorities* (4th ed.). Dubuque, IA: Brown & Benchmark.

Bowser, B. P., & Hunt, R. G. (Eds.). (1996). *Impacts of racism on White Americans* (2nd ed.). Thousand Oaks, CA: Sage.

Carter, R. T. (1995). *The influence of race and racial identity in psychotherapy: Toward a racially inclusive model.* New York: Wiley-Interscience.

Cose, E. (1993). *The rage of a privileged class.* New York: Harper Collins.

D'Andrea, M. (1992, October). The violence of our silence: Some thoughts about racism, counseling, and development. *Guidepost,* p. 14.

D'Andrea, M. (1996). White racism. In P. B. Pedersen & D. C. Locke (Eds.), *Cultural and diversity issues in counseling* (pp. 55–57). Greensboro, NC: ERIC/CASS.

D'Andrea, M. (in press). The evolution and transformation of a White racist. *Journal of Counseling and Development.*

D'Andrea, M., & Daniels, J. (1994). The different faces of racism in higher education. *Thought and Action, 10*(1), 73–87.

D'Andrea, M., & Daniels, J. (1995). Promoting multiculturalism and organizational change in the counseling profession: A case study. In J. G. Ponterotto, J. M. Casas, L. A. Suzuki, & C. M. Alexander (Eds.), *Handbook of multicultural counseling* (pp. 17–33). Thousand Oaks, CA: Sage.

D'Andrea, M., & Daniels, J. (1998). *Assessing the different psychological dispositions of White racism: An exploratory study.* Unpublished manuscript, University of Hawaii.

D'Andrea, M., Locke, D. C., & Daniels, J. (1997, April). *Dealing with racism: Counseling strategies.* Workshop presented at the annual meeting of the American Counseling Association, Orlando, FL.

Feagin, J. R., & Vera, H. (1995). *White racism: The basics.* New York: Routledge.

Gilligan, C. (1982). *In a different voice: Psychological theory and women's development.* Cambridge, MA: Harvard University Press.

Harvey, W. B. (1991). Faculty responsibility and racial tolerance. *Thought and Action, 7*(2), 115–136.

Jones, J. M. (1997). *Prejudice and racism* (2nd ed.). New York: McGraw Hill.

Jones, J. M., & Carter, R. T. (1996). Racism and White identity development. In B. P. Bowser & R. G. Hunt (Eds.), *Impacts of racism on White Americans* (2nd ed., pp. 1–23). Thousand Oaks, CA: Sage.

Kohlberg, L. (1978). Revisions in the theory and practice of moral development. *New Directions for Child Development, 2.*

Lewis, J., Lewis, M., Daniels, J., & D'Andrea, M. (1998). *Community counseling: Empowerment strategies for a diverse society.* Pacific Grove, CA: Brooks/Cole.

Locke, D. C. (1992). *Increasing multicultural understanding: A comprehensive model.* Newbury Park, CA: Sage.

Loevinger, J. (1976). *Ego development: Conceptions and theories.* San Francisco: Jossey-Bass.

Magner, D. K. (1989, April). Blacks and Whites on campuses: Behind ugly racist incidents, student isolation and insensitivity. *Chronicle of Higher Education,* p. 1.

McIntosh, P. (1989, July/August). White privilege: Unpacking the invisible knapsack. *Peace and Freedom,* pp. 10–12.

Perry, W. G. (1970). *Forms of intellectual and ethical development in the college years.* New York: Holt, Rinehart, & Winston.

Scheurich, J. J., & Young, M. D. (1997). Coloring epistemologies: Are our research epistemologies racially biased? *Educational Researcher, 26,* 4–16.

Skillings, J. H., & Dobbins, J. E. (1991). Racism as a disease: Etiology and treatment implications. *Journal of Counseling and Development, 70,* 206–212.

Southern Poverty Law Center. (1997, Summer). *Intelligence Report, 87,* 19–27.

Sue, D. W., Arredondo, P., & McDavis, R. J. (1992). Multicultural competencies/standards: A pressing need. *Journal of Counseling and Development, 70* (4), 477–486.

Sue, D. W., Ivey, A. E., & Pedersen, P. B. (Eds.). (1996). *A theory of multicultural counseling and therapy.* Pacific Grove, CA: Brooks/Cole.

Sue, D. W., & Sue, D. (1990). *Counseling the culturally different: Theory and practice* (2nd ed.). New York: Wiley.

Washington, J. M. (1986). *A testament of hope: The essential writings of Martin Luther King, Jr.* San Francisco: Harper & Row.

Welsing, F. C. (1970). *The Cress theory of color-confrontation and racism (White supremacy).* Washington, DC: C-R.

5 R. A. C. E.—Racial Affirmation and Counselor Educators

Michael Mobley in collaboration with Harold Cheatham

During the past three decades the influence and role of culture has received increasing attention and legitimacy in counseling and psychotherapy literature. Much of this attention has been accorded under the contemporaneous title of cultural diversity or multiculturalism. This shift is evidenced in the plethora of writings (Pedersen, 1991; Ponterotto & Casas, 1991; Ponterotto, Casas, Suzuki, & Alexander, 1995) and conference themes addressing multicultural issues in the profession (American Counseling Association, American College Personnel Association, American Psychological Association), as well as in training programs' policies, procedures, practices, and clinical experiences (Allison, Crawford, Echemendia, Robinson, & Knepp, 1994; Hills & Strozier, 1992; Pope-Davis & Nielson, 1996; Ridley, Mendoza, Kanitz, Angermeier, & Zenck, 1994). Moreover, the surge in attention to multiculturalism has been accompanied by similar attention to revising and extending the cultural identity development models advanced in the late 1950s and early 1960s (Cass, 1979, 1996; Cross, 1971, 1995; Thomas, 1971).

The critical role and function of cultural identity development models rests in their utility for advancing our understanding of self-identification processes employed among the many diverse cultural groups, including racial and ethnic groups, women, gay men, and lesbian women. Another unique capacity of cultural identity development models resides in their emphasis on the individual within the context of the social environment; that is, an individual's self-understanding and self-concept are highly influenced by his or her interpretations or perceptions of and interactions with significant others comprising his or her social-cultural milieu.

Study of cultural identity development models such as racial, ethnic, gender, and sexual orientation identity has been broadly incorporated into training programs to assist counselors to achieve greater (ideally, maximum) effectiveness in working with culturally diverse clients. It can be argued that cultural identity development models represent a critical tool for fostering increased levels of cultural understanding not only in counseling but also in society, in general. For example, Helm's racial identity model (1990, 1995, 1996) and Atkinson, Morten, and Sue's (1998) minority/majority models (generally regarded as derivative of Cross's [1971, 1991] origin postulation) are among the most frequently relied upon frameworks for examining potential effects of race and ethnicity in the therapeutic relationship. Others include Carter (1990), Gim, Atkinson, and Kim (1991), Helms and Carter (1991), and Parham and Helms (1985). In addition, Cass's (1979, 1996) and Gilligan's (1982) models are equally relevant in understanding sexual orientation identity and gender identity development, respectively.

This application of cultural identity development models is laudable. Indeed, recently the models have has been further extended to examine the supervisory relationship between counselor educators and counselors in training. Many researchers and scholars have emphasized the importance of supervisors and supervisees exploring how cultural variables may effect all levels of the clinical service delivery process. These researchers have noted that cultural influence emanating from the client, counselor, and supervisor need to be considered (Ashby & Cheatham, 1996; Constantine, 1997; D'Andrea & Daniels, 1997; Fong & Lease, 1997; Gonzalez, 1997; Martinez & Holloway, 1997; Stone, 1997).

The foregoing progress notwithstanding, one domain that has not received much attention encompasses the relationships fostered between counselor educators and counselors in training, relationships that parallel teacher-student, adviser-advisee, and mentor-mentee dyads. As efforts continue to improve the training and functioning of multicultural counselors and therapists, it seems vital that cultural identity development models also inform the training of faculty members to serve in their roles as teacher, adviser, and mentor as well as colleague. This latter role pinpoints a second domain in which cultural identity development models applicable: the working relationships among counselor educators.

General consensus (based on available research evidence) is that individuals work best when they feel or are affirmed within their cultural identities as unique, contributing members of a relevant or reference group. Because multiculturalism essentially derives from acknowledging and graciously incorporating culture, we cannot afford to offer hollow respect for differences and similarities. We must instead provide genuine concern for both counselors in training and our colleagues by valuing and appreciating the heart and soul of each individual and his or her cultural being.

To further this objective, this chapter focuses on the utility of racial identity development models in assisting counselor educators in their roles and responsibilities as cultural guardians of the counseling profession. A conscious decision has been made to focus on race while recognizing that other facets of cultural identity, such as gender and sexual orientation, are equally important. Two levels of intersections between counselor educators and racial identity development models are specifically addressed: (1) self-awareness and exploration of counselor educators' racial identity development and (2) understanding of interactional dynamics between counselor educators and counselors in training (and, in some cases, among counselor educators themselves). The chapter's intention is to explicate critical issues relevant to how counselor educators' racial identity influences their role and actions in training programs, their professional and interpersonal relationships with counselors in training both in didactic and experiential phases of training programs, and their working relationship with colleagues.

SELF-AWARENESS AND EXPLORATION OF RACIAL IDENTITY DEVELOPMENT

Sue, Arredondo, and McDavis (1992) articulated a definition for the culturally skilled counselor that we believe is transferable to counselor educators. Thus, to expand and paraphrase, the culturally skilled counselor educator is one who is aware of his or her own assumptions, values, biases, and limitations; understands the worldview of the multicultural pluralistic counselors in training; and develops appropriate and culturally sensitive strategies in working with culturally diverse counselors in training as well as other counselor educators.

Self-Awareness for Multiculturally Oriented Counselor Educators Model

How can counselor educators become culturally skilled? One of the best ways is to explore their level of awareness about their own "emic"—that is, their own culture-specific assumptions, values, biases, and limitations—and engage in active self-reflection using existing racial identity development models. The self-awareness for multiculturally oriented counselor educators model, which is based on Bowman's (1996) multicultural training model as well as issues and dynamics espoused by Ashby and Cheatham's (1996) perspective on multicultural supervision, assist in this self-reflection process.

In utilizing the model, the primary objective is for counselor educators to gain increased awareness, sensitivity, and knowledge about their own racial-cultural heritage as well as the racial-cultural heritage of the counselors in training and the other counselor educators they interact with. A secondary objective is for counselor educators to increase their range of skills in interacting with culturally diverse students and counselor educators. The self-awareness for multiculturally oriented counselor educators model, which is defined in the context of race and ethnicity, has three components: learning about self, learning about others, and learning about how the self relates to others. In the first component, energy and attention are dedicated to the counselor educator learning more about his or her own racial identity. In the second component, time and focus are geared toward counselor educators' learning about the cultural background and sociopolitical influences of others, including both students and colleagues. In the third component, the counselor educator reflects on how he or she relates to counselors in training or colleagues based upon level of racial identity development.

As a framework for understanding the objective and goals of each three components in the self-awareness for multiculturally oriented counselor educators model, a grasp of racial identity development models (e.g., Cross, 1991, 1995; Helms, 1990, 1995, 1996; Rowe, Behrens, & Leach, 1995) is important. Essentially, racial identity development models explicate the critical function of "self-in-relation" interpersonal dynamic espoused by Ivey, Ivey, and Simek-Morgan (1997). The concept of self-in-relation emphasizes a sociocultural interaction dynamic between one's self and others in society.

Helms' Black and White Racial Identity Models

Helms' Black and White identity models (1990, 1996) are utilized in the self-awareness for multiculturally oriented counselor educators model to explicate potential interaction dynamics between counselor educators and counselors in training. Helms' models have broad demonstrated utility across field (e.g., counseling and psychotherapy, higher education, K-12 schools, business) and offer a perspective on how members of the two dominant racial groups in U.S. society tend to interact and respond to one another.

In her model Helms has identified cognitive, affective, and behavioral responses likely to be exhibited by Blacks and Whites in relation to each other. Recently, Helms (1996) has referred to the notion of culturally characteristic response patterns as "ego statuses." That is, every individual represents a composite set of ego statuses across his or her racial cultural identity. Helms emphasized that each of these ego statuses is related to a specific form of information-processing strategy, that is, the way "people encode, analyze, react to, and retrieve racial information" (p. 155). Furthermore, she noted that observable behaviors or "schema" may be associated with each ego status.

In the Black identity model there are five unique ego statuses: Conformity (Preencounter), Dissonance (Encounter), Immersion/Emersion, Internalization, and Integrative Awareness (Internalization/Commitment). Table 5-1 provides for each ego status a description, information-processing strategy, and sample schema.

In the White identity model, there are six unique ego statuses: Contact, Disintegration, Reintegration, Pseudo-independence, Immersion/Emersion, and Autonomy. Table 5-2 provides for each ego status a description, information-processing strategy, and sample schema.

UNDERSTANDING INTERACTIONAL DYNAMICS: HOW TO USE THE SELF-AWARENESS FOR MULTICULTURALLY ORIENTED COUNSELOR EDUCATORS MODEL

Suggestions for how counselor educators can use the self-awareness for multiculturally oriented counselor educators model are presented in this section.

Actions/steps, questions, and examples are provided for each of the model's three components: learning about self, learning about others, and learning about how the self relates to others.

Learning About Self

Many counselor educators may not consciously consider how their own level of racial identity development process impacts their roles and responsibilities. In this first component, counselor educators should dedicate energy and attention to hearing about their social identity.

A first step is to perform a cultural self-assessment of your racial identity ego statuses. Use Tables 5-1 and 5-2. As you think about your racial cultural identity, recall critical incidences that forged your self-understanding of yourself as a Black or White racial being. Try to reflect upon the messages you have received as a result of the socialization process in your family, in your religious/spiritual faith, and in your educational and residential communities. What are the earliest memories you have of consciously recognizing that you were different from another individual on the basis of your race? Did this cultural awareness occur during childhood, adolescence, or perhaps early adulthood either in college or the military? Take time to record these memories. Write down what happened, what other people were involved, and what your relationship was with these people. How old you were? What feelings do you recall experiencing? Did you feel powerful or powerless? In the case of powerless, did you think that your presence or perspective was not fully appreciated or validated by the other(s) in your environment who were different from yourself? How does this understanding and/or perception of yourself as a racial-cultural being affect relationships with others in your life today, specifically counselors in training and colleagues?

Do you find that your racial ego status is appreciated and valued in your relationship with counseling students? Have you been able to openly discuss ways in which your race impacts the dynamics in your working relationship with counseling students? For example, do your students perceive you as being culturally sensitive, culturally encapsulated, or culturally skillful? What critical behaviors or schema as identified by Helms (1996) could you document to provide support for your perception of how your race is perceived by counseling students? Equally important, how do your colleagues respond to you?

If you perceive your racial ego status within the Integrative Awareness (of Black racial identity) or Autonomy (of White racial identity) statuses, complete your racial cultural self-assessment profile by recalling critical incidences that forged your self-understanding in relation to equally influencing aspects of your cultural identity such as gender and sexual orientation. If there are gray areas in characterizing your primary racial ego status, eliciting help from a trusted family member, friend, or colleague may be helpful.

A second step in learning about yourself involves self-reflection on your time as a graduate student in training, specifically in regard to yourself as a racial being.

How has your race influenced your graduate training process? Do you recall how you were experienced as a racial being by your own professors, supervisors, and/or mentors? Is it possible that given White privilege (McIntosh, 1989) your identity as a White racial being was consciously inconsequential? As an African American graduate student, was your racial identity acknowledged in your training interactions with faculty, supervisors, and/or staff? How do you characterize your racial ego status during this significant period in your professional development? In this process of increasing your racial self-awareness level, recalling the level of racial diversity within your training program, department, and/or across campus may be helpful.

During the learning process all students, both young and old, desire to experience cultural affirmation—with *cultural affirmation* defined as a genuine acceptance and appreciation of the essence of one's cultural heritage and toward developing multiple facets of cultural identities. During your graduate training experience were you afforded cultural affirmation?

A third step in learning about yourself involves thinking about how you have responded to major sociopolitical and cultural events in society. In understanding your own racial-cultural heritage, think about your cognitive, affective, and behavioral reactions to the following historical events: the civil rights movement (march on Selma, Million Man March, Million Woman March), the gay rights movement (Stonewall riots, 1987 and 1993 marches on Washington), religious gatherings (Promise Keepers). Did you participant in any of these major events? Did you observe them from the sidelines or from TV coverage? Do you recall talking to love ones, family, relatives, neighbors, and others about your reaction to these events? In particular, do you recall having talked about these events in your role as counselor educator with your counseling students? More importantly, how has your identity as a racial-cultural being influenced your perspective about these major sociopolitical and cultural events?

Time has not expired. Discussing your understanding and perspective on one or two of these major sociopolitical and cultural events in society with your counseling students and/or colleagues may be fruitful. The objective is to explore one another's reaction to an event in the context of your racial ego status. For example, discuss the Million Woman March in regard to simply being a woman or being a man in regard to being a racially/ethnically identified woman or man. What feelings arise in you as you consider your unique cultural identity in relationship to this event? Equally important, how do (did) your cognitive, affective, and behavioral reactions to this event influence your relationships with counseling students, colleagues, or those different from yourself?

You may also focus on your reactions to the associations of famous historical figures in our society, such as Martin Luther King, Jr., Robert and John F. Kennedy, and Medger Evers; or to the deaths of Elvis, Princess Diana, John Wayne, and Mother Teresa. In addition, there have been well-publicized legal hearings, such as on Lorena Bobbit's assault on her husband, Michael Jackson's alleged sexual inappropriateness, O.J. Simpson's involvement in the death of his ex-wife and friend, the Anita Hill and Clarence Thomas Senate hearings, or President Clinton's relations with Paula Jones or Monica Lewinsky.

A personal example that I vividly recall is a White female supervisor's reaction to the verdict delivered in the O. J. Simpson trial. When she approached me, an African American male graduate student, and asked what my response to the verdict was, I informed her that I had not actually heard the verdict and indeed, had stopped watching the TV court drama several weeks prior. My White female supervisor seemed surprised but informed me that O. J. Simpson was found not guilty. I did not display any visible behavioral reactions. My supervisor appeared perplexed and asked me if I could believe this outcome considering all the evidence presented against O. J. Simpson for the death of his ex-wife, Nicole, and her friend, Ron Goldman. One of my vivid memories at the time was that I was truly disinterested in this American legal drama. My supervisor finally stated that "as a woman I can not believe this happened! How could he get off?" My supervisor also commented about the press release the National Organization for Women made in protest of the verdict. I felt that my supervisor wanted me to share her worldview about this historical event. I distinctly remember feeling that a distance had formed between us, if only for the moment that followed this sociopolitical dialogue.

Learning About Others

Counselor educators should gear time and focus in this second component of the self-awareness for multiculturally oriented counselor educators model toward learning about the cultural background and sociopolitical influence of others, including their students as well as their colleagues.

Now that you have been engaged in a cultural self-reflection process of yourself as a racial being, it is time to focus on learning about others. To be an effective multicultural counselor educator, gaining increased knowledge both experiential and didactic about racial-cultural groups different from your own is essential. Racial identity development models represent a lens to increase your understanding consciously about those who are different from yourself.

Numerous books, articles, and literary writings offer invaluable knowledge about the four dominant racial/ethnic cultural groups (African American, Asian American, Hispanic American, and Native American) in the United States (Atkinson, Morten, & Sue, 1998; McGoldrick, Pearce, & Giordano, 1982; Sue & Sue, 1990). These readings serve as a method toward increasing your general understanding about individuals from differing racial backgrounds. Recognizing both within-group and between-group differences as you seek to learn about others is important.

After reading about differing cultural groups, a method for learning more specifically about various racial/ethnic cultural groups is to find out about the culturally diverse college students, faculty, and staff on your own campus. What percentages of culturally diverse students attend your institution? Are within your college? Are

within your department and program? What have you learned about these particular students based upon your present level of contact and interactions?

Multiple campus resources are available to counselor educators as they pursue
learning about others. For example, many institutions of higher education provide
summary statistical data about culturally diverse students attending the campus.
This information provides a basic perspective of cultural representation within
your collegiate environment. How might this information be important? When
you interview prospective culturally diverse students, verbally communicating
this simple factual information will be duly noted, and you may be perceived as a
counselor educator who is informed about the presence of diverse students in your
environment. Further, many counselor educators often do not know how many
culturally diverse students are being served by their institution. By sharing such
information, you are likely to be perceived as a multiculturally oriented counselor
educator.

Another example of a campus resource is the student newspaper. Counselor
educators who dedicate time to reading the campus student newspaper often find
stories and articles that address issues, topics, and events in the life experiences of
racial/ethnic culturally diverse students. Feature stories about cultural holidays
and celebratory occasions describe students' preparation, involvement, and experience of these time-honored cultural traditions. By reading the campus student
newspaper you gain an increased and more specific knowledge about how cultural
diverse students feel, think, and act within your collegiate environment.

As you absorb information about the experience of various racial/ethnic
groups, assessing what racial identity ego status domains may be reflected, based
upon these students' affective, behavioral, and cognitive reactions to university
life, is helpful. An article talking about a Martin Luther King, Jr., celebration taking place at the African American Student Cultural Center may, for example,
provide insights about the ego status domains of students attending this event. In
addition, notice that *African American* is the reference group identified within the
name of this student gathering place. What if the name of center utilized *Black* as
the reference group label for the student center? Might our understanding of
Helms' Black racial identity model suggest a potential ego status domain for this
particular organization? What if the name of the center was the Multicultural
Resource Center? In such a case, we might expect to find the representation and
service of all diverse racial/ethnic groups of students, including White college students. And when was the last time you actually entered such a building on campus and interacted with the culturally diverse students on campus? This is
another example of an excellent resource for learning about others.

As you increase your experiential and didactic knowledge about differing cultural groups, thinking of yourself as engaging in an anthropological inquiry may be
helpful. Your objective is to gather culturally relevant contextual information
about diverse students. Your own pattern of interaction across groups or particular individuals is not the central focus. You want to adopt a spectator position and
develop a skillful level of "objective subjectivity" in your information-processing

strategy for encoding racial interaction dynamics. Objective subjectivity should be used to account for your observed or identified perspective of another individual (similar or dissimilar to your own racial identity) in relationship to the influence of your own racial identity ego status (which controls your information-processing strategy for any given stimuli, whether observed, identified, or informed). Objective subjectivity reinforces the self-in-relationship dynamic affecting all racio-cultural human interactions.

If for example, you as an African American counselor educator are predominantly in the Immersion/Emersion ego status within the Black racial identity model and you observe that a group of White students have organized to form a pro-White student association, your affective, behavioral, and cognitive reactions will be quite different from those of an African American counselor educator predominantly in the Conformity (Preencounter) ego status or a White counselor educator predominantly in the Reintegration ego status. As an African American counselor educator with an information-processing strategy defined by the Immersion/Emersion) ego status, you act to promote empowerment of your own racial group but are likely to denigrate or go against White racial group efforts. In this example, I hope that you as a racially identified counselor educator may understand how your racial ego status acts as a filter for all incoming stimuli. Again, although you are aware of how your information-processing strategy is mediated by your racial ego status, it is important to note that as an anthropological spectator using objective subjectivity, you are more focused on the affective, behavioral, and cognitive responses of those culturally different from yourself.

Learning About How the Self Relates to Others

The first two components of the self-awareness for multiculturally oriented counselor educators model assist counselor educators in developing skills for learning about their own cultural/racial identity and that of their students and colleagues. The third component builds on these skills and assists counselor educators in increasing their awareness, sensitivity, and cutural skills in interacting with others. These increases are accomplished through reflecting on how they relate to students, colleagues, and others based on racial identity ego statuses (see Tables 5-1 and 5-2) and through developing a conscious awareness of the cultural infuences operating in their relationships with students, colleagues, and others.

In this final component of the self-awareness for multiculturally oriented counselor educators model, you are asked to focus on self-in-relationship to others. More specifically, you are asked clearly to identify and recognize how your racial ego status impacts your reaction to and experience of counseling students culturally different from yourself. This component of the self-awareness for multiculturally oriented counselor educators model also requires that, after careful self-exploration of your culturally oriented response style, you seek feedback from counseling students and possibly other counselor educators about their perceptions of you as a racially cultural being. In essence, you want to engage in Buber's I-Thou relational style.

Investigating and learning about how you relate to others requires a moderate to high level of risk taking on your part as a counselor educator. You need to exercise careful consideration of the when, where, who, what, and how in regard to

Table 5-1 | Black Racial Identity Ego Statuses, Information-Processing Strategy, and Sample Schema Items

Status Descriptions	Black Ego Statuses
Status 1—Acceptance of societally imposed racial characterizations and rules for dispensing societal resources *Information-Processing Strategy:* denying, distancing, own-group blaming, individualistic	**Conformity (Preencounter)**—External self-definition that implies devaluation of Whites and White standards of merit. *Sample Schema:* "I feel uncomfortable around Black people."
Status 2—Confusion concerning one's racial group commitment and ambivalence in racial self-definition. *Information-Processing Strategy:* disorientating, repressive, vacillating	**Dissonance (Encounter)**—Ambivalence and confusion concerning one's role relative to one's own racial group and the White group *Sample Schema:* "I feel guilty or anxious about some of the things I believe about Black people."
Status 3—Idealization of one's group and use of external standards to define oneself and the contrast group, resistance to outgroup oppressive forces. *Information-Processing Strategy:* hypervigilant, judging, dichotomizing, combative	**Immersion/Emersion**—Idealization of one's own racial group, denigration of that which is perceived to be White, emphasis on group empowerment *Sample Schema: "I frequently confront the system and the (White) man."*
Status 4—Resolution of intrapsychic conflict with contrast racial group and internalization of positive racial characteristics *Information Processing Strategy:* analytic, flexible, intellectualizing	*Internalization*—Intellectualizing, capacity objectively to assess and respond to members of the White group, and use of internal criteria for self-definition. *Sample Schema:* "People regardless of their race have strengths and limitations."
Status 5—Questioning, analysis, and comparison of racial group status relative to other socioracial groups, universal resistance to oppression *Information-Processing Strategy:* probing, restructing, integrating	**Integrative Awareness** (Internalization/Commitment)—Capacity to value one's own collective identities as well as recognize similarities between oneself and other oppressed people *Sample Schema:* I involve myself in social action and political groups even if there are no other Blacks involved.

Note. From "Toward a Methodology for Measuring and Assessing Racial as Distinguished from Ethnic Identity," by J. E. Helms, in *Multicultural Assessment in Counseling and Clinical Psychology*, edited by G. R. Sodowsky and J. C. Impara, 1996, Lincoln, NE: Buros Institute of Mental Measurements. Adapted with permission.

Table 5-2 | White Racial Identity Ego Statuses, Information-Processing Strategy, and Sample Schema Items

Status Descriptions	White Ego Statuses
Status 1—Acceptance of societally imposed racial characterizations and rules for dispensing societal resources *Information-Processing Strategy:* denying oblivious, naive	**Contact**—Satisfaction with racial status quo, obliviousness to racism and one's participation in it *Sample Schema:* "I wish I had a Black friend."
Status 2—Confusion concerning one's racial group commitment and ambivalence in racial self-definition *Information-Processing Strategy:* disorientating, suppressive	**Disintegration**—Disorientation caused by racial moral dilemmas which force one to choose between commitment to one's racial group and principles of humanity *Sample Schema:* "I do not feel that I have the social skills to interact with Black people effectively."
Status 3—Idealization of one's group and use of external standards to define oneself and other groups *Information-Processing Strategy:* minimizing, selectively percepting, outgroup distorting	**Reintegration**—Idealization of one's own racial group, denigration of other racial groups, championship of own-group entitlement *Sample Schema:* "I get angry when I think about how Whites have been treated by Blacks."
Status 4—"Good-bad" dichotomization of racial groups and imposition of own group's standards as condition for acceptance *Information-Processing Stategy:* rationalizing, selectively percepting	**Pseudo-independence**—Rationalization of commitment to own racial group and of ostensible liberalism toward other groups. *Sample Schema:* "I feel as comfortable around Blacks as I do around Whites."
Status 5—Questioning, analysis, and comparison of racial group status relative to other groups *Information-Processing Strategy:* hypervigilant, probing, analyzing	**Immersion/Emersion**—Search for an understanding of how one benefits from and contributes to racism *Sample Schema:* "I am making a special effort to understand the significance of being White."
Status 6—Self-affirming commitment to one's societally assigned racial group; flexible standards for perceiving other racial group *Information-Processing Strategy:* integrating, intellectualizing	**Autonomy**—Informed, integrated positive racial-group commitment, use of internal standards for self-definition, capacity to relinquish the privileges of racism *Sample Schema:* "I involve myself in causes regardless of the race of the people involved in them."

Note: From "Toward a Methodology for Measuring and Assessing Racial as Distinguished from Ethic Identity," by J. E. Helms, in *Multicultural Assessment in Counseling and Clinical Psychology*, edited by G. R. Sodowsky and J. C. Impara, 1996, Lincoln, NE: Buros Institute of Mental Measurements. Adapted with permission. These tables are reprints from Helms (1996).

processing raciocultural human interactions. Effective movement in this component of the model also requires that you have become culturally responsive and
capable of adequately perceiving the dominant racial ego status influencing the
counseling students you interact with. You also need to be confidant about the
racial ego statuses impacting your affective, behavioral, and cognitive response
style. The ability to engage effectively in racially oriented cultural communication
with counseling students and colleagues reflects a counselor educator's level of
multicultural competence. Multicultural competence in this context is defined as
a set of perceived and demonstrated culturally oriented skills used for enhancing
cultural affirmation of self and another.

For example, a Black counselor educator in the Immersion/Emersion ego status may tend to maintain distance between him- or herself and White counseling
students and colleagues and seek more contact with other Black counselor educators. He or she may tend to value offering support and advisement to Black
students as opposed to White students. This does not mean that the Immersion/
Emersion ego status counselor educator ignores White colleagues and counseling
students, but that he or she simply does not choose to or desire to establish
strong working relationships with Whites. Individuals in this status tend not to
trust White people. Further, because the Immersion/Emersion ego status counselor educator might be perceived as hypervigilant, judging, combative, and
dichotomizing, he or she may not achieve an open trusting relationship with
Whites.

Given this Black ego status orientation, the counselor educator needs to work
hard at finding avenues to forge closer connections with White colleagues and
counseling students. The Immersion/Emersion ego status counselor educator
needs to seek experiences and encounters that would allow him or her to increase
the level of trust and respect for White colleagues and counseling students. It
seems imperative for this individual to engage in collaborative work with White
counselor educators and/or counseling students that provides evidence that
White colleagues and/or students not only understand but also support (work to
eliminate) the oppressive forces impacting Blacks in America. Further, this type
of interpersonal interaction with White colleagues and students affords change
within the Immersion/Emersion ego status counselor educator's information-
processing strategy (Helms, 1996), so that over time, he or she may be propelled
into Helms' Internalization ego status.

For another example, a Pseudo-Independence ego status White counselor educator may exhibit a "rationalized commitment to [his or her] own racial group and
. . . ostensible liberalism toward other groups" (Helms, 1996, p. 157). Thus it
is with great comfort and ease that the Pseudo-Independent ego status counselor
educator provides support and encouragement to other White counselor educators and counseling students. As long as other Whites in the environment hold
values, beliefs, and attitudes similar to those of the Pseudo-Independent ego status counselor educator, their position and perspective will be supported and
advanced by the Pseudo-Independent ego status counselor educator. In addition,

the Pseudo-Independent ego status counselor educator will act as a strong advocate for Black colleagues and counseling students as long as they, too, adopt and
display those values, beliefs, and attitudes defined as appropriate majority group
norms or standards (Helms, 1996).

Difficulty arises when a Pseudo-Independent ego status White counselor educator encounters Black colleagues or students who challenge the justness of certain White norms or standards. The Pseudo-Independent ego status White
counselor educator may strongly resent the indication that his or her norms or
standards are inappropriate—or inaccurate from the perspective of cultural diversity. Again, difficulty also arises when a Pseudo-Independent ego status counselor
educator perceives other Black colleagues and students as being "too pushy" or as
rebels. These types of Blacks may also be characterized as being "bad people,"
"troublemakers," or "whistle blowers." Indeed, other White counselor educators
or counciling students who espouse similar grave concerns about White norms or
standards may be characterized in this manner as well.

Most beneficial for the White Pseudo-Independent ego status counselor educator will be to broaden his or her information-processing strategy beyond ratio-
nalizing and selectively perceiving (see Table 5-2). The Pseudo-Independent ego
status counselor educator needs to recognize subtle shades of differences resulting
from intracultural diversity and accept the reality that not all Black students or
colleagues experience his or her "liberal" concern and care as being genuinely supportive. This may be disconcerting for the Pseudo-Independent ego status counselor educator because he or she expects many Blacks, if not all, to have similar
political perspectives, worldviews, socioeconomic status, religious/spiritual orientation, sexual orientation. In fact, these shades of differences among Blacks as a
unique cultural group are not often portrayed in popular press and media. Thus
the Pseudo-Independent ego status White counselor educator does not perceive
what Cross (1991) has noted in his title, *Shades of Black: Diversity in African-
American Identity*.

These two examples illustrate potential raciocultural human interactions
among counselor educators, counseling students, and colleagues and emphasize
the importance of racial identity ego statuses in learning about how counselor
educators, students, and colleagues may relate to each other.

Given your progression through the first two components of the self-awareness
for multiculturally oriented counselor educators model, you are now prepared to
assess how you relate to others racially different as well as similar to yourself.
Think about a highly charged positive and negative interaction you experienced
with a counseling student. Think about racial identity development. For both of
these encounters, identify the primary racial ego status(es) influencing your affective, behavioral, and cognitive response style with this counseling student. Can
you also hypothesize the racial ego status(es) influencing the student during these
interactions? Based on your professional and clinical judgment, what assumptions
might you draw about how you and the student are relating to one another?
Determining the degree and manner to which racial ego status may be affecting

how you relate to others, as well as how others may consequentially perceive you, may be beneficial. Exploration through the self-awareness for multiculturally oriented counselor educators model may, as stated earlier, involve a moderate level of risk taking, but if you have a solid working relationship with the student and he or she seems willing, engage in open dialogue about your perceptions and experiences to ascertain the student's perspective. Remember that as a counselor educator in a culturally diverse society, it is important not only that you develop multicultural competence but also that you role model for students successful ways to integrate racial identity into faculty-student, mentor-mentee, adviser-advisee, and supervisor-supervisee working relationships.

SUMMARY

Racial identity has been defined as "the psychological or internalized consequences of being socialized in a racially oppressive environment and the characteristics of self that develop in response to or in synchrony with either benefiting from or suffering under such oppression" (Helms, 1996, p. 147). Counselor educators need to be mindful of the impact of intentional and unintentional forms of oppression that may affect socioracial relationships with counseling students. Critical understanding of racial identity serves as a powerful conceptualization that increases our levels of awareness, sensitivity, knowledge, and skills in relationship to socioracial human interactions.

The counseling profession has made extensive use of racial identity development models in seeking to enhance the counselor/client dyad and, recently, the supervisor/supervisee dyad. It seems important and timely for us to examine more closely the multiple roles and relationships within the counselor educator/counselor-in-training dyad. Counselor educators are charged with multifaceted roles and responsibilities as cultural guardians of the counseling profession, and as such we are training future counselors to provide critical interventions within a multiculturally pluralistic society. Are we effectively modeling how to explore and manage racial dynamics in our working relationships within the training environment?

The self-awareness for multiculturally oriented counselor educators model is recommended as a process for assessing counselor educators achievement of increased multicultural competence in working relationships with counseling students. The model addresses three component areas: learning about self, learning about others, and learning about how the self relates to others. Although this model may be utilized to explore various facets of cultural identity variables affecting counselor educator and counseling student interactions, the salience of race has been the focal point in this chapter.

Understanding primary issues affecting Blacks and Whites in regards to racial identity development is critical (Helms, 1996). Helms noted that for Blacks, as a less powerful sociocultural group, a primary socioracial identity issue is to overcome the internalized negative stereotyping associated with membership. For Whites, a more dominant sociocultural group, primary issues include overcoming the entitled stereotyping associated with membership and learning to appreciate one's group and oneself as a member of the White socioracial group. For better or worse, in many ways we still live in a polarized society. Information-processing strategies emerging from racial ego status(es) drive individual responses, sometimes consciously, sometimes unconsciously. In efforts to serve as cultural change agents, the counselor educators must seek to promote cultural affirmation—the experience of having the various facets of cultural identity validated by others in the environment. Movement through the self-awareness for multiculturally oriented counselor educators model has strong potential to foster racial cultural affirmation within and among counselor educators and consequently their students and colleagues.

REFERENCES

Allison, K. W., Crawford, I., Echemendia, R., Robinson, L., & Knepp, D. (1994). Human diversity and professional competence: Training in clinical and counseling psychology revisited. *American Psychologist, 49,* 792–796.

Ashby, J. S., & Cheatham, H. E. (1996). Multicultural counseling and supervision. In J. L. DeLucia-Waack (Ed.), *Multicultural counseling competencies: Implications for training and practice* (pp. 47–59). Alexandria, VA: Association for Counselor Education and Supervision.

Atkinson, D., Morten, G., & Sue, D. W. (1998). *Counseling American minorities: A cross-cultural perspective.* Dubuque, IA: Brown.

Bowman, V. E. (1996). Counselor self-awareness and ethnic self-knowledge as a critical component of multicultural training. In J. L. DeLucia-Waack (Ed.), *Multicultural counseling competencies: Implications for training and practice* (pp. 7–30). Alexandria, VA: Association for Counselor Education and Supervision.

Carter, R. T. (1990). Does race or racial identity attitudes influence the counseling process in Black and White dyads? In J. E. Helms (Ed.), *Black and White racial identity attitudes: Theory, research, and practice* (pp. 145–164). Westport, CT: Greenwood Press.

Cass, V. C. (1979). Homosexual identity formation: A theoretical model. *Journal of Homosexuality, 4,* 219–235.

Cass, V. C. (1996). Sexual orientation identity formation: A western phenomenon. In R. Cabaj & T. Stein (Eds.), *Textbook of homosexuality and mental health* (pp. 227–252). Washington, DC: American Psychiatric Press.

Constantine, M. G. (1997). Facilitating multicultural competency in counseling supervision: Operationalizing a practical framework. In D. B. Pope-Davis & H. L. K. Coleman (Eds.), *Multicultural counseling competencies: Assessment, education and training, and supervision* (pp. 310–324). Thousand Oaks, CA: Sage.

Cross, W. E. (1971). The Negro-to-Black conversion experience: Toward a psychology of Black liberation. *Black World, 20*(9), 13–27.

Cross, W. E. (1991). *Shades of Black: Diversity in African-American identity.* Philadelphia: Temple University Press.

Cross, W. E. (1995). The psychology of nigrescence: Revising the Cross model. In J. G. Ponterotto, M. Casas, L. A. Suzuki, & C. M. Alexander (Eds.), *Handbook of multicultural counseling* (pp. 93–122). Thousand Oaks, CA: Sage.

D'Andrea, M., & Daniels, J. (1997). Multicultural counseling supervision: Central issues, theoretical considerations, and practical strategies. In D. B. Pope-Davis & H. L. K. Coleman (Eds.), *Multicultural counseling competencies: Assessment, education and training, and supervision* (pp. 290–309). Thousand Oaks, CA: Sage.

Fong, M. L., & Lease, S. H. (1997). Cross-cultural supervision: Issues for the White supervisor. In D. B. Pope-Davis & H. L. K. Coleman (Eds.), *Multicultural counseling competencies: Assessment, education and training, and supervision* (pp. 387–405). Thousand Oaks, CA: Sage.

Gilligan, C. (1982). *In a different voice.* Cambridge, MA: Harvard University Press.

Gim, R. H., Atkinson, D. R., & Kim, S. J. (1991). Asian American acculturation, counselor ethnicity and cultural sensitivity, and ratings of counselors. *Journal of Counseling Psychology, 38,* 57–62.

Gonzalez, R. C. (1997). Postmodern supervision: A multicultural perspective. In D. B. Pope-Davis & H. L. K. Coleman (Eds.), *Multicultural counseling competencies: Assessment, education and training, and supervision* (pp. 350–386). Thousand Oaks, CA: Sage.

Helms, J. E. (1990). *Black and White racial identity: Theory, research, and practice.* Westport, CT: Greenwood Press.

Helms, J. E. (1995). An update of Helm's White and people of color racial identity models. In J. G. Ponterotto, M. Casas, L. A. Suzuki, & C. M. Alexander (Eds.), *Handbook of multicultural counseling* (pp. 181–198). Thousand Oaks, CA: Sage.

Helms, J. E. (1996). Toward a methodology for measuring and assessing racial as distinguished from ethnic identity. In J. C. Impara (Series Ed.) & G. R. Sodowsky & J. C. Impara (Vol. Eds.), *Multicultural assessment in counseling and clinical psychology* (pp. 325–343). Lincoln, NE: Buros Institute of Mental Measurements.

Helms, J. E., & Carter, R. T. (1991). Relationships of White and Black racial identity attitudes and demographic similarity to counselor preferences. *Journal of Counseling Psychology, 38,* 446–457.

Hills, H. I., & Strozier, A. L. (1992). Multicultural training in APA-approved counseling psychology programs: A survey. *Professional Psychology: Research and Practice, 23,* 43–51.

Ivey, A. E., Ivey, M. B., & Simek-Morgan, L. (1997). *Counseling and psychotherapy: A multicultural perspective.* Needham Heights, MA: Allyn & Bacon.

Martinez, R. P., & Holloway, E. L. (1997). The supervision relationship in multicultural training. In D. B. Pope-Davis & H. L. K. Coleman (Eds.), *Multicultural counseling competencies: Assessment, education and training, and supervision* (pp. 325–349). Thousand Oaks, CA: Sage.

McIntosh, P. (1989, July/August). White privilege: Unpacking the invisible knapsack. *Peace and Freedom,* 10–12.

McGoldrick, M., Pearce, J. K., & Giordano, J. (Eds.). (1982). *Ethnicity and family therapy.* New York: Guilford Press.

Parham, T. A., & Helms, J. E. (1985). Relation of racial identity attitudes to self-actualization and affective states of Black students. *Journal of Counseling Psychology, 32,* 307–322.

Pedersen, P. B. (1991). Introduction to the special issue on multiculturalism as a fourth force in counseling. *Journal of Counseling and Development, 70,* 4.

Ponterotto, J., & Casas, M. (1991). *Handbook of racial/ethnic minority counseling research.* Springfield, IL: Charles C Thomas.

Ponterotto, J., Casas, M., Suzuki, L. A., & Alexander, C. M. (Eds.). (1995). *Handbook of multicultural counseling.* Thousand Oaks, CA: Sage.

Pope-Davis, D. B., & Nielson, D. (1996). Assessing multicultural counseling competencies using the multicultural counseling inventory: A review of the research. In J.C. Impara (Series Ed.) & G. R. Sodowsky & J. C. Impara (Vol. Eds.), *Multicultural assessment in counseling and clinical psychology* (pp. 325–343). Lincoln, NE: Buros Institute of Mental Measurements.

Ridley, C. R., Mendoza, D. W., Kanitz, B. E., Angermeier, L., & Zenck, R. (1994). Cultural sensitivity in multicultural counseling: A perceptual schema model. *Journal of Counseling Psychology, 41,* 125–136.

Rowe, W., Behrens, J. T., & Leach, M. M. (1995). Racial/ethnic identity and racial consciousness: Looking back and looking forward. In J. G. Ponterotto, M. Casas, L. A. Suzuki, & C. M. Alexander (Eds.), *Handbook of multicultural counseling* (pp. 218–235). Thousand Oaks, CA: Sage.

Stone, G. L. (1997). Multiculturalism as a context for supervision: Perspectives, limitations, and implications. In D. B. Pope-Davis & H. L. K. Coleman (Eds.), *Multicultural counseling competencies: Assessment, education and training, and supervision* (pp. 263–289). Thousand Oaks, CA: Sage.

Sue, D. W., Arredondo, P., & McDavis, R. J. (1992). Multicultural counseling competencies and standards: A call to the profession. *Journal of Counseling & Development, 70*(4), 477–486.

Sue, D. W., & Sue, S. (1990). *Counseling the culturally different: Theory and practice* (2nd ed.). New York: Wiley.

Thomas, C. (1971). *Boys no more.* Beverly Hills, CA: Glencoe.

6 | Confronting Racism Through Increased Awareness, Knowledge, and Skill as a Culture-Centered Primary Prevention Strategy

Paul Pedersen

No matter how highly skilled or trained, if counseling professionals make wrong or inappropriate culturally learned assumptions they will not be accurate in their assessment or appropriate in their treatment interventions. By the time individuals enter multicultural training in counselor education most have developed some form of ethnocentric, racist and/or prejudicial behaviors and/or attitudes. Increasing the student's self-awareness of these cultural misunderstandings early in the training process, rather than through remediation after training when working with culturally different clients, is an example of how multicultural training can be viewed as a primary prevention strategy. The knowledge about counseling and the skills to deliver counseling services can then be mediated by a culturally sensitive self-awareness by the counselee trainee.

The inaccuracy or misattribution resulting from wrong assumptions translates into defensive disengagement by both the provider and consumer of counseling, each trying to protect the truth as he or she perceives it. Multicultural training is too often classified as a secondary or tertiary prevention strategy. This chapter examines multicultural training as a primary prevention strategy in mental health services and describes a three-stage developmental sequence that uses a culture-centered approach and moves from multicultural awareness to knowledge/comprehension to skill/applications. In the first stage, auditing the assumptions being made by counselors and increasing the level of cultural self-awareness in both the provider and consumer of counseling services challenges the culturally encapsulated descriptions of key concepts in health, illness, change, safety, respect, trust, and other commonly shared expectations or values. In the second stage, documenting facts and knowledge for increased comprehension is essential to meaningful understanding of a presenting problem in its cultural context and provides

or constructs a receptive site for treatment and change. In the third stage, generating appropriate treatment skills for bringing about change so that the provider
is appropriate and effective in matching the skill to the cultural context builds on
a common ground of shared positive expectations and values. These areas of common ground may be expressed differently in the behaviors of culturally different
people. The provider and consumer can then express their shared positive values
in their own culturally different ways.

The three-stage developmental sequence of awareness, knowledge, and skills
is based on Sue, Bernier, Durran, Feinberg, Pedersen, Smith, and Vasquez-Nuttall
(1982) and on more recent expansion of this model by Sue, Arredondo, and
McDavis (1992). When the National Institute of Mental Health (NIMH) project
Developing Intercultural Skilled Counselors, which was based in Hawaii,
reviewed program designs across the country, it found that programs failed typically for one of three reasons (Pedersen, 1994). The first reason was that a program overemphasized awareness and participants became sick and tired of a
search for awareness that did not seem to be productive because an emphasis on
knowledge and skill was lacking. The second reason for failure was that a program
overemphasized knowledge and information and participants, lacking awareness
and skill, could not see how all that information was relevant. The third reason
for failure was that a program jumped directly to teaching skills, but the participants, lacking awareness and knowledge, could not tell if their skills were making
things better or worse! Thus the three-stage developmental sequence from awareness to knowledge to skill that is described in this chapter provides a convenient,
comprehensive, and balanced approach to culture-centered training.

Much training and most education skip over the first stage of developing multicultural awareness. It is difficult to know the culture of others until and unless
we have an awareness of our own culturally learned assumptions as they control
our lives. We dare not assume that we or our colleagues have already achieved a
high level of cultural self awareness because this is an ongoing developmental
process. The importance of these unexamined underlying assumptions is frequently underestimated.

Once we have achieved some degree of self-awareness, both as we perceive
ourselves and how we are perceived by others and have become clear about our
underlying assumptions, we also know more about the facts and information we
need to acquire and it is appropriate to move to the second stage. Increased
awareness helps us ask the right questions in the right way at the right time.
Increased awareness also helps us find both similarities and differences between
and among the population being served.

Once we have accomplished both cultural self awareness and knowledge we
are ready to move to the third stage and identify the skills we need. The same
behavior that is appropriate in one culture may be completely inappropriate in
another culture. Because every test and theory was developed in a specific cultural context, each is likely to reflect assumptions implicit in that context and, to
a greater or lesser extent, be biased. Culture-centered skill is the ability to use

data from culturally biased tests or theories and apply them appropriately, meaningfully, and helpfully in a variety of different cultural contexts.

STAGE 1—CULTURE-CENTERED AWARENESS

Culture is emerging as one of the most important and perhaps one of the most misunderstood constructs in contemporary counseling literature. Culture may be defined narrowly as limited to ethnicity and nationality or defined broadly to include any and all potentially salient ethnographic, demographic, status, or affiliation variable. This chapter presumes the broad and inclusive definition of culture to those variables that are salient at a particular point of time, recognizing that this salience is always changing as the context changes. Given this broader definition of culture, it is possible to identify at least a dozen assets that are exclusively available through increased cultural awareness:

1. Because all behavior is learned and displayed in a cultural context, accurate assessment, meaningful understanding, and appropriate interventions are culturally contextual constructs. When I encounter colleagues opposed to multiculturalism, I ask them if they consider accuracy to be important, which they always do. Then I suggest that we are on the same side in our search for accuracy.

2. The common ground of shared values or expectations, such as Respect, Trust, Success, and Safety, can be expressed by culturally learned "contrasting" behaviors that are different from one culture to another. Not everyone who smiles at us is our friend, and not everyone who shouts at us is our enemy. Reframing conflict in a culture-centered perspective allows two people or groups to "apparently" disagree in their behaviors while accurately expressing agreement on their shared values. In some cultures a student is rewarded by giving that student a lot of public attention and credit. In other cultures singling out a student for public and attention is a very negative experience for that student. If we prematurely judge another's behavior out of context, we are likely to turn potential friends into enemies. If we begin by increasing our awareness of the shared positive values and expectations, we can both teach and learn about which behavior is best in each cultural context.

3. The visual image I have of culture is a thousand people sitting with me in my chair or wherever I am day and night. These thousand culture teachers, accumulated from relatives, friends, enemies, and fantasies, whisper advice, reward, and scold as they celebrate our accomplishments and mourn our losses. Our internal dialogue with these culture teachers is a frequently underutilized resource in our decision-making and hypotheses-forming processes.

4. A healthy socioecosystem requires a diversity of cultural perspectives just as a healthy biosystem requires a diverse gene pool. Utopian or cult groups that have cut themselves off from their cultural context to create perfect little worlds by eradicating cultural alternatives in their society have failed throughout history. Superpowers that have failed to recognize and acknowledge their interactive dependence on smaller nations have fallen. Culture is a growing, changing, interdependent, and always emerging force that resists capture and incarceration by language, power, or influence.

5. A culture-centered perspective protects us from inappropriately imposing our own culturally encapsulated self-reference criteria in the evaluation of others. By comparison, culturally encapsulated counselors define everyone's reality according to their own cultural assumptions, minimalize cultural differences, impose a self-reference criterion in judging the behavior of others, ignore proof that disconfirms their position, depend on techniques and strategies to solve their problems, and disregard their own cultural biases (Wrenn, 1962).

6. Contact with culturally different groups provides an opportunity to rehearse adaptive functioning for our own future survival in the global village. We know the future is so different that it is beyond our imagination, and we know that some of us will not survive because we will not be ready. By seeking out people and groups who do *not* think, dress, eat, play, work, or talk like ourselves and by learning to interact with people or groups who are different, we will acquire the facility for our own survival in that beyond-imagination future.

7. Understanding social justice and moral development in a multicultural context helps us differentiate necessary absolutes from culturally relative principles. Social justice typically requires an inclusive rather than an exclusive perspective, and moral exclusion has consistently resulted in classifying society according to the oppressed and the oppressors (Opotow, 1990). Cultural relativism has failed because it prevents discussion of social justice across cultures. Cultural absolutism has also failed because those who are in power are not always right. A more culturally interactive and relational ethic is needed.

8. A culture-centered perspective reflects the complementarity of the quantum metaphor (that light is both a particle and a wave) by emphasizing both the similarities and differences between and among us. Overemphasizing differences erects barriers and leads to hostile disengagement. Overemphasizing similarities results in a melting pot where the person or group that is in power makes the rules.

9. All learning and change involve some degree of culture shock to the degree that they influence our basic perspectives. Much can be learned through culture shock that cannot be learned in any other way. Culture provides a metaphorical model for education and the social change process

generally, by recognizing and accepting the pain or discomfort and reframing the experience in a positive perspective.

10. A culture-centered perspective enhances our spiritual completeness by linking culturally different spiritual perspectives to the same shared reality. The mystery of our being cannot be comprehended by any religion in isolation. In many cultures the only really important questions are the questions about where we originated and what happens after our death.

11. A culture-centered perspective builds pluralism as an alternative to authoritarianism or anarchy in our social organization. However, pluralism has never really been tried successfully. We have not developed the skill, or perhaps the ultimate necessity, to survive with one another. With population growth, pollution, and rapid utilization of limited global resources, we will be forced to one of these three choices, however; and learning to live together is much preferred to chaos.

12. A culture-centered perspective strengthens contemporary theories of humanist, behavioral, or psychodynamic psychological intervention rather than weakens or displaces them. The only reality we have is the one we perceive through our senses, and the rules for perceiving are themselves culturally learned. By making culture central rather than marginal to our psychological theory of choice, that theory functions more effectively in a variety of different cultural contexts.

The Intrapersonal Cultural Grid (see Figure 6-1) is an attempt to demonstrate how (1) each behavior is based on (2) expectations as expectations are based on (3) values and as values are learned from (4) culture teachers from the various social systems in our lives. By understanding each behavior in the cultural context of consequent expectations, values, and culture teachers, it becomes possible to better understand that behavior. The Cultural Grid (Pedersen & Pedersen, 1985, 1989) provides a personal-cultural orientation in a heuristic framework for discussing and understanding same and different behaviors in their cultural context.

The categories of the Intrapersonal Cultural Grid, shown in Figure 6-1, provide a conceptual framework for demonstrating how cultural and personal factors interact in a combined context and link each behavior to expectations, each expectation to values, and each value to those social systems in which that value was learned.

Each cultural context is complicated and dynamic, influenced by many culture teachers from social systems that take turns being salient. Our cultural identity results from identifying the link between behaviors, expectations, values, and culture teachers. The Intrapersonal Cultural Grid is intended to show the complex relationship across cultures. Each behavior has many different expectations. Each expectation can express many different values. Each value is learned from many different culture teachers.

Figure 6-1 | The Intrapersonal Cultural Grid

	Role Behavior	Expectation	Value/Meaning
Demographic Race Gender Age Other			
Ethnographic Ethnicity Nationality Language			
Status Level Economic Social Educational			
Affiliation Formal Nonformal Informal			

The following vignette illustrates an application of the Intrapersonal Cultural Grid:

A middle school boy at a large Syracuse city school got into fights, threw chalk, and was disruptive every day about 3:00 p.m. until he was sent home. Every day followed the same routine until the teachers were ready to send the young man to a "custodial school" for hopeless youth. The counselor followed the young man home and discovered he was living with his single-parent mother. Every day about 3:00 p.m. the mother's boyfriend came to visit, usually a little bit drunk, and beat up the mother . . . unless the middle school son was home. If the son was home the mother would not get beaten up. The middle school boy knew he had to get home around 3:00 p.m. every day to protect his mother from being assaulted. If we apply the Interpersonal Cultural Grid to this situation, it is easy to see how it might be useful for counselors. First, the teachers were interpreting the boy's BEHAVIOR "out of context" without regard for WHY the young man was getting into fights every afternoon at 3:00 p.m. Second, although the young man's behaviors might be unacceptable, his values were heroic! Third, once the teachers and counselor identified the young man's motive, to protect his mother, then it was possible to discuss which behavior was most likely to result in the EXPECTATION shared by counselors, teachers, and the young man for protecting his mother. This situation would be in cell two—different behaviors but shared expectation—and was moving toward cell three, where the teachers could force the boy to behave differently but lose his trust entirely. The Interpersonal Cultural Grid provides a framework to interpret client's behaviors in the context where those behaviors were learned and displayed.

STAGE 2—CULTURE-CENTERED KNOWLEDGE

Cultures have negotiated their similarities and differences throughout history, and a comprehensive review of multicultural knowledge needs to go back to the beginning of recorded society. We know relatively little about the role of culture or counseling in prehistorical Asia, Africa, and other ancient civilizations. The social construct of culture has evolved from academic disciplines in Europe and areas colonized by European powers. In many cases the study of cultural differences was motivated by the need to justify social, economic, and political colonization of less industrialized cultures (Miles, 1989).

In 16th century Europe, there was much concern with social development and distinguishing "civilized" European from "savage" or "primitive" people outside the European context. European colonial powers sent scholars, philosophers, naturalists, and physicians on scientific expeditions to study cultural and physiological differences among primitive people, so as to provide a rationalization for colonization. By the 20th century, German scholars had taken the lead in studying the mentality of primitives, and the disciplines of psychology, anthropology, and sociology began to emerge influenced by the cultural context of 19th- and 20th-century Europe.

Psychology assumed a single universal definition of normal behavior whatever the cultural context. Thus the psychological study of cultures assumed a fixed state of mind, observation of which was obscured by cultural distortions, with culture seen as a deviation from the norm. A contrasting anthropological position assumed that cultural differences were clues to divergent attitudes, values, or perspectives that differentiated one culture from another and that were based on culture-specific factors. The anthropological perspective assumed that different groups or individuals had somewhat different definitions of normal behavior as a result of their own unique cultural contexts. Anthropologists have tended to take a relativist position when classifying and interpreting behavior across cultures; psychologists, by contrast, have linked social characteristics and psychological perspectives with minimum attention to the different cultural contexts. Only recently has there been a serious attempt to reconcile these two polarized positions.

A multicultural theory (Sue, Ivey, & Pedersen, 1996) seeks to provide a conceptual framework that acknowledges the complex cultural diversity of a plural society. The ultimate multicultural theory is a contextual understanding. As stated by Segall, Dasen, Berry, and Poortinga (1990), "there may well come a time when we will no longer speak of cross-cultural psychology as such. The basic premise of this field—that to understand human behavior, we must study it in its sociocultural context—may become so widely accepted that all psychology will be inherently cultural" (p. 352). That is not, however, the present situation.

The Basic Behavioral Science Task Force of the National Advisory Mental Health Council (1996), in their national plan for behavioral science research, identified several areas where social and cultural factors were evident in the research literature about mental health. Although this report is focused on mental health and mental illness, the implications for other fields of applied psychological intervention are clear. First, anthropological and cross-cultural research has demonstrated that cultural beliefs influence the diagnosis and treatment of mental illness. Second, the diagnosis of mental illness differs across cultures. Third, research has revealed differences in how individuals express symptoms in different cultural contexts. Fourth, culturally based variations in diagnosis vary according to the diagnostic categories relevant to the majority population. Fifth, most providers come from a majority culture whereas most clients are members of minority cultures.

A culture-centered perspective is central to the content and process of our knowing and comprehension. Sue et al. (1996) have attempted to describe a multicultural theory based on six propositions to demonstrate the fundamental importance of a culture-centered perspective.

1. Each Western or non-Western theory represents a different worldview.
2. The complex totality of interrelationships in client-counselor experiences and the dynamic changing context must be the focus of counseling, however inconvenient that may become.
3. A counselor or client's racial/cultural identity influences how problems are defined and dictate or define appropriate counseling goals or processes.
4. The ultimate goal of a culture-centered approach is to expand the repertoire of helping responses available to counselors.
5. Conventional roles of counseling are only some of the many alternative helping roles available from a variety of cultural contexts.
6. Multicultural theory emphasizes the importance of expanding personal, family, group, and organizational consciousness in a contextual orientation.

As these multicultural theory propositions are tested by counselors, new questions will emerge and lead to a more comprehensive culture-centered understanding of counseling and discussion of outcomes resulting from appropriate or inappropriate counseling (Gielen, 1994). Under what circumstances and in which culturally circumscribed situation does a given psychological theory or methodology provide valid explanations for the origins and maintenance of behavior? What are the cultural boundary conditions potentially limiting the generalizability of psychological theories and methodologies? Which psychological phenomena are culturally robust in character, and which phenomena appear only under specified cultural conditions?

There is a pervasive awareness of change in the social sciences generally and counseling in particular that will require rethinking of our culturally learned assumptions. Smith, Harre, and Van Langenhove (1995) have contrasted the new and old paradigms. The new paradigms emphasize applied understanding more than abstract measurement, finding meaning more than causation, social significance more than statistical significance, explanation more than numerical reductionism, holistic rather than atomistic perspectives, particularities more than universals, context-based more than context-free perspectives, and subjectivity more than objectivity. The old and new rules are seemlessly connected in the cultural context of counseling as alternative perspectives of the same phenomena. There needs to be a closer connection between theories about counseling and the practice of counseling in a necessarily multicultural context.

Counseling has been characterized by the culturally learned assumptions in which counseling originated and which must now be tested and modified as appropriate. Ten examples of these assumptions demonstrate this cultural dependency (Pedersen, 1994):

1. **We all share the same single measure of what is normal behavior.** There is a frequent assumption that describing a person's behavior as normal reflects a judgment both meaningful and representative of a desired pattern of behaviors across social, cultural, economic, and political contexts.
2. **Individuals are the basic building blocks of society.** The presumption is that counseling is primarily directed toward the development of individuals rather than units of individuals or groups such as the family, the organization, or society.
3. **Only problems defined within a framework of the counselor's expertise or academic discipline boundaries are of concern to the counselor.** There is a tendency to separate the identity of the counselor from that of other professionals, even though multicultural problems wander across these boundaries freely.
4. **There is a superior quality judgment attached to abstractions.** In our use of professional jargon, we all attach the same meaning to the same words across contexts. Although this assumption is typical of a low-context culture it will not apply to cultures where all words are contextually mediated.
5. **Independence is desirable and dependence is not desirable.** As part of our emphasis on individualism, there is a belief that individuals should not be dependent on others nor should individuals allow others to be dependent on them. This is not the case in a more collectivistic culture.
6. **Clients are helped more by formal counseling than by their natural support systems.** Family and peer support is the primary resource in many

cultures in which counseling is a last resort when everything else has failed. The long-term positive effect of counseling may require family and peer support.

7. **Everyone thinks the same way, moving linearly from cause to effect.** It is not just the content of our thinking that is culturally mediated but the process of thinking itself. Nonlinear thinking, typical of many cultural groups, will seem illogical to linear thinkers.

8. **Counselors need to change clients to fit the system and not change the system to fit the client.** Much of counseling relates to client adjustment, sometimes even when the system is wrong and the client is right.

9. **History is not relevant for a proper understanding of contemporary events.** Counselors are more likely to focus on the immediate events that created a crisis and consider historical background a distraction at best and a defensive evasion at worst.

10. **We already know all of our culturally learned assumptions.** Each time we discover something new about ourselves, we disprove this assumption. As we increase our contact with persons and groups from other cultures this process of self discovery is accelerated.

All counseling is, to a greater or lesser extent, multicultural. As we increase our contact with other countries and cultures, we can expect to learn a great deal about ourselves. We can expect to challenge more of our unexamined assumptions about ourselves as we learn to know and comprehend the world around us. We can expect to move beyond the parochial concerns of our culturally limited perspective to see the world around us in a new and more comprehensive perspective. The primary argument for increasing our multicultural knowledge and comprehension is to enhance our accuracy and effectiveness as counselors across the great variety of cultural contexts before us.

STAGE 3—CULTURE-CENTERED SKILL

The ability to listen consciously and intentionally to our own internal dialogue is positively correlated to counseling performance (Fiske & Taylor, 1991; Kimberlin & Friesin, 1980; Montgomery & Haemmerlie, 1987; Shorter, 1987). Unfortunately self-communication is difficult to access. There have been think-aloud approaches or thought-listing methodologies for assessing internal dialogue, but they are intrusive and distorted. There is, however, a teachable/learnable relationship between a trainee's thinking and behaving that contributes to competence (Richardson & Stone, 1981). Self-control, self-instruction, and mental imagery are all part of self-talk. Hypotheses formulation skills that occur through self-talk are positively related to facilitative performance. Self-talk has been used to reduce trainee anxiety. Self-talk mobilizes mental imagery, expressed belief, and culturally learned assumptions (Kline, 1988). Competence requires that we learn more about how our inner speech mediates our self-consciousness and inhibits our culturally encapsulated perspective. Research on self-talk suggests that it is the quality rather than the quantity of self-talk that is most important (Kurpius, Benjamin, & Morran, 1985).

There are a number of ways that managing self-talk contributes to competency (Nutt-Williams & Hill, 1996):

- Self-talk focuses attention on the task, self-evaluation, and perspective taking.
- Self-talk leads to higher levels of self-awareness.
- Self-talk permits the internalization of others' perspectives.
- Self-talk contributes to self-observation in a continuous communication loop.
- Guilt reactions are mediated by an internal thought process.
- By changing our self-talk, we can change our feelings and actions.
- Internal voices influence intrapersonal and interpersonal relationships.

Research on self-talk has indicated a number of ways that it influences the therapy process (Nutt-Williams & Hill, 1996):

- Self-talk is related to perceptions of therapy.
- Therapists who think negatively about themselves are perceived as less helpful.
- Self-talk changes the environment, finds meaning, and directs behavior.
- Self-evaluation provides motivation.
- Clients hide their true feelings through self-talk.
- Therapists focus more on their own self-talk than the client's self-talk.
- Therapists can use self-talk to manage anxiety and hear the client's internal dialogue.

Counseling occurs as a dialogue between the counselor and client where self and society are not discrete conceptions. The dialogue is constructed and reconstructed with input from others both within and outside the self (Hermans & Kempen, 1993). The complexities of decision making best demonstrate our multivoiced selves interacting in a sociocultural context. If self is a multiplicity of voices more than a unitary thought process, then this polyphonic interpretation of self has more than one theme.

Every counseling interview includes three simultaneous conversations. First, the client and counselor have a verbal conversation, which they can both monitor. Second, the counselor has his or her own internal dialogue exploring related or sometimes unrelated factors, which the counselor can also monitor. Third, the client has her or his own internal dialogue, exploring related and sometimes unrelated thoughts, which the client can monitor but the counselor cannot. The counselor does not know what a client is thinking, but the counselor does know that some of the client's internal dialogue is positive and some of the client's internal dialogue is negative. These three interacting conversations have led to the development of the Triad Training Model (Pedersen, 1997) for counseling and counselor education.

The Triad Training Model is a simulation to make explicit the internal dialogue that the client might be thinking but not saying. The more culturally different the counselor is from the client, the less likely that counselor is to know what the client is thinking. Although we do not know what the client is thinking, we can assume some of what the client is thinking is positive and some is negative. The counselor trainee is matched with three resource persons in a culturally matched team, different from the counselor trainee's culture. One resource person is in the role of a coached client who presents the problem for which he or she is seeking help from counseling. A second resource person is in the role of a coached anti-counselor who articulates the negative internal messages that the client might be thinking but not saying. The anticounselor will attempt to sabotage the counseling process by emphasizing and exaggerating these negative messages. The third resource person is in the role of a coached procounselor who articulates the positive internal messages that a client might be thinking but not saying. The procounselor will facilitate the success of the counselor and the counseling process.

The resulting four-way conversation between the counselor, the client, the procounselor, and the anticounselor provides the counselor access to the client's internal dialogue during the simulated counseling interview. As the counselor becomes more familiar with the positive and negative messages that a culturally different client might be thinking but not saying, the counselor will be able to incorporate those messages into the counseling interview itself (Pedersen, 1997). The four-way interaction is typically videotaped, and the videotape is reviewed in the debriefing session following each role-play to provide feedback to the counselor trainee.

The Triad Training Model simulates a force field of positive and negative messages from the client's cultural context articulated by the procounselor and the anticounselor. For the model that seems to work best:

- there should be both positive and negative feedback to the counselor during the interview;
- the simulated interview should reflect actual events in realistic ways;
- the simulated interview should occur under conditions that the counselor considers safe;
- procounselors and anticounselors should be carefully trained to be effective;
- the feedback to the counselor and client should be immediate and explicit during the actual interview;
- the resource persons should be articulate as well as authentic to the client's background;
- the counselor should learn how to focus on the client while listening to the anticounselor and the procounselor all at the same time;

- the interview should be spontaneous and not scripted;
- the interaction should be videotaped to ensure a more effective debriefing; and
- the actual simulated interview should be brief (8 to 10 minutes) to avoid overwhelming the counselor with information during or after the interview.

Potential advantages of including an anticounselor in the simulated cross-cultural counseling interview are that the anticounselor

- forces the counselor to become more aware of the client's cultural context;
- articulates the negative, embarrassing, and impolite comments that a culturally different client might not otherwise make;
- forces the counselor to examine her or his own defensive prejudices;
- points out a counselor's inappropriate interventions immediately during the interview while the counselor still has time to recover; and
- attempts to distract the counselor and thereby trains the counselor to focus on the client under battlefield conditions.

Advantages contributed by the procounselor in the simulated counseling interview are that the procounselor

- is a resource person to consult when the counselor is confused or in need of support;
- makes explicit information about the client that might facilitate the counselor's success;
- provides a partner for the counselor to work with on the problem rather than the counselor having to work alone;
- helps the counselor stay on track and avoid sensitive issues so as to decrease client resistance; and
- provides beneficial feedback to the counselor to avoid mistakes and build on successful strategies.

As an example of the resource teams at work, let us consider a situation in which a White American male counselor is working with a 24-year-old Japanese American female client who is troubled about whether or not to move out of her parent's home. The procounselor and anticounselor are also Japanese American women who articulate the positive or negative messages the client is thinking but not saying:

Client: What do you think I should do? I mean, what's correct? Do you think. . . .
Procounselor: That's right, trust him! He wants to help you!
Anticounselor: He's White and he's male! How can anyone that different from us be any help?
Counselor: Well, I guess if you are going to play by your parents' rules staying home and suffering, I think. . . .

Anticounselor: See! He thinks you're suffering at home and that you should move out! Remember your parents and your obligations to them!

Client: Do you think I'm suffering at home?

Procounselor: Something is certainly wrong, and he is trying to help you find out what it is.

Counselor: Well, I think something brought you here to talk to me about the dilemma you're in about wanting to move out and being very uncomfortable . . . having a rough time bringing it up to your folks in such a way that . . . uh . . . you can do that?

Anticounselor: Ask him when he moved out. When did he move out of his parents' home?

Client: Yeah, when did you move out of your parent's home?

Procounselor: Keep the focus on yourself. Attacking him is not going to help you.

Counselor: I moved out of my folk's home when I was 16.

Anticounselor: Why did he move out so young? You know? He moved out at 16! After all that his parents did for him and everything! You know? He moved out at 16! Such disrespect!

Counselor: Well, I went away to school and it was important to live at school. The school was in another town.

Procounselor: Keep the focus on your problem or he will never be able to help you. He wants to help you! Let him!

Client: Didn't your parents get mad that you went to another school?

Procounselor: His family rules may be different, but they still loved one another. Focus on the positive part!

Counselor: No, they wanted me to go to school. Education was pretty important to them.

Anticounselor: See!!! He's saying that your parents don't think education is important! He's insulting your parents!!!

This brief transcript illustrates the internal dialogue in action within the client's mind, how the client is focusing on positive, common-ground expectations but at the same time is also aware of different and possibly negative behaviors. Culture-centered competency in counseling requires the ability to monitor both the client's positive and negative internal dialogue.

SUMMARY

Competence in culture-centered counselor training and education is more than following a list of rules. Competence requires a more comprehensive change of perspective in the competent person and about the counseling process as a whole. Without such a change in perspective, a counselor in training can develop a high level of performance on skills in the classroom setting but fail to generalize that expertise to the outside world. Many of the most important elements of culture-centered counseling cannot be taught, but they can be learned if a favorable context is provided. The three-stage developmental sequence that begins with awareness, then moves to knowledge and finally to skills is one example of a favorable training context. The primary teachers of culture are inside ourselves, speaking to us—if we will listen to them. We accumulate the best and the brightest talent we can discover throughout our lives, and we add those voices to our own personal collection. If and when we are competent it is because those inside-the-person voices are guiding us toward competence.

In addition to hearing our own voices, we need to become more aware of the client's voices. Competence is measured by our ability to know what our client is thinking but not saying. To the extent that a client and counselor are culturally different, the task of hearing the client's voices is more difficult, but just as important. The Triad Training Model provides one way to hear what a culturally different client may be thinking but not saying, both positively and negatively. Feedback from an anticounselor and a procounselor helps counselors break out of their culturally encapsulated self-reference criterion. This culture-centered foundation of awareness, knowledge, and skill provides a basis for developing competence in counseling and counselor education/training.

REFERENCES

Basic Behavioral Science Task Force of the National Advisory Mental Health Council (1996). Basic behavioral science research for mental health: Sociocultural and environmental processes. *American Psychologist, 51*, 722–731.

Fiske, S. T., & Taylor S. E. (1991). *Social cognition* (2nd ed.). New York: McGraw Hill.

Gielen, U. P. (1994). American mainstream psychology and its relationship to international and cross-cultural psychology. In A. L. Comunian & U. P. Gielen, *Advancing psychology and its applications: International perspectives* (pp. 26–40). Milan, Italy: Franco Angeli.

Hermans, H. J. G., & Kempen, H. J. G. (1993). *The dialogical self: Meaning as movement.* New York: Academic Press.

Kimberlin, C. L., & Friesen, D. D. (1980). Sex and conceptual level empathic responses to ambivalent affect. *Counselor Education and Supervision, 19*, 252–258.

Kline, W. B. (1988). Training counselor trainees to talk to themselves: A method of focusing attention. *Counselor Education and Supervision 22*(4), 296–302.

Kurpius, D. J., Benjamin, D., & Morran, D. K. (1985). Effects of teaching a cognitive strategy on counselor trainee internal dialogue and clinical hypothesis formulation. *Journal of Counseling Psychology, 32*(2), 263–271.

Miles, R. (1989). *Racism.* New York: Routledge.

Montgomery, R. L., & Haemmerlie, F. M. (1987.) Self-perception theory and heterosocial anxiety. In J. E. Maddux, C. D. Stoltenberg, & R. Rosenwein (Eds.), *Social process in clinical and counseling psychology* (pp. 139–152). New York: Springer Verlag.

Nutt-Williams, E., & Hill, C. E. (1996). The relationship between self-talk and therapy process variables for novice therapists. *Journal of Counseling Psychology, 43*, 170–177.

Opotow, W. (1990). Moral exclusion and injustice: An introduction. *Journal of Social Issues, 46*(1), 1–20.

Pedersen, P. (1994). *A handbook for developing multicultural awareness.* Alexandria, VA: American Counseling Association.

Pedersen, P. (1997). *Culture-centered counseling interventions: Striving for accuracy.* Thousand Oaks, CA: Sage.

Pedersen, A., & Pedersen, P. (1985). The cultural grid: A personal cultural orientation. In L. Samovar & R. Porter (Eds.), *Intercultural communication: A reader* (pp. 50–62). Belmont, CA: Wadsworth.

Pedersen, P., & Pedersen, A. (1989). The cultural grid: A complicated and dynamic approach to multicultural counseling. *Counseling Psychology Quarterly, 2*(2), 133–141.

Richardson, B., & Stone, G. L. (1981). Effects of a cognitive adjunct procedure within a microtraining situation. *Journal of Counseling Psychology, 28*(2), 168–175.

Segall, M. H., Dasen, P. R., Berry, J. W., & Poortinga, Y. H. (1990). *Human behavior in global perspective: An introduction to cross-cultural psychology.* New York: Pergamon Press.

Shorter, J. (1987). The social construction of an "us": Problems of accountability and narratology. In R. Burnett, P. McGhee, & D. Clarke, *Accounting for relationships* (pp. 225–247). New York: Methuen.

Smith, J. A., Harre, R., & Van Langenhove, L. (1995). *Rethinking psychology.* London: Sage.

Sue, D. W., Arredondo, P., & McDavis, R. J. (1992). Multicultural counseling competencies and standards: A call to the profession. *Journal of Counseling and Development, 70,* 477–486.

Sue, D. W., Bernier, J. E., Durran, A., Feinberg, L., Pedersen, P., Smith, C. J., & Vasquez-Nuttall, G. (1982). Cross-cultural counseling competencies. *The Counseling Psychologist, 19*(2) 45–52.

Sue, D. W., Ivey, A., & Pedersen, P. (1996). *Multicultural counseling theory.* Belmont, CA: Brooks/Cole.

Wrenn, G. (1962). The culturally encapsulated counselor. *Harvard Educational Review, 32,* 444–449.

7 | Ways of Knowing/Oppression and Privilege

Mary E. Swigonski

Ways of knowing are intrinsic elements of systems of prejudice and oppression. Ways of knowing are also intrinsic elements of movements for social and economic justice and empowerment. As a consequence, knowledge and education are never politically neutral. What we know, what we teach, and how knowledge is employed and applied, influences and shapes the distribution of power and resources in our world. Teaching cultural diversity and multicultural training can open the door to the possibility of creating a learning community: a place were differences can be acknowledged, where we can finally all understand, accept, and affirm each other (hooks, 1994). For genuine communities to be created, however, our understanding, acceptance, and affirmation of each other must be based on knowledge that is as complete and accurate as possible. Complete and accurate knowing is elusive. It is even more so in contexts of diversity.

This chapter discusses a set of strategies to help students explore how ways of knowing are woven throughout relations of power. The awareness, knowledge, and skill that students acquire through their work with these strategies prepare them for multicultural work that both celebrates differences and works to end prejudice and oppression. Students are helped to learn to practice solidarity characterized by a spirit of intellectual openness that celebrates diversity, welcomes dissent, and rejoices in a collective dedication to truth (hooks, 1994). This process is facilitated by providing students with strategies and opportunities to explore the differences and similarities in the experiences, needs, and beliefs of people, and the dynamics and consequences of social and economic injustice. It is further facilitated by helping students to acquire the knowledge and information to analyze and understand the dynamics of forms of oppression and discrimination, and the diverse beliefs, values, roles, and norms of culturally different clients.

This chapter thus presents a conceptualization of teaching that goes beyond merely sharing information. This view of multicultural training incorporates contributing to the intellectual and spiritual growth of students as an essential component of the process (hooks, 1994). In this process, education becomes a practice of freedom, creating strategies for "conscientization"—the creation of critical awareness—and engagement, including praxis—action and reflection upon the world in order to change it (hooks, 1994). Those who choose to engage in this process should recognize that working to help students recognize cultural diversity, rethink ways of knowing, and deconstruct old epistemologies leads to significant and substantive transformations in our classrooms, in how we teach and what we teach. Helping students recognize the politics of racism, sexism, and heterosexism, and how they inform the process and content of what we teach and learn, is to engage in a political process. That is not always easy. It is not always immediately appreciated, but it is always important and life affirming.

The task of constructively engaging students in the process of learning about racism can be daunting. The thought of attempting to engage students in the process of learning about the prejudices of racism, sexism, and heterosexism can be down right overwhelming. It means engaging students in the examination of truths that much of our culture works to deny. It means asking students to discuss frustrating and sometimes painful facts about our culture and our ways of living. It calls on students to rethink some of their taken-for-granted assumptions about social institutions and how those institutions operate. This chapter first discusses the use of standpoint theory to provide students with a set of conceptual tools to understand how racism, sexism, and heterosexism constrain our ways of knowing. Two activities for students to help them in the process of learning to take different standpoints are outlined. The chapter next addresses oppression and privilege by considering how to develop awareness of oppossion and prejudice through understanding their characteristics and recognizing their pervasiveness; and then by exploring ways to understand anger and diversity through looking at the presence of anger in multicultural situations and presenting strategies to address that anger. Two additional acitivities for students to help them as they learn to understand and address oppression and anger are outlined. Throughout all activities, skills in critical thinking and developing a critical consciousness are key components.

WAYS OF KNOWING: STANDPOINT THEORY

The axioms of standpoint theory work effectively as strategies to challenge students to recognize the contingency and standpoint specificity of master narratives, the "truths," and their supporting analytical categories. Thinking within the parameters of standpoint theory leads us to examine how

> knowledge claims must be assessed from a variety of standpoints that unmask the conditions under which knowledge is produced. It is necessary to constantly scrutinize the presuppositions and foundation of knowledge claims while inexorably moving to the idea that acting on information which contradicts and overturns orthodox knowledge involves political engagement. (Schmidt & Patterson, 1995, p. 13)

Justifications for standpoint theory typically begin with Hegel's insight into the relationship between the master and the slave. Hegel (see Harding, 1991) observed that the master might well be quite ignorant of the daily realities of the slave's life, with no adverse consequences. If the master is a person of conscience, that ignorance might serve a self-protective function, allowing the master to retain the delusion that the condition of slavery is not all that bad for the slave. The slave, however, is quite aware of the conditions of his or her own life, and also has to be knowledgeable about the realities of the master's life conditions. All of that knowledge is essential to the slave's survival. Knowledge of differential life conditions is common among the oppressed. The transformation of that knowledge into a standpoint that supports political engagement, however, must be developed through education such as Paulo Freire's (1993) *conscientization* (see chapter 3). Knowledge is one thing. The meanings we make of it are (or can be) quite another. Marx, Engels, and George Lukacs (see Harding, 1991) have developed Hegel's perceptions into a proletarian standpoint. They argued that human activity, or "material life," not only structures but sets limits on human understanding: "What we do shapes and constrains what we can know" (Harding, 1991, p. 120). Nancy Hartsock (1983) further elaborated the basis of standpoint theory:

> If human activity is structured in fundamentally opposing ways for two groups [Whites/Blacks, men/women, heterosexuals/homosexuals] one can expect that the vision of each will represent an inversion of the other. In systems of domination the vision available to the rulers will be both partial and perverse. (p. 285)

Standpoint Axioms

The grounds of standpoint theory have been developed by Patricia Hill Collins (1986, 1989, 1990), Sandra Harding and Merrill B. Hintikka (1983), Sandra Harding (1987, 1991), Nancy Hartstock (1983), Hillary Rose (1983), and Dorothy Smith (1987). Their works have suggested six key axioms of the theory:

1. Life experiences structure an individual's understanding.
2. Members of the most and the least powerful groups potentially have opposed understandings of the world.
3. Less powerful groups' standpoints have to be developed through education for critical consciousness and political action.
4. The standpoint of those who are outside the dominant group develops from their daily activities.
5. The appropriate standpoint for research activities is from the conditions of everyday life.
6. Members of marginalized groups are valuable strangers to the social order, especially as they function as outsiders within the social order.

Applying Standpoint Axioms

The axioms are fairly abstract. Students can be helped to conceptualize them through two activities: analyzing a story in terms of the standpoint axioms and undertaking a research critique assignment to uncover researcher standpoints.

A story that concretely illustrates the axioms.   N'Gugi wa Thiongo, a Kenyan scholar, provides concrete illustration of the standpoint axioms in the following story:

> There once was a short-sighted farmer, who on Sunday mornings would stand on the prostrate bodies of his gardeners to look through the window and enjoy the sight of his vast tea plantation that spread out from the manor house. "What at a beautiful day, so peaceful" he would murmur, genuinely moved by the apparent stability all around. So absorbed was he by the peace that he could not hear the rumblings of the gardener's tummies or their silent groans of discontent. "A peaceful country, don't you think?" he would say to the house servants who stood by ready to serve him his breakfast. And the house servants would also stand on some of the prostrate bodies, but at a respectful distance from the master, and they would chorus back, "yes, master, peace." (N'Gugi wa Thiongo, 1993, p. 116)

The story powerfully illustrates the way in which the farmer's material life structures and limits his understanding of reality. His view of the material circumstances, that comprise his world is notably partial. He holds no awareness of the conditions, circumstances, or desires of his gardeners, and his view is certainly perverse when juxtaposed with that of the gardeners. Discussing the story with students in this first activity can open the door to examining the grounds of standpoint theory and to using it as a tool for understanding how patterns of oppression have influenced our knowledge, our ways of knowing and thinking, our ways of perceiving the world and relationships.

Provide students with a copy of the story and a list of the six axioms of the theory. Divide the class into small work groups, and have each group analyze the story to find examples that illustrate each of the six axioms. Students often struggle with axioms 5 and 6. As the students consider axiom 5, ask them to consider how research projects from the standpoint of the plantation owner and from the standpoint of the gardeners might differ: What research questions might each group ask? What data might each group choose to gather? As the students work with axiom 6, ask them to consider how the house servants, as outsiders within, can work with the owner to transform the oppressiveness of that social order. Then have the groups come together as a whole to discuss their respective analyses. The groups can also draft their own stories to provide additional illustrations of the axioms of standpoint theory.

This activity helps students challenge the simplifications and distortions that support the persistence of prejudice and oppression. Through it they begin to become aware that they may not always have the whole picture about social interactions. The activity introduces students to the importance of developing a critical consciousness that seeks out and exposes the contradictions existing within local communities, and between themselves, the state, and their environment (Schmidt & Patterson, 1995). Standpoint theory demonstrates to students that one way to accomplish this is by learning to search for and attend to multiple viewpoints so as to provide different explanations of the present day power relations embedded within these isms.

A *research critique assignment.* In this second activity to illustrate standpoint axioms, students are challenged to uncover the implicit traces of prejudice and oppression in professional literature. This assignment directs students' attention to three elements of the research process: the resource base of the research, the purpose of the research, and the self-awareness of the researcher.

Direct students to complete the following tasks. Tell them to be prepared to present the results in writing and in classroom discussions.

1. Identify and read three research articles that relate to the topic of your term paper.
2. Briefly summarize the findings of the research, and then answer the following questions for each article. It may be necessary to "read into" the articles to develop answers.
   - What is the resource base of the research project?
     — Look carefully at the categories used to structure the research project. Whose categories are they? Whose life experiences do they illuminate? Whose life experiences are ignored or rendered ambiguous or invisible? Do the data collected with these categories function to deny the presence or importance of certain groups?
     — Whose voice is allowed to speak and given veracity? Whose voice is silenced or ignored throughout the research project?
   - What is the hypothesis/research question within each article?
     — How did these phenomena get defined as social problems?
     — For whom are these issues problematic? (A problem is always a problem *for* someone.)
     — If viewed from a different standpoint, how else might this problem be defined?
   - What is the purpose of this research?
     — What groups will benefit from its findings?
     — How might these findings contribute to the perpetuation of stereotypes or the oppression of other groups?
   - What are the effects of the social location of the researcher on the research project?
     — (Are the sources of the researcher's social power examined (personal and socio-structural)?

3. Select one of the articles and briefly discuss how it could be redesigned from the standpoint of an oppressed or marginalized group whose voice is excluded in the current project. How might that change the research question, research design, and data analysis and interpretation?

The goal of this assignment is to have the students carefully determine whose reality, whose standpoint, provides the structure of the research projects they are reading about. Students consider how else the problems might be defined, what other variables might have been used to construct the hypothesis. In discussing their analyses, the students consider how the issues might look from the reality of particular marginalized groups, such as African Americans, Hispanic Americans, Asian and Pacific Rim Americans, Native Americans, women, and lesbians and gay men.

Thinking about research questions in this way, in terms of standpoint axioms, helps students call into question the norms and values used in generating research questions and in interpreting the findings generated through the application of those questions. For example, students may suggest that beginning research from the lives of clients can lead to asking questions about how the limitations of welfare benefits perpetuate homelessness rather than about how the homeless are different from middle class persons. Or students in critiquing research about child abuse may pose alternative research questions about how the isolated, autonomous nuclear family permits the continuation of undetected child abuse.

Through this assignment, students interested in an issue as a potential research problem learn the need to explore answers to these questions: For whom is this issue a problem? What are the conditions of her life? What are the determining causes, the features of the social structure, that contribute to creating those life patterns? How does the world look from the perspective of those who live this experience? The students also learn to look at the choices that members of a group make, and think about why group members believe those are good things to do. This research critique assignment helps student focus on the strengths of oppressed groups, see their behaviors as coping strategies in the face of prejudice and oppression, and begin to consider the connections among ways of knowing, power relations, prejudices, and oppression.

OPPRESSION AND PRIVILEGE

Oppression and privilege are two sides of the same coin. Oppression denies individuals access to resources and opportunities as a consequence of their membership in a particular group, typically as an accident of birth. Privilege provides special access to resources and opportunities—advantages—that accrue to individuals as a consequence of their membership in a particular group, typically as an accident of birth.

Oppression and privilege are both unearned. To those who enjoy privilege, it feels right and natural. It is a taken-for-granted characteristic of status. Those who suffer oppression can also come to regard it as a taken-for-granted characteristic of status (internalized oppression). For those who enjoy privilege, it is simply the way of being. For those who suffer oppression, it too becomes the way of being. For those who are denied access to privilege, the denial signifies the lesser value of their way of being, of their very being. For those absolved from oppression, that absolution signifies the greater value of their way of being and of their being. An important pedagogical goal is to help students recognize that neither interpretation holds veracity.

Oppression is a system of interrelated barriers and forces that reduce, immobilize, and mold people who belong to certain groups and effect their subordination to other groups (Frye, 1983, p. 33). Frye explained that systems of oppression presuppose that there are two categories of persons that are both distinct and fairly easy to identify. Systems of oppression require that the categories or groups of persons be well defined. Racism, as we know, divides the world into categories based on racial characteristics, particularly skin color, with darker skinned persons subordinated to white or lighter skinned persons. Sexism divides the world into categories based on biological sex, with women subordinated to men. Heterosexism divides the world into categories based on sexual orientation, with heterosexuals claiming dominance.

Privilege safeguards the levels of social acceptance that can be presumed across the multiple contexts of life. Peggy McIntosh (1995) extensively discussed the parallels between White privilege and male privilege. Within her analysis she has identified a number of characteristics of privilege. She noted that privilege ensures that some people have the freedom to associate exclusively or primarily with members of their own group. Privilege guarantees some people the ability to see members of their group in a positive light and as role models in historical records, texts, and the media. Privilege carries a freedom from the adverse consequences of stereotyping and an ability to be oblivious of other groups. Privilege adds up to an enhanced ability for some people to feel at home in the world because it is their world, and they are soundly in the center of it. Access to privilege functions as a protection from frustrations and anger. Denied access to privilege not only means denied access to respect, advantages, security, and safety but also increased insults and injuries.

Developing Awareness of Oppression and Prejudice

The first two activities (N'Gugi's story and the research critique) have helped students begin to develop their awareness of the pervasiveness of oppression and prejudice, including racism, sexism, and heterosexism, throughout their lives and the lives of their clients. Students now need to be helped to understand that racism, sexism, and heterosexism have common characteristics as well as unique aspects.

Elements of oppression.   Susan Pharr (1988) has identified four common elements of oppression:

1. **defined norms:** The defined norms become the standard of rightness against which all others are judged and held accountable. Institutional and economic power, violence (institutional and physical), and the threat of violence all serve to support defined norms.
2. **definition of those outside the norms as other:** Those outside the norm, the others, are rendered unknown, unknowable, or invisible. What is known about those who are other is presented in ways to highlight negatives and stereotypes.
3. **assignment of blame for their oppression of the victims:** Blaming the victim is a vicious process that identifies a problem and then studies those who have the problem to see how they are different from those who do not have the problem. Social programs are typically devised to make those with the problem more like those who do not have it. When these programs fail, those with the problem are blamed for not changing. The fallacy within this process is the omission of study and change of the sociostructural factors that give rise to and support the problematic circumstance. Two consequences of blaming the victim are internalized oppression (believing the lies of the oppressor, letting others define the truth of the situation, and personal deprecation) and horizontal hostility (directing anger, resentment, and hostility at other members of the victim's own group rather than toward members of those groups with more power).
4. **isolation of the oppressed groups and individuals from each other:** When oppressed groups and individuals are isolated from each other, they become more susceptible to blaming themselves for their circumstances, and to feeling powerless in their situation.

Vignettes for exploring prejudicial assumptions.   An additional way to help students recognize and appreciate the pervasiveness of prejudiced and oppressive presumptions throughout our ways of perceiving and evaluating interactions is an in-class activity applied to sexism—but easily adaptable to racism and heterosexism.

Begin the activity by conceptually introducing sexism as the hierarchical ordering of the world, of relationships and socioinstitutional preferences based on gender. In our world, the male gender is given higher priority and power. Although sexism is manifest in interpersonal relationships, it is also important to remember that the locus and power of sexism are in the system of social institutions and cultural mores, not in a particular act (Frye 1983). Sexism, like racism, pervades our daily life as water does that of fish. Frye has suggested that each of us should monitor our behavior for a period of time. The reason, she observed, is that

> In everything one does, one has two complete repertoires of behavior, one for interactions with women, and one for interactions with men. Greeting, storytelling, order

giving and order receiving, negotiating, gesturing deference or domination, encouraging, challenging, asking for information: one does all of these things differently depending upon whether the relevant others are male or female. (1983, p. 20)

Students often hear this definition rather dispassionately. Some may even comment that the women's movement has changed (or is changing) all of that. This activity helps them reevaluate that belief.

Divide students into small working groups (three to five students per group). Students are asked to write a one-to-two page vignette describing in some detail the process and interactions associated with an event or set of events that are common consequences of sexism. Such events include on-the-job sexual harassment, rape, spouse abuse, a corporate board meeting with 90% of the participants of the same gender, and home care responsibilities—as well as others brainstormed by the class. Assign one event to each group. Ask student groups first to describe the event as it might typically unfold. Next ask the student groups are asked to write a second description of a similar event, this time switching the gender of the key actors. Each group then reads their second vignette aloud to the class. At first the stories seem silly and absurd. After the reading has concluded, it is important to help the students thoughtfully process their reactions. Why were the reversals so funny? Because what they describe is unthinkable. And that is the proof of how pervasive the values and assumptions of sexism are throughout our culture.

Five questions, adapted from Susan Pharr's (1988) Catechism of Patriarchy, to help students further process their experience of and thoughts about this exercise:

1. Who benefits from the subordination of women (or persons of color, or gay men and lesbians)?
2. In what ways do they benefit?
3. Who suffers from each of these forms of subordination?
4. How are these forms of subordination maintained (economics, violence, fear)?
5. What would the world be like without sexism (racism, heterosexism)? Consideration of this possibility helps to disabuse students of the false belief that pervasiveness equals necessity and inevitability.

Engaging in this work with students is difficult enough on a conceptual level. However, teaching from a standpoint that develops student awareness of the oppressions and privileges associated with race, sex, class, and sexual orientation is likely to spark emotions and passions that are not traditionally part of the classroom venue. As students discuss this material, they inevitably become engaged not only cognitively but also emotionally. Students experience the frustration of being misunderstood and of not knowing as much as they thought they knew. They experience what they perceive to be insults in other students' sometimes insensitive modes of expression. They become increasingly aware of the injustices they experience (and sometimes perpetuate). All of this can lead to anger in the classroom. If we as counselor educators want to go beyond sharing information and seek to contribute to the intellectual and spiritual growth of students, then we must be prepared to help them develop the skills to understand and work with their own emotions as well as those of their clients.

Understanding Anger and Diversity

There is often a concern that teaching from a standpoint that includes awareness of race, sex, class, sexual orientation will be uncontrollable, that emotions and passions will not be contained (hooks, 1994). Counseling and human services professors may be more likely than our colleagues in the cognate disciplines to possess skills and strategies for dealing with antagonism and anger. As we engage students in this work, we need to be prepared to bring those skills into the class-room. Often approaches to anger management focus on the issue of safety—in the sense of providing students with strategies to protect themselves (and others) from expressions of anger. But, as bell hooks (1994, p. 40) argued, building a sense of community with a shared sense of commitment and a common good that binds us can create a climate of openness and intellectual rigor. That sense of commu-nity affords an even more powerful context for confronting oppression and addressing anger than mere management strategies. An important point to take from hooks is that the goal is not the elimination of anger. A more powerful goal is understanding and using anger to confront and challenge oppression. A shared sense of community provides a context in which that process can occur on an ongoing basis; a shared sense of community provides a context in which compas-sion and commitment can be developed.

Anger in multicultural situations.   Compassion and commitment are important to develop because ambiguity, and ambivalence are common in multicultural sit-uations. Difficulties, obstacles, ambiguity, and ambivalence all generate feelings of frustration. Contacts between different cultural groups produce experiences in which personal or cultural insults emerge from differing cultural values and behavior patterns. Current and historical patterns of resource distribution and privilege perpetuate overt and covert, intentional and unintentional, expressions of social injustice. Frustrations, insults, and injustices are three of the most com-mon categories of events and experiences that produce anger (Tavris, 1989). Nearly by definition, multicultural training is likely to engender feelings of anger.

Persons of color feel anger in connection with a history of experiences of deval-uation (Pinderhughes, 1989). Pinderhughes noted that people of color need to be persistently on guard for "micro aggressions," for small subtle acts, often out of awareness, that exploit, degrade, put down, and express aggression. Experiences of micro aggressions are subtle, yet pernicious. Audre Lorde (1984, p. 124) detailed the sources of her anger in response to racism: experiences of exclusion, assumptions of unquestioned privilege at her expense, being silenced, being used, stereotyping, defensiveness, misnaming, betrayal, and co-optation as well as racist attitudes, actions, and the presuppositions that arise from them. The persistent unwillingness of White Americans to accept people of color as fellow human beings is a root cause of anger (Grier & Cobbs, 1968).

European Americans experience feelings of anger in reaction to feelings of guilt or in response to confronting feelings of bigotry or prejudice that they have kept hidden or suppressed (Pinderhughes, 1989). Some European Americans experience anger in relationship to affirmative action programs, or experiences of "reverse discrimination" believing those programs to be sources of injustice and inequitable resource distribution. European Americans have enjoyed the privilege of having their culture stand as the dominant, taken-for-granted standard against which all others are evaluated. Diversity challenges that hegemony. Diversity calls on European Americans to relinquish the privileges of ethnocentrism. That loss of privilege is frustrating, insulting, and feels unjust. In response to that loss, European Americans are likely to become angry unless they have the skills to understand the sources of their anger (and they may still become angry even with those skills).

For members of groups that have experienced oppression, persistent vigilance against prejudice is necessary for self-protection. This vigilance can appear to be hypervigilance to those whose lives do not require them to keep a constant check on the level of prejudice, and can be experienced as hypersensitivity (Rodwell & Blankebaker, 1992). Where persons of color see the need to monitor insults, frustrations, and social injustices constantly to ensure their safety, European Americans find themselves asking, "When will enough be enough?" This pattern of divergent perceptions is fertile ground for angry confrontations. These patterns of experience also illustrate how frustrations, insults, and injustices interact to generate multiple and complex sources of anger.

Contexts of diversity are also fertile grounds for the spawning of feelings of anger. Remembering past experiences of oppression can produce anger. Confronting feelings of guilt and incompetence can engender anger. The frustrating effort required to understand each other across different cultures, values, and goals can spread anger. And the expression of anger largely remains taboo. Except within certain ritualized social situations, such as sporting events and war, angry expressions are either denied or ignored. Anger is erroneously regarded as a negative emotion. Anger can have positive functions if it is managed effectively. Although anger can promote fear and create distance, those are not universally undesirable byproducts. Distance can mean protection in contexts of prejudice or oppression (Rodwell & Blankebaker, 1992). Anger can also be a profound source of motivation for actions confronting injustice and leading to social change.

Anger is often regarded as a negative, dangerous, damaging emotion. We fear anger because we do not know what to do with it, because it seems to signal a person out of control (or at least out of social control), and because we confound anger, rage and aggression. We are less likely to perceive anger as a resource or strategy in relationships and social action. Yet anger serves important social functions. It can be a preferred response over fear and insecurity because it allows the individual to retain a sense of power and control (Pinderhughes, 1989). Anger functions to protect the social order, warning individuals or groups not to violate cultural rules or roles. Anger can provide the motivation to work for social change in the face of injustices.

Strategies for addressing anger.   Becoming aware of sources of anger helps students deal with feelings of anger. Knowing the sources of their anger provides them with a base from which they can understand, evaluate, and intentionally choose how they will respond to their feelings of anger and the contexts that produce them. Recognizing that some anger-producing acts are unintentional can allow them to relinquish some of their anger. Recognizing that some sources of injustice and anger are covert can empower them to amplify their anger as a source of motivation for social action.

As they learn to work in multicultural situations, students need to develop their self-awareness, to monitor their emotions, and to choose their course of action in response to their anger so that they can express it effectively and appropriately. Students need three layers of skill and ability to work with feelings of anger. They need to be able to:

- feel anger and recognize its sources;
- control actions in response to those feelings; and
- choose and plan an appropriate course of action to address the source of anger.

Journal keeping is a powerful tool to support students' progress in working with their anger. Initially, students simply monitor their anger, noting in their journals episodes of anger. In the next stage, they select one anger episode each day, and write more extensively on its sources (intrapsychic, interpersonal, and sociocultural). They can then analyze (within their journals or in small discussion groups) their actions in response to anger-provoking events and consequences of their actions. In-class role-plays additionally provide students with a forum for planing and practicing alternative actions and response patterns.

SUMMARY

This chapter presents a set of classroom activities that enable students to apply the axioms of standpoint theory so as to understand more effectively the pervasiveness of oppression and privilege in structuring our ways of knowing. The goals of this set of activities ultimately is to help students develop the awareness, knowledge, and skill to engage in a critical examination of our professional paradigms and to demystify the patterns of power inherent in social relations and professional practices.

In the work of Marilyn Frye (1983) and Maria Lugones' (1990) are three useful summary concepts: arrogant perception, loving perception, and world traveling. Arrogant perception is the failure to remember and allow for the fact that individuals in other groups are independent and fully human beings. Arrogant perception expects others to be what we expect them to be and to behave as we expect them to behave (often in our service). Arrogant perception fails to seek out and include the standpoint of others and perpetuates systems of prejudice, oppression, and privilege. Loving perception knows the independence of other individuals and pays attention to learn the uniqueness of the others' human dignity and suffering. It is a way of knowing that intentionally and explicitly includes the voices and standpoints of others so as to build communities that celebrate the diversity of our multicultural world. The *world* of world traveling is used suggestively and it refers to a place inhabited by flesh-and-blood people, but not necessarily a whole society, as well as to a structured, coherent set of social institutions and relationships that act to construct the dailiness of life. Many of us live in and travel among multiple worlds, such as the worlds of work, family, and ethnic or other identity groups. Lugones (1990, p. 396) observed that world travelers have the experience of being different in different worlds, that they experience themselves differently and have the experience of being perceived and treated differently, in their different worlds. World travelers engage in learning to know from the standpoint of others so that their own world is transformed.

When we are members of dominant groups, we are more likely to perceive others arrogantly. The task for and challenge to students is to learn to perceive others with loving perception. This is akin to empathy. Loving perception requires learning to travel to the other person's world and viewing it from his or her standpoint. This is not a romantic idealization. It is a profound commitment to compassion and engaged action for social and economic justice.

REFERENCES

Collins, P. H. (1986). Learning from the outsider within: The sociological significance of Black feminist thought. *Social Problems, 33*:514–523.

Collins, P. H. (1989). The social construction of Black feminist thought. *Signs: The Journal of Women in Culture, 14*:745–773.

Collins, P. H. (1990). *Black feminist thought: Knowledge, consciousness, and the politics of empowerment.* London, UK: Harper Collins Academic.

Freire, P. (1993). Pedagogy of the oppressed (Rev. 20th anniversary ed., M. B. Rames, Trans.). New York: Continuum.

Frye, M. (1983). The politics of reality. Freedom, CA: Crossing Press.

Grier, W. H., & Cobbs, P. M. (1968, 1992). *Black rage.* New York: Basic Books, Harper Collins.

Harding, S. (Ed.). (1987). *Feminism and methodology.* Bloomington: Indiana University Press.

Harding, S. (1991). *Whose science? Whose knowledge?* Ithaca, NY: Cornell University Press.

Harding, S., & Hintikka, M. (1983). *Discovering reality.* Dordrecht, Holland: Reidel.

Hartsock, N. (1983). The feminist standpoint: Developing the ground for a specifically feminist historical materialism. In S. Harding & M. Hintikka, *Discovering reality* (pp. 283–310). Dordrecht, Holland: Reidel.

hooks, b. (1994). *Teaching to transgress: Education as the practice of freedom.* New York: Routledge.

Lorde, A. (1984). *Sister outsider.* Freedom, CA: Crossing Press.

Lugones, M. (1990). Playfulness, "world" traveling, and loving perception. In G. Anzaldua, *Making face, making soul haciendo caras: Creative and critical perspectives by women of color* (pp. 390–402). San Francisco: Aunt Lute Foundation.

McIntosh, P. (1995). White privilege and male privilege: A personal account of coming to see correspondences through work in women's studies. In M. Anderson & P. H. Collins (Eds.), *Race, class, and gender: An anthology* (pp. 76–86). Belmont, CA: Wadsworth.

N'Gugi wa Thiong'o. (1993). *Moving the center: The struggle for cultural freedoms.* Portsmouth, NH: Heinemann.

Pharr, S. (1988). *Homophobia: A weapon of sexism.* Inverness, CA: Chardon Press.

Pinderhughes, E. (1989). *Understanding race, ethnicity, and power: The key to efficacy in clinical practice.* New York: Free Press.

Rodwell, M. K., & Blankenbaker, A. (1992). Strategies for developing cross-cultural sensitivity: Wounding as a metaphor. *Journal of Social Work Education* 28(2):153–165.

Rose, H. (1983). Hand, brain, and heart: A feminist epistemology for the natural sciences. *Signs,* 9:73–90.

Schmidt, P. R., & Patterson, T. C. (Eds.). (1995). *Making alternative histories: The practice of archeology and history in non-western settings.* Santa Fe, NM: School of American Research Press.

Smith, D. (1987). *The everyday world as problematic: A feminist sociology.* Boston: Northeastern University Press.

Tavris, C. (1989). *Anger: The misunderstood emotion.* New York: Touchstone.

8 | Reducing Prejudice: The Role of the Empathic-Confrontive Instructor

Mark S. Kiselica

Few, if any, educational endeavors are as challenging and unique for both instructor and students as the process of helping counseling students develop multicultural sensitivity. The instructor of a multicultural education course is charged with the task of helping students explore in front of one another their cultural values and biases, divest themselves of harmful stereotypes about the culturally different, and develop an appreciation for other cultures. This task requires the instructor and students to make a shift from the traditional model of didactic instruction, which emphasizes the dissemination of facts that are processed cognitively, to a group process model of teaching in which information is processed both affectively and cognitively through experiential exercises and discussions centered on highly personal and emotionally charged issues, such as racism, sexism, homophobia, and ableism.

For many students, this shift represents a new and frightening learning experience prompted by several instructional challenges. The instructor, as the facilitator of this new learning process, asks the students to change from being passive to active participants in the classroom. It is also common for the instructor to ask students to describe the effects of prejudicial behavior on their lives. In addition, the instructor usually challenges the students to confront their rigid and biased stereotypes about the culturally different—their isms. Thus the students are expected to take an active role in examining how they are both the victims and perpetrators of prejudicial thinking and behavior, subjects that many prefer to avoid addressing in public, especially when they are in the presence of other people they may not know well.

Students tend to avoid the subjects of racism, sexism, homophobia, and ableism for several reasons. Students who have been the victims of several forms of oppression fear that their experiences will not be affirmed but rather glossed over by the instructor and classmates alike; consequently, some wonder why they should even bother to disclose experiences that are truly significant to them. Most students worry that they will offend someone else by stating their beliefs and that they will be accused of being a racist, a sexist, a homophobic, or an ableist; and they often decide it is better to play it safe and keep quiet rather than risk stating their opinions. On an unconscious level, many students are anxious about discovering their own prejudicial practices, so they find ways to avoid talking about forms of prejudice altogether. Nearly all students are guarded about what might be said about their particular cultural group; some are doubtful that they will be able to control their defensiveness and anger when they perceive their classmates making unfair characterizations about their culture; and some attempt to control their reactions by remaining silent until they can hold back no longer and explode with intense emotions that frighten other classmates from saying anything further.

At the same time that these forces are at work, there is a strong opposing expectation by the instructor that students engage in dialogue about issues of race, gender role, sexual orientation, and physical ability and disability. Somehow, the instructor must help the students move beyond their fears so that substantive discourse about these issues can be achieved. In the words of Craig Rooney, Lisa Flores, and Chantele Mercier, three graduate students of counseling from the University of Missouri, participating in this process can be daunting for students. It also demands that the instructor guide the students through unfamiliar and uncharted waters:

> The role of the educator in a multicultural class is an enormous undertaking in resocialization. As students, we are being asked to do something that we have not done and many of us have not seen. Thus, instructors need to be willing to show what the process feels and looks like and the decisions that are made along the way. (Rooney, Flores, & Mercier, 1998, p. 24)

But how does an instructor show what the process looks and feels like? How can an instructor prepare students for the strong emotions they are about to experience while they make disturbing discoveries about themselves? How can a multicultural educator teach trainees to recognize and overcome the defense mechanisms that prevent them from realizing their biases about people who are different from themselves? How does the teacher help students confront their prejudices in spite of their fears of doing so? How does the trainer inspire students to persist with, rather than withdraw from, the uncomfortable aspects of the training process so that students will discover the benefits and joys of multiculturalism, such as the pleasures of experiencing different cultures and developing multicultural awareness and sensitivity?

This chapter answers these questions by proposing that the multicultural instructor must be a deeply caring and highly committed educator who sensitively guides students through the process of multicultural training. The educator must also possess and demonstrate particular qualities in order to be an effective facilitator of his or her students' multicultural development. Specifically, the trainer should serve as an empathic-confrontive instructor who

- discloses his or her own struggles and joys associated with trying to develop multicultural sensitivity;
- empathizes with the fears and accomplishments of all students, including those from oppressed groups and nonoppressed groups alike;
- demonstrates that he or she is still striving to enhance his or her multicultural awareness;
- mentors students outside of the classroom; and
- lovingly confronts students to explore their ethnocentrism and prejudicial thinking.

Above all else, the empathic-confrontive instructor fully brings his or her self to the training process in order to join his or her students in the profoundly human endeavor of developing multicultural awareness and sensitivity. Thus the focus of this chapter is on "the person" that the multicultural trainer presents in the classroom to his or her students rather than on specific training exercises that have been developed for multicultural training. (For a representative sample of multicultural training activities, see, for example, Brislin & Yoshida, 1994; Cushner & Brislin, 1997; Dillard, 1983; McGrath & Axelson, 1993; Parker, 1988; and Weeks, Pedersen, & Brislin, 1986.)

This chapter first focuses on self-disclosing multicultural struggles and joys, empathizing with the fears and joys of oppressed and nonoppressed students, demonstrating ongoing strivings to enhance multicultural awareness, and mentoring students outside the classroom. The chapter then discusses confronting ethnocentrism and prejudice through the instructor's use of the caring skill of confrontation, maintenance of a loving perspective, and confrontation of extreme prejudice as well as White students and oppressed students.

SELF-DISCLOSING MULTICULTURAL STRUGGLES AND JOYS

Acquiring multicultural awareness and sensitivity is "a developmental process that unfolds over time" (Kiselica, 1998, p. 9). A central aspect of this development involves transformations in the students' identities as ethnic and racial beings, a process known as ethnic and racial identity development. According to several theories of ethnic and racial identity development, individuals who are stimulated by life experiences to examine their conceptions of themselves as ethnic and racial persons proceed through a series of stages of identity development (Atkinson, Morten, & Sue, 1993; Cross, 1991; Hardiman, 1982; Helms, 1990b; Kim, 1981; Phinney, Lochner, & Murphy, 1990; Ponterotto, 1988). Although the terms used to describe these stages vary from model to model, they each predict that ethnic and racial identity growth involves dilemmas that the individual must resolve, a process that provokes powerful emotions and significant psychological changes for the individual. Although it is beyond the scope of this chapter to describe in detail each of these dilemmas and their psychological and emotional features, a review of several common ethnic and racial identity developmental events will illustrate why it is important that the instructor be an individual who is, or has been, in the process of examining his or her own racial identity and developing a multicultural identity (Ponterotto, 1998).

In general, according to Ponterotto and Pedersen (1993), during the early stages of ethnic and racial identity development the individual strongly identifies with the values and norms of the White culture that dominates American society. For people of color, this includes a prejudice against their own cultural group, whereas for Whites there is an acceptance of prevailing stereotypes about minorities. Exposure to new information and engaging in encounters with people over matters of race provide the individual with a new perspective about his or her ethnic and racial identity. Previously held prejudices are questioned, and individuals face a conflict as to whether or not to examine more carefully their prejudicial attitudes about their own or different cultural groups, or to continue to accept their biases. This conflict is marked by confusion, anger, guilt, fear, and embarrassment. If the person chooses continually to confront and discard harmful stereotypes, however, he or she begins the gradual process of formulating a new identity in which there is an appreciation for his or her own culture as well as different cultures. Furthermore, the individual experiences a gradual movement beyond unsettling, negative feelings to a sense of cultural pride, self-worth, and joy associated with the discovery and celebration of different cultures. Throughout this movement toward multicultural appreciation, there may be repeated conflicts centered around retreating to former ways of thinking or proceeding with the difficult task of confronting ethnocentric and racist views. These conflicts are predicted to diminish in frequency and power once the individual reaches a state in which he or she can embrace the good found within his or her own culture while recognizing and combating various forms of prejudice.

Students entering multicultural education classes vary in terms of where they are in their cultural identity development: some are relatively ethnocentric; others are more multicultural and culturally sensitive. Consequently, disagreements and heated discussions are bound to emerge as students in different stages of their cultural identity development express differences of opinion regarding issues pertaining, for example, to race, ethnicity, gender roles, and sexual orientation. These conflicts evoke strong emotions that may be uncomfortable but also have the potential to stimulate significant growth if they are managed successfully and utilized constructively throughout the training.

Because the process of developing multicultural awareness and sensitivity is a journey marked by fears, painful self-reflection, and joyful growth, it is best led by a person who has experienced the struggles and joys of this journey and is willing to share these experiences with his or her students. For example, Julianne Lark and Brian Paul, doctoral students of counseling psychology at Western Michigan University, reported that one of their instructors had the courage to reveal his personal biases and struggles regarding his own racial identity development (see Lark

& Paul, 1998). This sharing by the professor was extremely effective in creating a safe environment in which the students could address their own issues. As Brian Paul explained,

> I remember sitting in class and being taught by my doctoral chair and listening to him self-disclose about the struggles in his own racial identity journey. It was an incredible relief to hear about his struggles. It validated my own experience and eased my discomfort and shame of my own racist behaviors and thoughts. It also helped me to openly discuss my own uncomfortable experiences and emotions around racism that had been bottled up inside of me, such as using derogatory names or stereotypes when referring to racial/ethnic minorities or participating in racist jokes. My doctoral chair's self-disclosure around his difficulties with race and racism allowed space for other White students to discuss and share their problems concerning the issue. (Lark & Paul, 1998, p. 38)

Brian Paul's experience illustrates that self-disclosure by the instructor gives students the courage to confront their own isms. This courage is rooted in the students' realization that the teacher keenly understands the painful aspects of examining one's biases. But it is also rooted in their recognition that the instructor is someone who has moved forward in his or her multicultural development and, consequently, has celebrated many of the joys inherent in the process. These joys include developing a multicultural identity and experiencing and appreciating the beauty of other cultures. As I have stated elsewhere, enthusiastically and genuinely describing these intangible payoffs in class demonstrates for students that multicultural training is worthwhile and filled with rewards that can enrich one's life and spirit (see Kiselica, 1998). For example, I have found it useful to share with my students the happiness I experienced feeling and understanding the *personalismo* and physical touch, such as a warm and vigorous handshake, of two Hispanic American parents as I helped them to bring their son's drug abuse under control; the deep affection I felt for an African American family who had expressed their gratitude to me for our work together in counseling by surprising me one day with a breakfast consisting of grits and sweet potato pie; and the warmth and awe I held for an Iranian client who showed me the intricate and colorful tapestries produced by people from his homeland. In addition, I tell my students that the process of experiencing different, fascinating cultures and their beautiful, courageous, and inspirational people changed me forever; that

> I have sensed myself being transformed from an individual constrained by, and locked within, my cultural perspective to a person who can more fully appreciate and celebrate culturally different perspectives, and that has been a truly uplifting and liberating experience. (Kiselica, 1998, p. 18)

Students who observe that their instructor has grown as a multicultural being, in spite of the hardships involved, are likely to believe that they, too, can benefit from multicultural training, and subsequently, they are apt to invest themselves fully in the training endeavor (Kiselica, 1998).

EMPATHIZING WITH THE FEARS AND JOYS OF OPPRESSED AND NONOPPRESSED STUDENTS

The instructor who has grappled with his or her own racial and cultural identity issues can respond empathically when students are scared and hesitant to share their own struggles. In a reassuring manner, the teacher can say, "I sense that you are scared to disclose how you feel about this issue, and I'm wondering what you are afraid of at this time." In response to such a supportive probe, students typically report that they are concerned that they might offend someone, or that they are too ashamed to describe what is currently running through their mind, or that their opinion will be disregarded or dismissed as unimportant. These are crucial moments because the manner in which the instructor reacts to these statements can make or break a student's trust in the instructor.

Timely, empathic self-disclosure by the instructor of his or her similar feelings can facilitate self-disclosure by students (Kiselica, 1998). For example, the instructor can relive with students a moment from his or her own experience as a trainee when he or she was scared to speak up in class. The instructor can describe his or her fears of making mistakes, appearing racist, offending someone, or being ignored. Furthermore, the instructor can model for the students the necessity of taking risks by telling a very personal story regarding his or her racist attitudes, what it was like to discuss them with others for the first time, the feelings that were involved, and how he or she coped with the situation. Alternatively, the instructor might relate an experience of having been a victim of prejudicial behavior and how scary it is to relive that experience when it is unclear that everyone will appreciate what one has to say. Through these measures, the students are likely to comprehend that the instructor is a person who profoundly understands the difficulties the students are experiencing and, therefore, is someone who will support them as they risk telling their own stories.

Empathic responding is also crucial during moments when students are inspired to describe enriching experiences prompted by their multicultural training. The instructor should be alert to share in the students' joy because this response communicates to the students that multiculturalism is much more than a training exercise designed to exorcise such demons as racism, sexism, homophobia, and ableism. Multicultural education is also an endeavor in diversity appreciation filled with discoveries of what is admirable and beautiful about other cultures as well as one's own culture. The instructor who fosters this appreciation will greatly enhance the educational endeavor for everyone involved.

DEMONSTRATING ONGOING STRIVINGS TO ENHANCE MULTICULTURAL AWARENESS

One of the biggest mistakes a multicultural educator can make is to present him- or herself as an all-knowing expert whose multicultural journey is complete. This is an ill-advised posture to take for two reasons. The first is that several scholars of multicultural counseling and development have argued that cultural identity development continues throughout the life span (see Kiselica, 1991, 1995, 1998, in press; Parham, 1989; Ponterotto & Pedersen, 1993). Although individuals may reach the highest levels of cultural identity development, they are likely to have ongoing experiences that cause them constantly to reexamine their cultural identity attitudes (Parham, 1989). Parham (1989) has proposed that people actually recycle through the stages of cultural identity development in response to significant life events. In light of these propositions, it is dangerous to give students a message that an individual can be complete in his or her cultural identity development. Such a message, whether communicated explicitly or implicitly, can lead students to make the erroneous conclusions that their multicultural awareness and development will be complete once they have successfully finished a course in multicultural education. On the contrary, a good multicultural course or training workshop should awaken students to the realization that they have just begun the process of exploring who they are as cultural persons and should inspire them to commit themselves to further multicultural education, both formal and informal, for the rest of their lives.

The second reason that it is a mistake for an instructor to behave as though he or she has achieved an ultimate level of multicultural awareness is that such a stance appears to discourage students from feeling safe in the classroom. Describing their reactions to professors who present themselves in this way, Rooney et al. (1998) stated that they and their fellow students were hesitant to reveal themselves to instructors who presented themselves as having "arrived" (p. 23) in their development because the students feared that these instructors were evaluating and judging their students, rather than sensitively sharing in their students' deeply personal and emotionally charged experiences. By contrast, the students preferred an instructor who had the courage to admit to his students on the first day of class that he struggled with racist, sexist, and homophobic attitudes that he had learned through his early socialization as a male reared in an isolated, rural, African American community. Rooney et al. elaborated on the value of learning from teachers who have not fully completed their multicultural journey:

> As graduate students, we view faculty as experienced mentors and often place them on a pedestal because of their accomplishments. In many ways, perhaps we like to see them as arrived, or finished, in their professional development. Having a faculty member who is vulnerable enough to share her or his struggles and mistakes is not only comforting but also provides us with a model of how to deal with owning our biases and the mistakes we will make in our multicultural education. It also validates our experiences as students *and illustrates that one's process of identity development does not stop* [italics added]. (p. 23)

Because students of multiculturalism prefer a teacher who is a coping, rather than a mastery, role model, multicultural educators are advised to scrutinize themselves constantly as cultural beings and to risk sharing their ongoing painful discoveries, their doubts, their fears, and their continued growth with their students.

MENTORING STUDENTS OUTSIDE OF THE CLASSROOM

Caring teachers extend themselves to students far beyond the domains of the classroom. Because multicultural training exercises commonly stir up strong emotions during classroom activities, the multicultural educator must be a dedicated and compassionate professional who is available outside of the classroom to help students process and clarify the confusing changes they are going through (Locke & Kiselica, in press). For example, the new information acquired in a multicultural class may prompt a student to move from a state of unquestioned and unconscious acceptance of racial stereotypes to a growing awareness that he or she has racist attitudes and beliefs. Similarly, diversity training can prompt other students to recognize how they are homophobic, or sexist, or ableist in their thinking. Some may be confronted with the disturbing realization that they harbor multiple isms. These sorts of discoveries about oneself can be very upsetting, and they can provoke an identity crisis for the student. The student must make a difficult choice: Do I fully acknowledge to myself that I am, at some level, a prejudicial person, and attempt to transform myself into becoming a more enlightened individual? Or do I deny, minimize, or rationalize my biases and avoid becoming a more culturally sensitive person? A student embroiled in this conflict may seek out his or her instructor during nonclassroom hours and show signs of this dilemma. In other instances, the instructor may sense the student's state of mind and proactively invite the student to see him or her outside of class. Often the student may not be able to articulate clearly what he or she is feeling but will appear upset, lost, and, in many cases, defensive. The instructor must be ready to handle the student gently and may have to probe the student delicately in order to ascertain what the student is experiencing. Above all else, what most students seek during such conflicts is reassurance from the instructor that they are accepted by, and worthy of, the respect of the instructor, even though it is clear that they are, at some level, racist, sexist, homophobic, and/or ableist. By communicating to the student that he or she is OK as a person in spite of isms, and by reliving with the student how he or she felt the first time he or she confronted his or her own prejudices, the instructor is likely to help the student move forward with his or her cultural identity development. Buttressed by this support, students tend to feel less threatened and join in, rather than withdraw from, continued multicultural training and self-examination (Kiselica, 1998, in press).

Effective multicultural educators mentor their students in many other ways. For example, it is productive with some students to join them for lunch at the student center on campus or to invite students to one's home for dinner. Alternatively, the instructor may attend events sponsored by ethnic student associations. These actions communicate acceptance and build rapport so that students feel safe approaching the instructor with their dilemmas. When such events are shared by an instructor and students who are culturally different, the instructor models how to initiate cross-cultural encounters.

Successful mentors also engage in scholarly activities pertaining to multiculturalism, they involve their students in related research, and they attempt to infuse current scholarship on multiculturalism throughout the entire curriculum (Locke & Kiselica, in press). These efforts provide students with a clear systemic message that multiculturalism is highly valued by the faculty member. In my experience, many students, especially students of color, seek departments with faculty who demonstrate such a broad commitment to multiculturalism because the students want to be taught by faculty who have the interest and ability to support student interest in multicultural topics and who are capable of understanding issues that are culturally salient to the students. Student enthusiasm for multiculturalism and diversity is heightened when faculty invite students to contribute to faculty research projects, supervise research investigations proposed by the students themselves, and copresent their findings at professional conferences and copublish their work in juried journals. Through such mentoring, an instructor can be responsible for inspiring some students to go on to become scholars of multiculturalism and multicultural educators themselves.

Joining students in a mutual service to society is another way faculty can mentor students. Social responsibility and activism are values that are central to the mission of multicultural education and the counseling profession (see chapter 4; Baker, 1997; Lee, 1997). The best way that multicultural educators can teach these values to their students is by demonstrating their involvement in organizations whose mission is, for example, to help oppressed groups, new immigrants to this country, impoverished families, and disabled children and adults. Recruiting students to work side-by-side with an instructor in such organizations helps students to experience fully the true spirit behind the multicultural movement while cementing a lasting bond between the instructor and his or her students.

Whether the instructor is chatting with a student about highly personal cultural identity issues, sharing a meal, conceptualizing a research project, or working for a service organization, the instructor forms a special mentoring relationship by expressing concern for the holistic needs of students. Students appreciate faculty who are concerned about their financial hardships, their difficulties juggling educational and personal responsibilities, the stress associated with graduate education and clinical work, and other matters. When a student encounters a faculty member who has taken the time to listen to students about their many worries, the student is likely to have a high degree of trust and respect in the instructor, conditions that facilitate student tolerance for, and acceptance of, being challenged.

CONFRONTING ETHNOCENTRISM AND PREJUDICE

Sometimes the process of providing students with information about the culturally different and supporting them as they recognize their own isms for the first time is insufficient for the task of helping students divest themselves of ethnocentric and prejudicial attitudes and beliefs. When this is the case, confrontation is in order.

Because confrontation has the potential to alienate students, it is crucial that the instructor understand how to challenge students constructively. Therefore, this section provides a brief but vital review of using the caring skill of confrontation and then addresses several considerations pertaining to the application of confrontation in the sometimes touchy domain of multicultural education, including the needs to maintain a loving perspective, confront extreme prejudice, and confront White students as well as oppressed students.

Use the Caring Skill of Confrontation

Confrontation (also known as challenging) is "an invitation to examine internal (cognitive) or external behavior that seems to be self-defeating, harmful to others, or both—and to change that behavior" (Egan, 1994, p. 158). As it is utilized in counseling and counselor education, confrontation is *not* an attack on a client or student (Gladding, 1992), nor is it a direct or harsh challenge (Ivey, 1994) or a way to ventilate or dump frustration (Cormier & Cormier, 1998). Instead, it is an educational technique designed to bring previously unknown, disregarded, or repressed information to the student's attention (Young, 1998). Confrontation "involves listening to the client carefully and respectfully" (Ivey, 1994, p. 190). Moreover, "a good, responsible, caring, and appropriate confrontation produces growth and encourages an honest examination of oneself" (Gladding, 1992, p. 211).

Confrontation produces constructive changes in thoughts and behaviors by creating cognitive dissonance. A confronted student experiences inconsistencies in his or her thoughts, feelings, and behaviors, which creates tension that the student becomes motivated to reduce. This tension is diminished by either denying that the inconsistency is important or by trying to change one of the incompatible elements (Young, 1998). For example, a student may claim that he or she is not a racist and yet admit to telling or laughing at racist jokes. By pointing out this discrepancy, the instructor creates an uncomfortable state of mind for the student, who faces the choice of either ignoring the inconsistency between his or her statement and behavior—in effect, denying that he or she is racist—or, preferably, working to reduce or eliminate the racist behavior.

The degree to which a person responds positively to a confrontation is greatly influenced by several factors. It is widely accepted that confrontation is more effective if there is a strong rapport and a high degree of trust between the two parties involved (Cormier & Cormier, 1998; Egan, 1994; Gladding, 1992; Ivey,

1991, 1994; Young, 1998). In addition, confrontation is tolerated better when the confrontee perceives the confronter to be a caring person who has the confrontee's best interests at heart (Kleinke, 1994). The effectiveness of a confrontation is enhanced when the confrontee is given ample time to react to and discuss the effects of the confrontation (Cormier & Cormier, 1998). Confronting the person in small steps with initial challenges about issues that are less threatening and easier for the client to address is also recommended (Cormier & Cormier, 1998).

Maintain a Loving Perspective

In order to be effective in challenging students about their prejudicial attitudes and behaviors, it is extremely important that the multicultural educator keep the preceding review in mind when it is time to confront a student. In such instances, it also can be helpful for the instructor to pause for a few seconds and try to recall what it was like when he or she was confronted by someone in the past regarding a personal shortcoming. For example, before attempting to confront a student I remind myself of those times I had behaved in an ethnocentric manner and how much I appreciated someone who confronted me gently and caringly about my behavior. Furthermore, I remind myself of a compassionate perspective held by one of my former colleagues, who stated that he always bears in mind that everybody is recovering from something, such as some form of neurotic behavior or a character flaw. Another colleague reminds herself that people espousing stereotypic beliefs are the victims of an unenlightened socialization and, therefore, warrant understanding during any attempt to confront and help them. Keeping these perspectives in mind makes it easier to challenge the prejudicial behavior of students lovingly and with the intention to teach rather than chastise.

Confront Extreme Prejudice

It must be acknowledged that maintaining such a positive mental stance is remarkably difficult with the rare student who is extremely rigid in his or her thinking. Deeply entrenched, stereotypic ideology is both difficult to change and offensive, even to a veteran multicultural educator. For example, some students hold on to their racist beliefs tightly, in spite of the presentation of accurate information about the culturally different, and despite the instructor's attempt to establish a trusting relationship through the practice of sharing his or her multicultural journey, expressing empathy for the students' experience, serving as a coping role model, and mentoring students. Regardless of all of these efforts, the blighted thinking of some students does not yield, and they typically respond with hostility to the instructor and their fellow students when they are confronted about their beliefs. It is common for these students to attack the instructor verbally and to accuse him or her of deliberately stirring up trouble.

Any educator facing such a situation should meet informally and privately with a colleague to discuss the problems the student is presenting and to solicit feedback about how the instructor has handled the matter thus far. This consultation can provide the instructor with much-needed emotional support and a fresh perspective regarding the student's behavior. It is also recommended that the instructor immediately schedule individual, face-to-face meetings with a problematic student to warn the student about the potential implications of his or her behavior, especially if a consulting colleague agrees that the student's behavior is unacceptable. Specifically, the instructor should inform the student that extremely prejudicial attitudes may prevent the trainee from adhering to ethical codes of professional conduct. For example, the ethical standards of both the American Counseling Association (1995) and the American Psychological Association (1992) require awareness of, and respect for, the cultural backgrounds of clients, including the clients' age, disability, ethnicity, gender, race, religion, sexual orientation, and socioeconomic status. According to these standards, counselors and psychologists are also expected to try to eliminate the effect on their work of biases based on these cultural factors. A student demonstrating unbendable stereotypes may not be able to live up to these standards and, therefore, may not be an appropriate candidate for a career in the helping professions. Reporting this observation will prompt some narrow-minded students to begin serious soul-searching, which may gradually lead to a reappraisal and altering of previously unyielding stereotypes.

In rare instances, however, even this measure is unsuccessful in effecting positive changes in the student. Some students may continue to attack the instructor and stand by their dysfunctional beliefs. Others may be so crushed by having their shortcomings pointed out to them they become psychologically unable to face the training experience any longer. Such responses may be suggestive of a character disorder (see Shea, 1988) that has the potential to render the student incapable of working as an effective counselor.

When confronted with these extreme reactions, the instructor should not have to stand alone. Academic departments and continuing education programs should have formal policies for addressing these types of students systemically. For example, the Department of Counseling and Personnel Services at the College of New Jersey (1997) has a student retention policy included in the student manual indicating that trainees who exhibit signs of being unable to meet their professional responsibilities will be referred to an ad hoc retention committee. This committee consists of several faculty members who review the student's performance and retention in the program. A common action taken by a retention committee after a review of a problematic situation is to require the student to complete successfully a remedial plan of study and supervision before he or she can enroll in a practicum or internship course. In more severe cases, the committee may recommend that the student take a leave of absence from the program, begin counseling designed to address the student's prejudicial attitudes, and provide the committee with progress reports from the student's counselor. In either case, the student must demonstrate an ability to abide by the ethical standards of the profession before advanced training is permitted. Failure to do so results in termination from the program, coupled with exit counseling designed to help the student explore alternative career options that are better suited to the student's particular strengths as a person. It is important to note that all meetings and correspondence with the student are guided by the sincere belief that this student needs help, and the actions of the committee are presented to the student as an intervention rather than as a punishment.

Retention committee interventions are seldom required when a careful screening of students is performed prior to admission into a training program, however. When such a process includes a thorough interview of applicants, inappropriate candidates can be weeded out before they enter graduate school. In addition, multicultural educators who practice the skills of an empathic-confrontive instructor are likely to have a good track record of inducing self-enhancing, characterological changes in most students, especially when the instructor pays attention to key issues pertaining to White students and students of color.

Confront White Students

The multicultural movement in the United States started as a reaction to the ethnocentrism and racism permeating our White-dominated society (Pedersen, 1991). Within the domains of counseling and psychology, much of the literature on multiculturalism and diversity has focused on raising awareness of the history of White racism and its effects on the practice of counseling and psychotherapy in this country. Concurrently, confrontation of White racism has become a common aspect of multicultural training, although little has been written about the process of addressing racism with Whites in a culturally sensitive manner (Kiselica, 1998).

There is no question that White racism remains one of the most urgent social issues of our time. Furthermore, there is evidence that White students of counseling are adversely influenced by the pervasive presence of racism in our society. For example, although empirical research findings reported by D'Andrea and Daniels (1998) suggested that few White students entering counselor education programs are hardened racists, their data also suggested that most White trainees exhibit various forms of racism ranging from a passive acceptance of racism to the active expression of racial stereotypes. These findings are consistent with those related to research on various models of White racial identity development proposed by Hardiman (1982), Helms (1984), Ponterotto (1988), and Sabnani, Ponterotto, and Borodovsky (1991), which predict that Whites in the early phases of White racial identity development demonstrate racial stereotypes in their thinking and behavior. (For an overview of this research, see Ponterotto and Pedersen, 1993.)

In light of these research findings, helping White students to examine racism in their lives remains a crucial challenge for counselor educators. This is especially true considering that Whites tend not to see themselves as racial beings and fail to recognize the scope, intensity, and detrimental impact of White racism (Helms,

1992). Examining White racism in class is also important because it is a salient issue for students of color who have been the direct targets and victims of White prejudice and discrimination. Addressing White racism communicates to ethnic/racial minority students that the instructor cares about this issue and that he or she is also likely to be sensitive to other concerns that might be important to the students.

Multicultural educators are urged to consult several excellent resources to guide them in their attempts to challenge Whites to examine their racist tendencies critically and constructively. A *Training Manual for Diagnosing Racial Identity in Social Interactions* by Helms (1990a) contains activities that are designed to help people recognize the racial identity style of Whites and that can also help educators understand the racial dynamics of White students in the classroom. Kiselica (1998) and Locke and Kiselica (in press) have presented ideas for addressing the fears and anxieties that Whites bring to racial encounters; these authors have also offered numerous suggestions for supporting White students to confront their own racism and commit themselves to the eradication of racism. Another publication by Helms, *Race Is a Nice Thing to Have* (1992), is a powerful workbook designed to raise awareness among Whites about how they are racial beings and how racism harms everybody. In addition, in chapter 4 in this book, D'Andrea and Daniels describe numerous strategies for working with Whites who express varying degrees of racism. These strategies are intended to foster more complex ways of thinking about racism, stimulate empathy for victims of racism, and promote skills that White persons can use to address the problem of racism in our modern society effectively.

Confront Oppressed Students

Some professors are quick to challenge White students about their racism but rarely if ever urge students of color and students from other oppressed groups to examine their prejudicial attitudes and behaviors (Rooney et al., 1998). Although White students certainly should be encouraged to examine racism in their lives—especially when the responsibility that Whites should shoulder for the history of racism in this country is considered—the practice of not challenging nonmajority students to do the same is *not* recommended for two reasons. The first is that this practice tends to have the effect of dividing the class along racial lines and engendering resentment between White and minority students. The second reason is that such behavior by the instructor is a manifestation of the questionable assumption that students from oppressed groups are inoculated from thinking or acting in ethnocentric and prejudicial ways. By not being challenged, minority students may be deprived of an important opportunity to grow in terms of their cultural sensitivity.

The latter point is illustrated by an experience reported by three graduate students who are members of oppressed groups. Rooney, Flores, and Mercier (1998), who are a White gay man, a Mexican American woman, and an African

American woman, respectively, reported that they were rarely challenged in some multicultural classes because of their status as members of different minority groups. They hypothesized that this practice reflects an unspoken assumption that students belonging to racial and other minority groups are developmentally advanced when it come to issues of multiculturalism. They argued that this assumption is dangerous because it continues to place pressure on specific minority individuals to be "experts" on issues regarding race and oppression rather than allowing them the same freedom to make mistakes and develop a broader appreciation for cultural diversity themselves. They clarified that they did not believe that minority students need to explore issues identical to those of White students (e.g., a racial minority does not have the same process of owning racist oppression), but they felt certain that minority students are socialized with biases worthy of exploration and evaluation. For example, Mercier courageously described how she benefited from the encouragement of a teacher who gently pushed her to address her biases about people who were not similar to her, such as those who were not African American, were not heterosexual, or who did not share her faith in Jesus Christ. As a result of her instructor's ability to balance confrontation with support, she felt comfortable examining the effects of her socialization as a Black, Christian, heterosexual female raised in the South. She gradually realized her prejudices, and she decided to alter her tendency to remain isolated from those who were different from her. Her experience illustrates that students of color may experience significant personal and professional growth when their instructors challenge them to examine their biases rather than assume that the students have entered a multicultural counseling course "as having arrived" (Rooney et al., 1998, p. 27) in their multicultural development.

As is the case with White students, multicultural educators must be careful to confront oppressed students supportively and with an understanding of the relationship between the cultural identity development of a student and his or her interactions with culturally different students in the classroom. To this end, several resources are recommended. Once again, *A Training Manual for Diagnosing Racial Identity in Social Interactions* by Helms (1990a) can be useful for learning how to recognize and understand racial dynamics in the classroom. Chapter 5 in this book by Mobley and Cheatham also provides numerous suggestions for addressing racial identity issues of students of color and how they get played out in multicultural classes. Locke and Kiselica (in press) have offered important observations about the emotions and perspectives of Black students involved in multicultural training, described several exercises designed to raise the comfort level of Black students during their training encounters with White students, and shared suggestions for helping Black students address issues of privilege in their lives. Lastly, Rooney et al. (1998) have written a very personal and highly informative account of the factors and training processes that helped them as members of oppressed groups to examine their biased forms of thinking and to grow in terms of their multicultural awareness and sensitivity.

SUMMARY

Multicultural education is a highly human experience often characterized by unsettling challenges and emotions. The role of the empathic-confrontive instructor is to join students in their multicultural journal in such a way that the students feel safe and supported as they are challenged to explore their imperfections and strive to become better human beings. Sharing in this experience with students is indeed a privilege and one of the most fulfilling endeavors that life has to offer.

REFERENCES

American Counseling Association (1995). *Code of ethics and standards of practice.* Alexandria, VA: Author.

American Psychological Association (1992). *Ethical principles of psychologists and code of conduct.* Washington, DC: Author.

Atkinson, D. R., Morten, G., & Sue, D. W. (Eds.). (1993). *Counseling American minorities: A cross-cultural perspective* (4th ed.). Dubuque, IA: Brown.

Baker, S. B. (1997). *School counseling for the 21st century* (2nd ed.). New York: Merrill.

Brislin, R. W., & Yoshida, T. (Eds.). (1994). *Improving intercultural interactions: Modules for cross-cultural training programs:* Vol. 1. Newbury Park, CA: Sage.

Cormier, W. H., & Cormier, L. S. (1998). *Interviewing strategies for helpers: Fundamental skills and cognitive-behavioral interventions* (4th ed.). Pacific Grove, CA: Brooks/Cole.

Cross, W. E. (1991). *Shades of black: Diversity in African-American identity.* Philadelphia: Temple University Press.

Cushner, K., & Brislin, R. W. (Eds.). (1997). *Improving intercultural interactions: Modules for cross-cultural training programs:* Vol. 2. Newbury Park, CA: Sage.

D'Andrea, M., & Daniels, J. (1998). *Assessing the different psychological dispositions of White racism: An exploratory study.* Unpublished manuscript, University of Hawaii.

Department of Counseling and Personnel Services, College of New Jersey. (1997). *Student manual.* Ewing, NJ: Author.

Dillard, J. M. (1983). *Multicultural counseling: Toward ethnic and cultural relevance in human encounters.* Chicago, IL: Nelson-Hall.

Egan, G. (1994). *The skilled helper: A problem-management approach to helping* (5th ed). Pacific Grove, CA: Brooks/Cole.

Gladding, S. T. (1992). *Counseling: A comprehensive profession* (2nd ed.). New York: Merrill.

Hardiman, R. (1982). *White identity development: A process-oriented model for describing the racial consciousness of White Americans.* Unpublished doctoral dissertation, University of Massachusetts, Amherst.

Helms, J. E. (1984). Toward a theoretical model of the effects of race on counseling: A Black and White model. *The Counseling Psychologist, 12,* 153–156.

Helms, J. E. (1990a). *A training manual for diagnosing racial identity in social interactions.* Topeka, KS: Content Communications.

Helms, J. E. (1990b). Toward a model of White racial identity development. In J. E. Helms (Ed.), *Black and White racial identity: Theory, research, and practice* (pp. 49–66). New York: Greenwood Press.

Helms, J. (1992). *Race is a nice thing to have.* Topeka, KS: Content Communications.

Ivey, A. E. (1991). *Developmental strategies for helpers: Individual, family, and network interventions.* Pacific Grove, CA: Brooks/Cole.

Ivey, A. E. (1994). *Intentional interviewing and counseling: Facilitating client development in a multicultural society* (3rd ed.). Pacific Grove, CA: Brooks/Cole.

Kim, J. (1981). *Process of Asian American identity development: A study of Japanese American women's perceptions of their struggle to achieve positive identities.* Unpublished doctoral dissertation, University of Massachusetts, Amherst.

Kiselica, M. S. (1991). Reflections on a multicultural internship experience. *Journal of Counseling and Development, 70,* 126–130.

Kiselica, M. S. (1995). *Multicultural counseling with teenage fathers: A practical guide.* Newbury Park, CA: Sage.

Kiselica, M. S. (1998). Preparing Anglos for the challenges and joys of multiculturalism. *The Counseling Psychologist, 26,* 5–21.

Kiselica, M. S. (in press). Confronting my own ethnocentrism and racism: A process of pain and growth. *Journal of Counseling and Development.*

Kleinke, C. L. (1994). *Common principles of psychotherapy.* Pacific Grove, CA: Brooks/Cole.

Lark, J. S., & Paul, B. D. (1998). Beyond multicultural training: Mentoring stories from two White American doctoral students. *The Counseling Psychologist, 26,* 33–42.

Lee, C. C. (1997, November). *Counseling Today, 40,* 5.

Locke, D. C., & Kiselica, M. S. (in press). Pedagogy of possibilities: Teaching about racism in multicultural counseling courses. *Journal of Counseling and Development.*

McGrath, P., & Axelson, J. A. (1993). *Accessing awareness and developing knowledge: Foundations for skill in a multicultural society.* Pacific Grove, CA: Brooks/Cole.

Parham, T. A. (1989). Cycles of psychological nigrescence. *The Counseling Psychologist, 17,* 187–226.

Parker, W. M. (1988). *Consciousness-raising: A primer for multicultural counseling.* Springfield, IL: Charles C Thomas.

Pedersen, P. B. (1991). Multiculturalism as a generic approach to counseling. *Journal of Counseling and Development, 70,* 6–12.

Phinney, J. S., Lochner, B. T., & Murphy, R. (1990). Ethnic identity development and psychological adjustment in adolescence. In A. R. Stiffman & L. E. Davis (Eds.), *Ethnic issues in adolescent mental health* (pp. 53–72). Newbury Park, CA: Sage.

Ponterotto, J. G. (1988). Racial consciousness development among White counselor trainees: A stage model. *Journal of Multicultural Counseling and Development, 16,* 146–156.

Ponterotto, J. G. (1998). Charting a course for multicultural counseling training. *The Counseling Psychologist, 26,* 43–68.

Ponterotto, J. G., & Pedersen, P. B. (1993). *Preventing prejudice: A guide for counselors and educators.* Newbury Park, CA: Sage.

Rooney, S. C., Flores, L. Y., & Mercier, C. A. (1998). Making multicultural education effective for everyone. *The Counseling Psychologist, 26,* 22–32.

Sabnani, H. B., Ponterotto, J. G., & Borodovsky, L. G. (1991). White racial identity development and cross-cultural counselor training: A stage model. *The Counseling Psychologist, 19*, 76–102.

Shea, S. C. (1988). *Psychiatric interviewing: The art of understanding*. Philadelphia: Saunders.

Weeks, W. H., Pedersen, P., & Brislin, R. W. (Eds.). (1986). *A manual of structured experiences for cross-cultural counseling*. Yarmouth, ME: Intercultural Press.

Young, M. E. (1998). *Learning the art of helping: Building blocks and techniques*. Upper Saddle River, NJ: Merrill.

9 | A Paradigm for Racial-Cultural Training in the Development of Counselor Cultural Competencies

Saundra Tomlinson-Clarke and Vivian Ota Wang

Counselor insensitivity and ineffective mental health service delivery outcomes of counseling training for culturally diverse populations have been shown to be based on culturally biased theoretical models (Carter, 1995; Ponterotto & Casas, 1991; Sue & Sue, 1977,1990). In this respect, Ridley (1986, 1995) has described five imperatives for the development of culturally relevant programs (professional, ethical, cultural-context, scholarly, and legal). Additionally, in recognizing the importance of multicultural counseling competence in meeting the diverse needs of racial-ethnic clients (Sue, Arredondo, & McDavis, 1992; Sue, Bernier et al., 1982), counseling scholars have provided leadership and direction in incorporating multicultural perspectives into counseling and psychology research and training by developing multicultural competency guidelines (Arredondo et al., 1996; Sue, 1998; Sue, Arredondo, & McDavis, 1992; Sue, Bernier et al., 1982; Sue, Carter et al., 1998), training programs, and evaluation instruments designed to assess multicultural counselor competencies (D'Andrea, Daniels, & Heck, 1991; LaFromboise, Coleman, & Hernandez, 1991; Pedersen, 1991, 1994; Ponterotto, Sanchez, & Magids, 1990; Ridley, Mendoza, & Kanitz, 1994; Sowdowsky, Taffe, Gutkin, & Wise, 1994). Ethical and professional mandates have emanated from these efforts resulting in required multicultural training designed to increase counselor sensitivity and competency in teaching, practice, and research in many counseling training programs (Atkinson, 1994; Ponterotto & Casas, 1991; Ridley et al., 1994). Although these convictions and genuine commitments exist, Ridley (1995) has argued that "graduate programs . . . have failed to prepare trainees for effective practice with clientele from culturally diverse populations" (p. 611). In fact, Allison, Crawford, Echemendia, and Knepp (1994) showed those who perceive themselves to be limited in multicultural counseling competence reported continuing to provide mental health services to clients representing racial and cultural diversity.

155

Criteria characterizing a multiculturally competent counselor (Sue, Bernier et al., 1982) and guidelines and standards identifying minimal multicultural counseling competencies and standards (Sue, Arredondo, & McDavis, 1992; Sue, Bernier et al., 1982; Sue, Carter et al., 1998) have provided a basis for integrating course work and practical experiences into training curricula. Revised and operationalized multicultural counseling competency objectives have been identified and designed to increase the awareness and knowledge needed to provide clinical skills and interventions to culturally diverse populations (Arredondo et al., 1996; Sue, Carter et al., 1998). However, comprehensive models for incorporating racial-cultural issues into counselor training curricula remain inconsistent (Allison et al., 1994; Hill & Strozier, 1992; Ota Wang, 1998; Ponterotto & Casas, 1987, 1991; Ridley et al., 1994) and often do not clearly state the training philosophy, goals, or the amount of training needed to develop professional multicultural competence (Carey, Reinat, & Fontes, 1990; Ridley et al., 1994).

Although counselor trainees have reported increased multicultural knowledge and skill development during follow-up interviews for multicultural training, some trainees felt that they lacked the appropriate level of awareness needed to further cultural self-knowledge and self-awareness (Ota Wang, 1998; Tomlinson-Clarke, 1998). In this respect, their experiences are not unlike those of many practicing mental health professionals who have reported their level of multicultural counseling competence in working with racial-ethnic clients as limited (Allison et al., 1994). Preparing counselors with an integrated multicultural counseling competence of awareness, knowledge, and skills needed to provide relevant and appropriate mental health services to a society that is becoming increasing diverse in culture, race, and ethnicity remains a professional challenge for the 90s and beyond.

The purpose of this chapter is to highlight discrepancies in multicultural training that influence the development and integration of multicultural awareness, knowledge, and skills into theory, practice, and research. After an overview of existing racial-cultural training models, this chapter discusses racial-cultural self-awareness and self-knowledge and then training climate as essential factors within a comprehensive training model. Both serve to decrease defensiveness and increase readiness and willingness to explore racial-cultural issues. The chapter then presents a model for training and evaluating counselor racial-cultural self-knowledge that includes didactic and experiential components as well as research and clinical practica.

OVERVIEW OF RACIAL-CULTURAL TRAINING MODELS

Professional competencies and standards proposed as necessary to address the needs of culturally diverse clients have focused on visible racial-ethnic groups, such as African Americans, American Indians, Asian Americans, and Hispanic

Americans (Sue, Arredondo, & McDavis, 1992). More recently, Arredondo and her colleagues (1996) have stated

> *Multicultural counseling* refers to preparation and practices that integrate multicultural and culture-specific awareness, knowledge, and skills into counseling interactions. The term *multicultural*, in the context of counseling preparation and application, refers to five major cultural groups in the United States and its territories: African/Black, Asian, Caucasian/European, Hispanic/Latino, and Native American or indigenous groups who have historically resided in the continental United States and its territories. It can be stated that the United States is a pluralistic or multicultural society and that all individuals are ethnic, racial, and cultural beings. (p. 43)

Educators and scholars have developed many multicultural training models that have incorporated a focused multicultural perspective and placed the training emphasis primarily within the cultural context of race and ethnicity. Within these multicultural counseling training models, multicultural counseling competency training has generally exposed students to multicultural diversity within the context of racial-ethnic groups through a single didactic course offering ancillary to existing curricula, with only a few scholars in training programs integrating multicultural course work and experiences throughout the curriculum (Carter, 1995; D'Andrea et al., 1991; Mio & Morris, 1990; Paul & Kavanagh, 1990).

In an attempt to develop more comprehensive training models designed to increase counselor multicultural counseling competencies, Ridley et al. (1994) conceptualized the process of developing a multicultural training program through a Multicultural Counseling Training Program Development Pyramid, a progressive five-stage model that includes training philosophy, instructional design, learning objectives, program designs, and evaluation (for a complete discussion of the development pyramid, see Ridley et al., 1994.) Researchers have identified the limited advantages and many disadvantages of single course offerings in training programs and are now emphasizing the importance of developing programmatic multicultural courses into a total curriculum in an attempt to achieve "meaningful training outcomes" (Ridley, Espelage, & Rubinstein, 1997, p. 132).

The cultural client has often become the point of analysis in teaching racial-cultural issues. A training focus on a racial client as the major distinguishing factor often results in tendencies to overgeneralize and homogenize members of various racial groups and ignore within-racial-group factors. Similarly, ethnic-focused training may result in ". . . the tendency to oversystematize and stereotype the notion of shared meanings by assuming the ethnocultural groups are more homogenous and stable than they actually are" (Falicov, 1995, p. 375). Some researchers have focused upon the needs of broader categories of racial-cultural people by studying a full range of differences inclusive of gender, religious affiliations, ability status, and sexual orientation (Fukuyama, 1990; Whitfield, 1994). However, a training strategy with a primary focus on clients' cultural beliefs and values may misguide attention to the visible racial-cultural "other" rather than inward toward self-understanding of the counselor's own cultural beliefs, values, and stereotypes that may remain largely ignored, unchallenged, and reinforced. Helms and Richardson (1997) have asserted that

> Most of the traditional counseling and psychotherapy theoretical orientations favored in the United States claim to honor the unique psychological characteristics of the client, but, in fact, ignore the differential psychological consequences to clients (and therapists) of being continuously socialized in a variety of sociodemographic groups. (p. 60)

Training programs have tended to ignore the influences of sociodemographic factors in developing models to assist counselors in exploring racial-cultural issues and developing multicultural counseling competence. Lacking in many training programs is a counselor-focused multicultural training philosophy that incorporates a multiculturally inclusive perspective that challenges a student's own beliefs, attitudes, and assumptions about race, ethnicity, gender, sexual orientation, disability, and human diversity, and that considers how these influence the socialization process of personal and professional counselor development and the complexities associated with developing counseling competence. In this regard, counseling professionals have been shown to be susceptible to clinical bias and to be influenced by individual client variables that include race (Luepnitz, Randolph, & Gutsch, 1982; Yarkin, Town, & Wallston, 1982), gender (Bowman, 1982), race and gender (Ota Wang & Briggs, 1997), and presentation of the presenting problem (Gelso, Prince, Cornfield, Payne, Royalty, & Wiley, 1985). In addition, Tomlinson-Clarke and Camilli (1995) found that social and demographic socialization experiences of counselors influence clinical judgments. Their study also suggested that counselor judgments are not affected by ethnicity and experience, but that they are influenced by counselor gender, with men and women counselors differing in their perceptions of client concerns.

The lack of focus upon counselor attitudes toward race and other aspects of human diversity, and the development of multicultural self-awareness and self-knowledge of the counselor as a racial-cultural person, have contributed to discrepancies between multicultural training, the acquisition of knowledge and skills, and the ability of individuals to integrate multicultural awareness and knowledge meaningfully into skills of practice. Sue and Sue (1990) have discussed in further detail the relationship between discrepancies in training and the acquisition of multicultural counseling competence, which are compounded by the low priority given to issues of culture and diversity within the counseling profession and the lack of racial/ethnic minorities entering into the profession.

Counselors' self-perceptions of limited competency may be due to the inability of training programs effectively to teach how the issues of race and culture are essential and related to the counseling skills needed to become multiculturally effective in practice and research. A cognitive, intellectual understanding of multicultural issues may not necessarily translate into the acquisition of adequate or sufficient counseling skills needed to address a culturally diverse clientele.

Thus a need exists for educators developing training programs to incorporate racial-cultural self-exploration as a goal in providing counselors with experiences to prepare for a variety of interactions with clients representing varying aspects of human diversity (Carter, 1995; Pinderhughes, 1989; Sue & Sue 1990). Clarifying ones own racial and cultural identities, and developing a sense of comfort and self-acceptance, are necessary prerequisites to developing the abilities to relate respectfully to people from differing racial and cultural groups and to function effectively within culturally diverse groups (Banks, 1997; Carter, 1995).

RACIAL-CULTURAL SELF-AWARENESS AND SELF-KNOWLEDGE

Common to many models of multicultural training are emphases on (a) understanding the influences of the individual's racial, ethnic, or cultural background on worldview and the way in which life and its circumstances are experienced; (b) learning about the worldview of individual's racial-cultural groups and how these groups experience and understand life and its circumstances; and (c) developing culturally sensitive and relevant counseling skills and interventions (Corvin and Wiggins, 1989). Richardson and Molinaro (1996), for example, have advocated self-awareness, inclusive of worldview, cultural values, and racial identity, as prerequisites for developing multicultural counseling competence among White counselors. Carter (1995), Corvin and Wiggins (1989), Johnson (1987), and Sabanani, Ponterotto, and Borodovsky (1991) are among multicultural training professionals who have developed models for exploring one's own race, issues of racism, and the development of racial identity for counseling professionals. Carter (1995) and Tatum (1992) have developed a training model for teaching the psychology of racism and race-based content and applying racial identity development theory through a systems-based approach for developing and integrating racial identity development into multicultural counselor training. Unfortunately, little research and few related multicultural training models exist that focus specifically on the importance of exploring one's own race, issues of racism, and racial identity development among White and visible racial-ethnic minority counselors. All counseling professionals, whether White or members of visible racial-cultural groups, must challenge assumptions, beliefs, and behaviors about race that may result in biases.

Researchers (Carter, 1995; Johnson, 1987; Ota Wang, 1994, 1995, 1998; Tomlinson-Clarke, 1998; Wang, 1993) have further emphasized self-exploration, a fundamental and often neglected area of training. Exploring one's own race, and understanding individual, cultural, and institutional racism (Jones, 1972), oppression (Pinderhughes, 1989), and White privilege (McIntosh, 1989) are critical elements in developing the level of self-awareness and self-knowledge needed to develop multicultural counseling competencies. Consistent with discussion of counselor self-knowledge, as presented by Weinstein and Alschuler (1985), a primary goal of counselor multicultural self-knowledge is to extend an existing stage of development to new areas. Sue and Sue (1990) also have suggested a direct relationship between exploring and understanding one's own values, biases, and assumptions and developing multicultural counseling competencies: ". . . very few counselor training programs have their students explore their values, biases, and preconceived notions in the area of racist attitudes, beliefs, and behaviors" (p. 76). The need for training programs to incorporate an inclusive multicultural perspective in which counselor values, biases, and preconceived notions of racism, sexism, heterosexism, homophobia, and other "isms" are explored is evident. However, exploring and understanding oneself as a racial-cultural person is the first major step in an ongoing process of personal and professional development.

Discussions of race and racism often result in "the conspiracy of silence about racism; as if not speaking about it will make it disappear" (Nieto, 1997, p. 392), however. Emotionally powerful feelings, potentially explosive situations, and feelings of guilt from members of racial groups who have intentionally or unintentionally benefited from who they are (e.g., White privilege) have often fueled this conspiracy of silence. Although a "racial veil of silence" may exist by the desire of some to deny the existence of racism in today's society, this silence also screams, begging to have issues of race and racism addressed—together with, the range of related feelings and emotions. Thus we as well as other educators (Carter, 1995; Ridley, 1995) believe that encouraging students to speak about their experiences as racial people and about their experiences with racism and other biases is one method of creating and developing an antiracist perspective. As Nieto has so aptly stated, "[W]hen students are given time and support for expressing their views, the result can be powerful because their experiences are legitimated and used in the service of their learning" (1997, p. 392). To this end, an antiracist perspective becomes an apparent part of the training curriculum as well as the overall counselor training program culture. In moving counselors beyond a cognitive and intellectual understanding of race and culture in society to a deeper understanding of the impact of racism and oppression, we propose a paradigm for teaching racial-cultural issues within a training climate that respects practitioners and clients alike as racial-cultural people within their sociopolitical contexts.

A "SAFE" TRAINING CLIMATE

Scholars have advocated the importance of the training environment as a major and often overlooked factor that influences student comfort levels in exploring racial-cultural content for themselves and their clients. Thus Ponterotto, Alexander, and Grieger (1995) developed the Multicultural Competency Checklist to describe and assess programmatic frameworks of training programs. Programs scoring high on the checklist have been associated with positive multicultural training outcomes (Ponterotto, 1997). More recently, Gloria and Pope-Davis (1997) examined the different cultural ambiences of various learning environments to which students are exposed (i.e., the college/university environment, student training and learning environment, classroom/curriculum environment, and the faculty environment). Subtle and covert messages within these various areas of the learning institution may result in defensiveness and unwillingness on the part of both faculty and students to explore racial-cultural issues in training. Reducing stress within the environment and creating a multicultural cohesive learning environment promote a safer climate for developing racial-cultural self-awareness and self-knowledge, for increasing racial understanding and promoting self-exploration. It is in such a climate that issues of race, racism, and oppression must be openly and thoughtfully discussed in order to address continually the full range of associated feelings and powerful emotions. Factors related to the climate of the learning institution and training program are among the power indicators of the institution's and the program's commitment to multiculturalism and multi-cultural counseling competence. Multiculturalism is more than a theoretical exercise; multicultural counseling is competent practices.

RACIAL-CULTURAL COUNSELING TRAINING MODEL

The racial-cultural counseling training model presented in this section is based upon Lewin's (1948) work on how conceptual frameworks of values and attitudes, or worldviews, affect thoughts and behaviors. Lewin suggested that an individual's feelings and behaviors are influenced by activities occurring in his or her "life space," which is comprised of all possible events. A person's individual psychological processes and his or her environmental ecology interact in a dynamic process from which values, feelings, and attitudes are formed. Within this context, power influences a person's worldview; and for those who experience "discrimination and prejudice, movement in the life space is more restricted. . . . [T]he same physical situation must . . . be described for different [groups of people] as a specifically different phenomenal and functional world" (Lewin, 1948, p. 73). Thus a worldview is a person's personal cultural reality from which he or she views and finds meaning (Ibrahim, 1991), and the complexity of an intrapsychic worldview is accounted for within a social, cultural, and political reality. (A multicultural counseling curriculum based on Lewin's perspective has already been developed, evaluated, and found to be successful in increasing multicultural counseling competence among counseling professionals—Ota Wang, 1995, 1998; Wang, 1993).

Added to the model based on Lewin (1948) is Brofenbrenner's (1986) ecological approach to understanding multicultural issues, which allows for a more inclusive model. This not only enables educators and scholars to conceptualize both White and visible racial-cultural people as equally valuable and responsible for multicultural issues in research, teaching, and practice (Ota Wang, 1998) but also grounds the programmatic racial-cultural counseling training model. Using

Brofenbrenner's approach, clients and counselors alike are understood and conceptualized in the four interlocking dynamic systems:

1. **microsystem:** includes individual psychological understandings of self and interactions between other individuals (e.g., family members);
2. **mesosystem:** includes the institutions that reside within communities in which individuals are directly influenced;
3. **exosystem:** consists of social, cultural, and political institutional structures that influence policies where the mesosystem resides; and
4. **chronosystem:** accounts temporally for the time in which the system is influenced. (For a more detailed discussion of ecological systems, see Brofenbrenne, 1986.)

Multicultural issues are typically taught and integrated in all classes; but in this model an additional multicultural program sequence of three different training experiences (didactic course, experiential course, and research and clinical practica) structurally supports the existing ecological training model. Using this combination of an integrative and structured sequence for multicultural training allows students to explore more meaningfully their own cognitive and affective understanding of themselves as racial-cultural people and how their worldviews influence their multicultural approach to research and practice.

Didactic Component

The didactic course provides knowledge and awareness of the chronosystem, exosystem, and mesosystem. Students are taught chronosystem issues concerning how racial group membership and racial politics have influenced the social, cultural, and political history of the United States. By understanding how institutional and group norms develop, are maintained, and shape current policies regarding accessibility and/or inaccessibility to a variety of educational opportunities and services, students are introduced to how chronosystems have systematically advantaged or disadvantaged groups of people depending on racial-cultural group affiliations. The mesosystem is examined within the history of psychology in terms of its theories, research, and practices. Students learn how the discipline and practices of psychology have been influenced by sociopolitical forces and how these forces impact the practice of psychology at the individual level. By introducing theories of racial and cultural identity, microsystems are examined within the perspective of integrating individual psychological understandings of self and interactions between other individuals (family members, friends, colleagues).

After completing the didactic course, students often express a need to extend their current stage of development to new areas. At this point in training, students generally recognize their limited racial-cultural knowledge base, particularly in the areas of self-awareness and self-knowledge (Tomlinson-Clarke, 1998). Students reach a readiness to explore and learn more about themselves as racial-cultural beings and how their identity influences interactions with others. Student readiness, willingness, and an openness to explore and understand one's own values, biases, and assumptions are factors that appear to moderate the level of multicultural competencies achieved as a student and as a professional.

Experiential Component

The experiential course builds upon the knowledge and beginning awareness of the didactic course by systematically focusing on students' self-examination and self-evaluation of themselves as a racial-cultural person and how their group affiliations influence their sense of self in relation to others. This structured experience is based upon the work of Johnson (1987) and Carter (1995). Through an in-depth group interview, students examine and identify their feelings and understandings of the ways in which (a) their own reference group identities influence who they are as racial-cultural people; (b) societal (chronosystem) and institutional (exosystem) disciplines (mesosystem) influence understanding of self and interactions with others; and (c) racial-cultural identity attitudes shape their understanding of who they are and the assumptions they make about themselves and to others. The underlying emphasis is upon valuing themselves as an integral and vital part of any multicultural dialogue by understanding how their reference group identities influence who they are as a helping professional. Using themselves as their own "cultural agent," students practice their multicultural counseling skills in simulated counseling sessions through evaluating both the content and process of multicultural counseling competency. The emphasis on competence, which is focused on reference group issues, is weighted

> on basic counseling competence such as the ability to listen; check perceptions; reflect thoughts, feelings, and experiences; focus and lead the interviewee; express and recognize emotions and feelings in oneself and others; show empathy; and receive and respond to feedback and supervision. . . . (Carter, 1995, pp. 264–265).

As students draw upon their prior life experiences and learning, it then becomes "possible to understand in one's self and others how race influences one's personality . . . perceptions of others and counseling interactions" (p. 265).

Practica

Research practicum   Students are introduced to multicultural research while they are involved in the didactic component of training. Students then learn the process of conducting research through a hands-on multicultural-focused research practicum in which they work closely with faculty mentors examining racial-cultural issues. Through the research practicum, students are able to (a) learn the process of conducting research (i.e., conceptualizing research problems, designing studies, completing literature reviews, collecting data, analyzing data, submitting manuscripts and papers for publication and presentation); (b) ethical multicultural research practices; (c) use diverse methodologies in studying a variety of sociocultural issues; and (d) integrate multicultural research training and multicultural practices in developing multicultural competencies. Students are encouraged to continue to work on multicultural research issues with faculty mentors throughout their training experiences.

Clinical practicum The practical application of the didactic and experiential courses is realized in multicultural counseling clinical practica in which students see a wide variety of clients from diverse background and experiences, presenting with a wide range of concerns. Receiving multicultural supervision allows students to understand, use, and trust themselves as meaningful racial-cultural conduits in their counseling interactions. The success of any clinical practicum assumes that both supervisor and student are continually challenging themselves, and that both are examining their feelings and understandings of the ways in which racial-cultural identity attitudes influence assumptions about self, interactions with others, and their ability to be effective in a helping relationship.

SUMMARY

A fundamental consequence of this chapter's ecological model of racial-cultural counseling for students in training is similar to that of Sue's (1998) dynamic sizing, a result of which ". . . the therapist has appropriate skills in knowing when to generalize and be inclusive and when to individualize and be exclusive" (p. 446). Thus the success of this programmatic racial-cultural counseling training model depends on the commitment of those who teach these courses continually to develop themselves as racial-cultural people coupled with institutional support that extends beyond blindness and tolerance of difference to a more accepting stance of the importance of understanding the influences of race and racism in education and training. Cultural competence, therefore, "is best acquired through observation of and interaction with skillful mentors (a social learning approach)" (LaFromboise & Foster, 1992, p. 473). Thus multicultural counseling competence becomes one of a lifestyle that lends itself to varying ideas, worldviews, and an openness to understanding who people are rather than what they are imagined to be.

REFERENCES

Allison, K. W., Crawford, I., Echemendia, R. L., & Knepp, D. (1994). Human diversity and professional competence. *American Psychologist, 49,* 792–796.

Arredondo, P., Toporek, R., Brown, S. P., Jones, J., Locke, D. C., Sanchez, J., & Stadler, H. (1996). Operationalization of multicultural counseling competencies. *Journal of Multicultural Counseling and Development, 24,* 42–78.

Atkinson, D. R. (1994). Multicultural training: A call for standards. *The Counseling Psychologist, 22,* 300–307.

Banks, J. A. (1997). *Teaching strategies for ethnic studies* (6th ed.). Needham Heights, MA: Allyn & Bacon.

Bowman, P. R. (1982). An analog study with beginning therapists suggesting bias against "activity" in women. *Psychotherapy: Theory, Research, and Practice, 19,* 318–324.

Brofenbrenner, U. (1986). Recent advances in research on the ecology of human development. In R. K. Silbereisen, K. Eyferth, & G. Rudinger (Eds.), *Development as action in context: Problem behavior and normal youth development* (pp. 287–309). Heidelberg and NewYork: Springer-Verlag.

Carey, J. C., Reinat, M., & Fontes, L. (1990). School counselors perceptions of training needs in multicultural counseling. *Counselor Education and Supervision, 29,* 155–169.

Carter, R. T. (1995). *The influence of race and racial identity in psychotherapy: Toward a racially inclusive model.* New York: Wiley.

Constantine, M. G., Ladany, N., Inman, A. G., & Ponterotto, J. G. (1996). Students' perceptions of multicultural training in counseling psychology. *Journal of Multicultural Counseling and Development, 24,* 241–253.

Corvin, S., & Wiggins, F. (1989). An antiracism training model for White professionals. *Journal of Multicultural Counseling and Development, 17,* 105–114.

D'Andrea, M., Daniels J., & Heck, R. (1991). Evaluating the impact of multicultural counseling training. *Journal of Counseling and Development, 70,* 143–150.

Falicov, C. J. (1995). Training to think culturally: A multidimensional comparative framework. *Family Process, 34,* 373–388.

Fukuyama, M. A. (1990). Taking a universal approach to multicultural counseling. *Counselor Education and Supervision, 30,* 6–15.

Gelso, C. L., Prince, J., Cornfield, J. L., Payne, A.B., Royalty, G., & Wiley, M. O. (1985). Quality of counselor's intake evaluations for clients with problems that are primarily vocational versus personal. *Journal of Counseling Psychology, 32,* 339–347.

Gloria, A. M., & Pope-Davis, D. B. (1997). Cultural ambiance: The importance of a culturally aware learning environment in the training and education of counselors. In D. B. Pope-Davis & H. L. K. Coleman (Eds.), *Multicultural counseling competencies: Assessment, education and training, and supervision* (pp. 242–259). Thousand Oaks, CA: Sage.

Helms, J. E., & Richardson, T. Q. (1997). How "multiculturalism" obscures race and culture as differential aspects of counseling competency. In D. B. Pope-Davis & H. L. K. Coleman (Eds.), *Multicultural counseling competencies: Assessment, education and training, and supervision* (pp. 60–79). Thousand Oaks, CA: Sage.

Hill, H. I., & Strozier, A. L. (1992). Multicultural training in APA-approved counseling psychology programs: A survey. *Professional Psychology: Research and Practice, 23,* 43–51.

Ibrahim, F. A. (1991). Contribution of cultural worldview to generic counseling and development. *Journal of Counseling and Development, 70,* 13–19.

Johnson, S. D. (1987). Knowing that versus knowing how: Toward achieving expertise through multicultural training for counseling. *The Counseling Psychologist, 15,* 320–331.

Jones, J. M. (1972). *Prejudice and racism.* Reading, MA:Addison-Wesley.

LaFromboise, T. D., Coleman, H. L., & Hernandez, A. (1991). Development and factor structure of the cross-cultural counseling inventory—revised. *Professional Psychology: Research and Practice, 22,* 380–388.

LaFromboise, T. D., & Foster, S. L. (1992). Cross-cultural training: Scientist-practitioner model and methods. *The Counseling Psychologist, 20,* 472–489.

Lewin, K. (1948). *Resolving social conflict*. New York: Harper.

Luepnitz, R. R., Randolph, D. L., & Gutsch, K. U. (1982). Race and socioeconomic status as confounding variables in the accurate diagnosis of alcoholism. *Journal of Clinical Psychology, 38*, 665–669.

McIntosh, P. (1989, July/August). White privilege. Unpacking the invisible knapsack. *Peace and Freedom*, 10–12.

Mio, J. S., & Morris, D. R. (1990). Cross-cultural issues in psychology training programs: An invitation for discussion. *Professional Psychology Research and Practice, 21*, 434–441.

Nieto, S. (1997). School reform and school achievement. A multicultural perspective. In J. A. Banks, & C. A. M. Banks (Eds.), *Multicultural education: Issues and perspectives* (3rd ed, pp. 387–407). Needham Heights, MA: Allyn & Bacon.

Ota Wang, V. (1994). Cultural competency in genetic counseling. *Journal of Genetic Counseling, 3*(4), 267–277.

Ota Wang, V. (1995). *Curriculum development and cognitive styles: Cultural competency in genetic counseling*. Unpublished doctoral dissertation, Columbia University, New York.

Ota Wang, V. (1998). Curriculum evaluation and assessment of multicultural genetic counselor education. *Journal of Genetic Counseling, 7*(1), 87–111.

Ota Wang, V., & Briggs, K. (1997, February). *The role of cognitive information processing and racial identity attitudes on causal attributions*. Paper presented at the 14th Annual Winter Roundtable on Cross-Cultural Psychology and Education, Teachers College, Columbia University, New York.

Paul, N., & Kavanagh, L. (Eds.). (1990). *Genetic services for underserved populations* (Birth Defects Original Article Series 26). Washington, DC: National Center for Education in Maternal and Child Health.

Pedersen, P. P. (1991). Multiculturalism as a generic approach to counseling. *Journal of Counseling and Development, 70*, 6–12.

Pedersen, P. (1994). *A handbook for developing multicultural awareness* (2nd ed.). Alexandria, VA: American Counseling Association.

Pinderhughes, E. (1989). *Understanding race, ethnicity, and power in clinical practice*. Chicago: Free Press.

Ponterotto, J. C. (1997). Multicultural counseling training: A competency model and national survey. In D. B. Pope-Davis & H. L. K. Coleman (Eds.), *Multicultural counseling competencies: Assessment, education and training, and supervision* (pp. 111–130). Thousand Oaks, CA: Sage.

Ponterotto, J. C., Alexander, C. M., & Grieger, I. (1995). A multicultural competency checklist for counseling training programs. *Journal of Multicultural Counseling and Development, 23*, 11–20.

Ponterotto, J. C., & Casas, J. M. (1987). In search of multicultural competence within counselor education programs. *Journal of Counseling and Development, 65*, 430–434.

Ponterotto, J. C., & Casas, J. M. (1991). *Handbook of racial/ethnic minority counseling research*. Springfield, IL: Charles C Thomas.

Ponterotto, J. G., Sanchez, C. M., & Magids, D. M. (1990). *The multicultural counseling awareness scale (MCAS): Form B; revised self-assessment*. New York: Fordham University.

Richardson, T. Q., & Molinaro, K. L. (1996). White counselor self-awareness: A prerequisite for developing multicultural competence. *Journal of Counseling and Development, 74*, 238–240.

Ridley, C. R. (1986, August). *The future of training in cross-cultural counseling*. Paper presented at the annual meeting of the American Psychological Association, Washington, DC.

Ridley, C. R. (1995). *Overcoming unintentional racism in counseling and therapy.* Thousand Oaks, CA: Sage.

Ridley, C. R., Espelage, D. L. & Rubinstein, K. J. (1997). Course development in multicultural counseling. In D. P. Pope-Davis & H. L. K. Coleman (Eds.), *Multicultural counseling competencies, assessment, education and training, and supervision* (pp. 131–158). Thousand Oaks, CA: Sage.

Ridley, C. R., Mendoza, D. W., & Kanitz, B. E. (1994). Multicultural training: Reexamination, operationalization, and integration. *The Counseling Psychologist, 22,* 227–289.

Sabnani, H. B., Ponterotto, J. C., & Borodovsky, L. G. (1991). White racial identity development and cross-cultural counselor training: A stage model. *The Counseling Psychologist, 19,* 76–102.

Sowdowsky, G. R., Taffe, R. C., Gutkin, T .B., & Wise, S. L. (1994). Development of the multicultural counseling inventory: A self-report measure of multicultural competencies. *Journal of Counseling and Development, 70,* 29–36.

Sue, D. W., Arredondo, P., & McDavis, R. J. (1992). Multicultural counseling competencies and standards: A call to the profession. *Journal of Counseling and Development, 70,* 477–486.

Sue, D. W., Bernier, J. E., Durran, A., Feinberg, L., Pedersen, P., Smith E. J., & Vasquez-Nuttall, E. (1982). Position paper: Cross-cultural counseling competencies. *The Counseling Psychology, 10,* 45–52.

Sue, D. W., Carter, R. T., Casas J. M., Fouad, N. A., Ivey, A. E., Jensen, M., LaFromboise, T., Manese, J. E., Ponterotto, J. G., & Vazquez-Nutall, E. (1998). *Multicultural counseling competencies: Individual and organizational perspectives.* Thousand Oaks, CA: Sage.

Sue, D. W., & Sue, D. (1977). Barriers to effective cross-cultural counseling, *Journal of Counseling Psychology, 24,* 420–429.

Sue, D. W., & Sue, D. (1990). *Counseling the culturally different: Theory and practice.* (2nd ed.). New York: Wiley.

Sue, S. (1998). In search of cultural competence in psychology and counseling. *American Psychologist, 53,* 440–448.

Tatum, B. D. (1992). Talking about race, learning about racism: The application of racial identity development theory in the classroom. *Harvard Educational Review, 62,* 1–24.

Tomlinson-Clarke, S. (1998). *Assessing multicultural training: A focus on counselor cultural self-awareness and self-knowledge.* Manuscript submitted for publication.

Tomlinson-Clarke, S., & Camilli, G. (1995). An exploratory investigation of counselor judgments in multicultural research. *Journal of Multicultural Counseling and Development, 23,* 237–245.

Wang, V. (1993). *Handbook of cross-cultural genetic counseling.* (Available from Vivian Ota Wang, College of Education, P.O. Box 870611, Tempe, AZ, 85287-0611.)

Weinstein, G., & Alschuler, A. S. (1985). Educating and counseling for self-knowledge development. *Journal of Counseling and Development, 64,* 19–25.

Whitfield, D. (1994). Toward an integrated approach to improving multicultural counselor education. *Journal of Multicultural Counseling and Development, 22,* 239–252.

Yarkin, K. L., Town, J. P., & Wallston, B. S. (1982). Blacks and women must try harder: Stimulus persons' race and sex attribution of causality. *Personality and Social Psychology Bulletin, 8,* 21–24.

II | RECOMMENDATIONS FOR MULTICULTURAL EDUCATORS

10 | Where Do We Go From Here? Some Observations and Recommendations for Multicultural Educators

Harold E. Cheatham

Over the years I have suggested that to the extent that traditional concepts of psychological theory and intervention ignore the cultural and con-textual specificity of nontraditional clients, these theories and related practices are inadequate for serving nontraditional clients. I have also contended, color, ethnicity, gender, or other distinguishing individual or group characteristics notwithstanding, that the goal of all counseling and therapy is to achieve long-term constructive outcomes (1990). That is, the vital goal is to achieve, through the therapeutic intervention, the integrated and fuller psychological functioning of the client. More than a decade ago (1985), I advanced the conclusion that existing psychological models have the potential, following some thoughtful revi-sions, to be used in providing effective service to the new clientele. Some years later in a revision of that conclusion, I wrote that the effective therapist moves beyond encapsulation to demonstrate cultural awareness that takes into account the client's sociocultural history and, further, that through genuine commitment to the client and the profession, the therapist is able to transcend the narrow argument regarding who can counsel whom.

> The revised model advocated here doesn't presume a "fourth force." [But] it does move dramatically beyond the rhetoric and stereotyped attack on counselors' and therapists' inadequacy to suggest the development of a paradigm that is respectful of the client and [that] replaces the pedestrian, detached, and intimidated treatment typically offered (1990, p. 389)

This historical perspective serves principally as backdrop for my appraisal of where we are in the development of a multicultural paradigm, and against which to note students' challenges and contributions to my own multicultural develop-ment. Among these students, one stands out for her persistent and poignant observation that indeed a revised psychological model presumes a fourth force in psychology—whether or not we term it as such. That student (and now practitioner) of multicultural counseling and theory contended at the outset of her training that no amount of retrofitting of the traditional models of counseling and theory could render them sufficient to the task of providing efficient and effective service to clients of other than Eurocentric sociocultural orientation and experience. The work of a large and growing number of theorists and practitioners, including the contributors to this book, support the contention (e.g., Atkinson, Morten, & Sue, 1979; Hilliard, 1985; Ivey, 1983; Ivey, Ivey, & Simek-Morgan, 1997; Kiselica, 1995; Lee, 1995; Locke, 1992; Lum, 1986; Paniagua, 1994; Pedersen, 1992; Ponterotto, Casas, Suzuki, & Alexander, 1995; Ponterotto & Pedersen, 1993; Ridley, 1991; Sue, Ivey, & Pedersen, 1996) and contribute to installing multicultural counseling theory as metatheory.

A range of explications and refinements to the theory and practice of multicultural counseling and therapy are offered in this book. The refinements address effective training and training methods and their measurement, supervision, issues in research, recognition and beneficial managing of prejudice and racism in the classroom, and trust as a critical dimension of psychological interventions. The preface advances the hope that other practitioners and educators who deal with issues of prejudice among trainees will find benefit in the propositions offered. However, my review suggests that many of the concepts and strategies are offered rather exclusively in the language and context of our profession and as such may not be readily accessible to practitioners outside of psychology and related disciplines. What an irony it would be to prepare a text for improving human interactions and functioning beyond cultural boundaries while erecting or leaving in place disciplined-based linguistic and cultural barriers! Failure to recognize and address discipline-bound barriers to the adoption and expansion of multicultural theory, in general, would retard our progress. In this chapter I chose to address commonalities among some of the conceptualizations advanced in this book and the portability of these psychology constructs to multicultural education in general.

CROSSING DISCIPLINE BOUNDARIES

The contributors to this book take as a given that prejudice and perhaps racism and its variants are likely to be present if not pervasive in the training setting and that the instructor or trainer is responsible for demonstrating awareness of the dimensions of this impediment to learning and for employing effective strategies to reduce or eliminate it by engaging the learner in development of productive behaviors. Ridley and Thompson in chapter 1 argue that racism and prejudice are both systemic and resistant to being reduced in the training environment because even otherwise intelligent people have been taught to manage the disparity between their recognition of inequity or injustice and their individual capacity—and, perhaps, obligation—to take constructive action. Ridley and Thompson adopt the term *dysconsciousness* to describe this disposition, suggesting that it may be effectively combated through assisting the learner to develop awareness or critical consciousness of his or her behavior as a byproduct of socialization in prejudiced and racist environments.

Although prejudice and racism comprise attitude and behavior components, it is the resistant behavior that should be the focus of the intervention, according to Ridley and Thompson. Moreover, resistance is rooted in and sustained by the individual's fears, anxieties, and sense of vulnerability as well as by the individual's estimate of the personal cost that results from relinquishing or retaining a behavior. To the extent that resistance or any behavior is rooted in and reinforced by experience, the behavior may be regarded as beneficial or of lower cost to retain than the cost to be paid for relinquishing the behavior. Thus the more foreign the behavior in which one is called upon to make a change (or the more radical the change called for), the greater may be the resistance. It is likely to be easier to change attitude and behavior regarding a convention of comparatively less social importance.

The implications for multicultural educators are that our students are products of their environs and of prevalent social conventions. The valence generally assigned to resistance in the psychological sense differs from that assigned to it in other contexts. Beyond the psychological training program setting, resistance might be regarded more generally as an expected and appropriate human response to the sense of threat. In multicultural education or diversity training setting, students may be called upon to disclose attitudes, and to do so in the face of lower tolerance than might be accorded in another academic classroom. Hence the expertise of the instructor is of critical importance in assessing the learner and the learning environment and then in constructing and implementing training that is consonant with the sophistication and needs of the learner. When explicating, in part, their model for diversity training, Ridley and Thompson, for simplicity, assume the highest level of racial identity development and consequent functioning at a high level of comfort and racial self-awareness. As the literature on supervision reveals, it is desirable that such levels of integration be demonstrated among those providing instruction and supervision; but in many instances, supervisors have not had the training or experiences that certify them as competent multicultural educators. Indeed, as this chapter notes, development of resistance management can be arduous and frustrating.

Kiselica in chapter 8, like Ridley and Thompson in chapter 1, addresses the challenges of guiding students' development as sensitive multicultural counselors. The active role that students are obligated to take in their own development with the instructor identifying structures and serving principally as a guide, is emphasized. Counseling students are disposed to avoid confronting and discussing the unsafe topics that are the focus of multicultural training—even in multicultural counseling classes—because (as several contributors noted) students have been permitted, and often reinforced in the general society and specifically in too many classrooms, to avoid the risk of offending or of revealing their ignorance and prejudice about ethnicity/race, gender, sexual orientation, and ableism.

The focus on the person who wants to be an effective multicultural trainer is both helpful and exportable because it de-emphasizes the theoretical in favor of demonstrating the effective trainer and training program as a work in progress. It is critical to convey, as it is in chapter 8, the notion that just as human development proceeds throughout life from meaning(s) attached to foundational events, so does development of multicultural competence. Equally critical to convey is that development of competence transcends the classroom setting and occurs in all venues. Chapter 8 characterizes the learning experience in terms of empathy, confrontation, self-reflection, and self-disclosure—terms that can be construed simultaneously in their psychological and their broader or more general meanings. Although the chapter chooses to elaborate the use of confrontation in counseling and counselor education, the explication serves the portability of this intervention to other disciplines.

Kiselica's notion of "lovingly confronting ethnocentrism and prejudice" in chapter 8 is compelling and in need of fuller development to acknowledge the level of skill and personal development that are implied for the person who wants to succeed in a transitive confrontation. Equally compelling (and I believe portable) is Kiselica's discussion of the trainer's obligation also to confront oppressed students as opposed to the damaging practice of assuming or acquiescing to the argument that as a function of their experiences they are inoculated from thinking and acting in ethnocentric and prejudicial ways. In main, however, I disagree with Kiselica's recommendation for confronting extreme prejudice. And I believe that his discussion of retention policies and committee intervention to recommend remediation for dysfunctional students bears elaboration for its portability to all training settings. It seems likely that the threat already inherent in the training environment is exacerbated by the instructor who informs the student that extremely prejudicial attitudes (or the behavior that Ridley and Thompson identify as the salient manifestation) may prevent the trainee from adhering to ethical codes of professional conduct. Regardless of the training context, it seems rather that the objective is less likely to be attained through invoking law-and-order principles than, again, through lovingly confronting. In this, I am reminded of the resistant, even disruptive, student in my general psychology class some years ago who proclaimed that he should not be required to take psychology because "it is nothing more than just common sense. Plus," he added, "all that we call psychology and are talking about in class is already in the Bible." Perhaps! But capturing his attention and interest (I know in retrospect) occurred through lovingly confronting/challenging him with discussion of the commandments and beatitudes and his apprehension of logical (or, perhaps, illogical) extensions of those that gave us psychology.

EMPLOYING EFFECTIVE MULTICULTURAL TEACHING STRATEGIES

All contributors to this book address effective teaching methodologies for multi-cultural counseling and education. All contributors also share the notion that effective training comprises a proper mix of didactic and experiential exercises. In chapter 5, Mobley specifically addresses the need for counselor educators to achieve integration of their cultural identity as a prerequisite to demonstrating concern, valuing, and appreciation of the differences and similarities between our-selves and counselors in training and, as well, between ourselves and our peers.

In chapter 9, Tomlinson-Clarke and Ota Wang, based on their research stud-ies, are critical of existing models for training and evaluating multicultural coun-seling competence despite mounting evidence of progress in counselors "knowing how versus knowing that" (Johnson, 1987). They note some continuing discrep-ancies in multicultural training. For example, although counseling students report gains in their levels of skill and knowledge, some trainees also report deficiency in awareness levels sufficient to promote their own cultural knowledge and aware-ness. Factors contributing to this deficient preparation include the attempts of some training programs to develop multicultural competence through a single didactic course or through training focused on a "racial client." The single-course approach is most likely to result in stunted development for lack of adequate exposure to a comprehensive model incorporating an experiential component. A further deficiency inherent in the single-course approach is that cognitive or intellectual comprehension does not necessarily translate as practical or practice skill. In addition, the racial-client approach may result in oversystematizing and stereotyping based on the fallacious assumption of stable and homogeneous char-acteristics among ethnocultural groups.

Tomlinson-Clarke and Ota Wang's observations in chapter 9 are consistent with Kiselica's notions in chapter 8 that regard the effective trainer and training program as a work in progress. Tomlinson-Clarke and Ota Wang's observations that understanding oneself as a racial-cultural being is the first major step in the ongoing process of multicultural development also resonate with mine and Mob-ley's in chapter 5. An integrative model complemented by a structured sequence of training experiences holds promise for effective cognitive and affective devel-opment of counselors in training; and an ecological model comprising didactic, experiential, and practica components as a complement to the typical approach of integrating multicultural issues into all course work is proposed. The exposition offered in chapter 9 of the didactic, experiential, and clinical training compo-nents, together with the observations of students' reported needs for further inte-gration between and among components, seems instructive for other training environments. Teacher training comes immediately to my mind. How much of the current controversy about teacher competence and classroom effectiveness (that those in certain quarters believe can be measured effectively with standardized tests) is owed to the failure of some training programs to provide sequenced train-ing experiences complemented by ecological models? Should those completing teacher training be expected to proceed directly from student teaching to consis-tent, competent, classroom performance?

Identity development models common to training programs are foundational to chapter 5's conceptualization: a self-awareness for multiculturally oriented counselor educators model for increasing awareness, sensitivity, and knowledge of the racial-cultural heritage of both instructors and trainees. Affirmation of self and others is proposed as a critical capacity of the culturally skilled trainer. Although the focus in chapter 5 is limited to the salience of racial characteristics, the model's components address learning about self, learning about others, and learning about self in relation(ships). Through exploration and experience in these dimensions, a counselor educator develops effectiveness and competence to explore and manage racial and (by extension) other distinguishing characteristics such as gender, ethnicity, and sexual orientation that may be present or pervasive in the training environment. Although the model has its origin and development in the psychology disciplines, through its practice exercises classroom teachers and others promoting learning can develop and export understanding of self, oth-ers, and self as countenanced by others.

The Freirean-based conceptualization of critical consciousness in counselor education described by Locke and Faubert in chapter 3, which also resonates with chapter 5, addresses states of awareness and openness to new knowledge or ways of understanding as a precursor to action. This postulation focuses on promoting the development of the counselor in training and considers development of criti-cal consciousness as an appropriate goal of counselor education. Locke and Faubert propose that an effective way for counselors in training to learn about themselves (and subsequently their own clients) is through dialogic education—that is, through listening to their personal stories. Students' personal stories or "authentic reflections on lived experience" can also be used as examples of how cultures and the dialogues within cultures may serve as an inspiration to others in a variety of situations and settings. This example of learning in the multicultural setting is rem-iniscent of the growth reported by a returning adult student. In the course evalua-tion the student noted that through the experience the class provided (multiple perspectives offered), he had a new way of listening to Rush Limbaugh. "I no longer listen to just what he says," the student wrote, "but to find out what he is up to." Fact is that the student probably never listened "just to" what Rush said; rather he listened and attended with a specifically or narrowly constricted perspective. His exclamation was about having learned to allow for the existence of an alternative perspective—or even multiple perspectives—on reality.

Of critical importance to the continuing development of the field of multicul-tural education are the ideas expressed in chapter 3—and implicit throughout this book—that a training program provides a vital, possibly unsurpassed, site for join-ing persons from traditionally privileged groups and persons from traditionally devalued groups, and that the cultural competence of the trainer cannot be assumed but must be demonstrated. Only upon such demonstration can the trainer be qualified to evaluate the cultural competence of the student or counselor in training. Teaching cultural competence is more than an intellectual activity, and it is only in an environment of trust, mutual support, and challenge that multicultural growth and development can be inspired and nurtured.

In chapter 7, Mary Swigonski critiques multicultural education from the perspective of movements for social and economic justice and empowerment. Her description of the enmeshment of knowledge and education with politics relates to the preceding discussion, particularly that touching on multiple perspectives and the possible salutary effects of multicultural education. Chapter 7 also amplifies the pervasive notion that the challenges of developing multicultural competence can be threatening for the counselor in training and reminds counselor educators that we need critical and conscious awareness that our objectives may require students to disclose painful facts before they are ready.

To arm trainees with conceptual tools to effect understanding of how racism and its variants constrain ways of knowing, the chapter proposes using standpoint theory. The axioms of the theory relate to an individual's actions and being, both from the individual's own and others' frames of reference. One axiom states that the standpoint of those who are outside the dominant groups develops from their daily activities. This axiom has also been expressed in the slave/master duality, and it seems to be a corollary to the challenge to our competence and suitability to provide counsel (particularly of the psychological variety) to those with whom we have not endured or enjoyed critical life experience. The challenge is expressed in the question, Who could (or can) counsel whom and under what circumstances?

The elegance of the model is in both its simplicity and its potential to engage the learner at the learner's present developmental stage and, through a series of related tasks, help the learner engage in systematic search for and attend to multiple viewpoints. Swigonski notes that standpoint theory introduces learners to the importance of developing critical consciousness that seeks and exposes contradictions. This can be accomplished through assignments in literature as well as through term papers, journals, and research projects. For example, in doctoral seminars in multicultural counseling, students have kept journals of their responses to and growth as a result of the various assignments and classroom discussions. These journals were submitted to and read only by a teaching assistant (an advanced level student, usually second year) who periodically offered in a seminar, without attribution, salient points from a student's journal. Curiously and refreshingly, as multiple perspectives were offered, invariably the writer self-disclosed and thereby generally enriched and extended the discussion.

In a similar approach, I have encouraged beginning students in multicultural training to discover the effects of subtle, everyday expressions of prejudice and power by having them list slogans for sharing in class discussion. A favorite exemplar of this task is "Go Hard Or Go Home!" As Swigonski suggests, learners' feelings of anger and frustration, and sometimes of being overwhelmed, when obligated to address their beliefs and prejudices can be assuaged through story-telling and similar exercises that provide insight with lessened threat.

WHERE DO WE GO FROM HERE?

Reviewing the conceptualizations of the contributors to this book and offering a critique of their implications for the future of multicultural counseling was my task in this chapter—and what a happy task! I began by reflecting on the age-old observation of deficiencies in traditional theory, and I added my perspective that we must not inadvertently erect or retain barriers to participation by all who strive to be multicultural educators. We must instead adapt and broadcast as widely as possible—that is, to every quarter where there is engagement in multicultural education—all that we have derived. At the end of this review, I am enriched and enjoying new confidence that significant progress has been made, that the fourth force is being safeguarded, sustained, and advanced by a cadre of committed scholars. Although less about ongoing research in multicultural counseling and education is revealed in this volume than is desirable, it is clear that scholarly research is underway. However, attention needs to be turned to ensuring the completion and publishing of research addressing constructs that are at the heart of multicultural theory and practice.

This book joins the stream of important literature that defines the field. I am deeply grateful for having been invited to participate.

REFERENCES

Atkinson, D. R., Morten, G, & Sue, D. W. (1979). *Counseling American minorities: A cross-cultural perspective*. Dubuque, IA: Brown.

Cheatham, H. E. (1985). *Crossing boundaries in counseling*. Unpublished manuscript, Pennsylvania State University.

Cheatham, H. E. (1990). Empowering Black families. In H. E. Cheatham & J. B. Stewart (Eds.), *Black families: Interdisciplinary perspectives* (pp. 373–393). New Brunswick, NJ: Transaction.

Hilliard, A. (1985). A framework for counseling the Afro-American man. *Journal of Non-White Concerns, 13*, 72–78.

Ivey, A. E. (1983). *Intentional interviewing and counseling: Facilitating client development in a multicultural society*. Pacific Grove, CA: Brooks/Cole.

Ivey, A, Ivey, M. B., & Simek-Morgan, L. (1997). *Counseling and psychotherapy: A multicultural perspective* (4th ed.). Boston: Allyn & Bacon.

Johnson, S. D. (1987). Knowing that versus knowing how: Toward achieving expertise through multicultural training for counseling. *The Counseling Psychologist, 15*, 320–331.

Kiselica, M. S. (1995). *Multicultural counseling with teenage fathers: A Practical Guide*. Thousand Oaks, CA: Sage.

Lee, C. C. (1995). *Counseling for diversity*. Boston: Allyn & Bacon.

Locke, D. C. (1992). *Increasing multicultural understanding: A comprehensive model.* Thousand Oaks, CA: Sage.

Lum, D. (1986). Social work practice with people of color. Monterey, CA: Brooks/Cole.

Paniagua, F. A. (1994). *Assessing and treating culturally diverse clients.* Thousand Oaks, CA: Sage.

Pedersen, P. B. (1991). Introduction to the special issue on multiculturalism as a fourth force in counseling. *Journal of Counseling and Development, 70,* 4.

Ponterotto, J. G., Casas, J. M., Suzuki, L. A., & Alexander, C. M. (Eds.). (1995). *Handbook of multicultural counseling.* Thousand Oaks, CA: Sage.

Ponterotto, J. G., & Pedersen, P. B. (1993). Preventing prejudice: A guide for counselors and educators. Thousand Oaks, CA: Sage.

Ridley, C. R. (1991). *Overcoming racism and prejudice in counseling and therapy: A practitioner's guide to intentional intervention.* Thousand Oaks, CA: Sage.

Sue, D. W. (1983). Ethnic minority issues in psychology: A reexamination. *American Psychologist, 38,* 583–592.

Sue, D. W., Ivey, A., & Pedersen, P. B. (Eds.). (1996). *A theory of multicultural counseling & therapy.* Pacific Grove, CA: Brooks/Cole.

11 | Challenging Our Profession, Challenging Ourselves: Further Reflections on Multicultural Counseling and Training

Amy L. Reynolds

Reading and reflecting on the important works shared in this book has been both a joy and a challenge. The joyful and exciting part has been that the entire focus of this book is addressing racism in multicultural counselor training when in-depth attention to these concerns has often been avoided and neglected in the multicultural counselor movement. Initially the multicultural counseling movement concentrated on raising awareness and content knowledge about people of color. Those early writings recognized the racism inherent in the counseling profession and soon began focusing on training issues. For the past several years a significant amount of writing in multicultural counseling has centered on multicultural competence. Although multicultural counseling authors often comment on the impact of racism on counseling, it is rare that we concentrate our energy on exploring racism as part of the solution.

Placing racism and prejudice and their influence on multicultural counseling at the center of effective multicultural training is a monumental step toward creating true change within individual counselors and supervisors as well as the counseling profession. The challenges inherent in exploring these significant issues occur on both a professional and personal level as all of us question ourselves and the counseling profession. Part of that challenge involves examining our own personal lives, values, and contradictions.

Based on the perspectives offered in the various chapters in this book and my own point of view and personal and professional experiences, I offer five core themes or ideas that I believe warrant further study, exploration, and understanding. These themes are:

- examining the conspiracy of silence surrounding racism within the counseling profession;
- examining the powerful role of multicultural trainer and how we best prepare ourselves to take on this responsibility;
- understanding where we fall short in our multicultural training efforts;
- exploring the influence of dualistic thinking in multicultural training; and
- taking a cognitive and phenomenological approach to multicultural training.

Although these themes are not ordered in terms of importance, one central notion offered and highlighted by Tomlinson-Clarke and Ota Wang in chapter 9 must be further highlighted: the conspiracy of silence about racism and oppression within the counseling profession. Sometimes it is easy to frame multiculturalism as being about understanding and appreciating cultures, gathering knowledge about different cultural groups, and learning to get along with those who are different from us. There is nothing wrong with those approaches. They are necessary to creating change; but they are not sufficient. This book does a good job of addressing this issue and acknowledging that the goal is not, and should not be, to make people more comfortable. Rather the goal is to help individuals understand the pervasive system of racism and how we, as individuals, have internalized that system. We must also understand how racism works as a self-perpetuating system within society and the counseling profession. The systemic issue, addressed by Tomlinson-Clarke and Ota Wang (in chapter 9) as well as Locke and Faubert (in chapter 3), must be addressed as part of our multicultural training efforts. Otherwise we are acting in codependent ways by not admitting or confronting the real and systemic, organizational realities that maintain racism and prejudice within the counseling profession. To use the common image used in addictions counseling, racism is often the huge elephant in the room that no one wants to discuss. This book makes the case that unless we address this often unnamed issue of racism, we cannot effectively and meaningfully create multiculturally competent counselors. When we only focus on increasing cultural sensitivity and knowledge and building effective multicultural counseling skills, we help to maintain the destructive system of racism. Sue (1995), Lee (1998), and others have offered suggestions as to how individuals can work within the counseling profession to produce social change. Sue suggested using the tools of multicultural organization development as a means of creating institutional change. Lee advocated empowerment and advocacy as part of a counselor's social responsibility. He stated that effective counselors must possess three levels of awareness: awareness of self, interpersonal awareness, and systemic awareness.

The tougher and more personal question that each of us who cares about these issues must ask is, How is our own conspiracy manifested in how we view multicultural counseling and how we teach or train around these issues? Lee (1998) acknowledged this work as risky business. Being the one who often raises multicultural issues and identifies the influence of racism in counseling, regardless of your own racial and ethnic background, can have detrimental professional consequences. This reality may be why many trainers and faculty instead choose to focus on multicultural competence and raising multicultural awareness. When we do not acknowledge racism and work to eradicate it, we all help to perpetuate racism within the counseling profession either consciously or unconsciously. Uncovering these biases and ways in which we are silent about racism is hard work, and there are no road maps to tell us where to go and how to get there.

A second theme, addressed by many chapters in this book, is the powerful role of the trainer/counselor educator. Keeping the spotlight on the trainer is especially meaningful considering how much easier it is to focus on the trainee/counseling student. Tomlinson-Clarke and Ota Wang (in chapter 9) focus on the importance of teacher as mentor. Others like Locke and Faubert (in chapter 3) as well as Kiselica (in chapter 8) focus on the centrality of self-disclosure and being genuine. But how do we prepare ourselves to teach and lead in this area? How do we learn to be role models? What must we do in our training and our life? Pedersen (in chapter 6) suggests listening to our inner voice as a means of developing skills. Tomlinson-Clarke and Ota Wang (in chapter 9) imply it is a lifestyle, a personal cultural reality. I agree with their point of view and have come to believe that truly embracing multiculturalism is about how we live our life. It is not enough to have a certain set of values and attitudes. I must constantly take the next step and look at my life in very tough ways. Who are my friends? What do I read? How do I spend my time and money? It has been said that we do what we value. So if my life is monocultural even though I talk multiculturalism, then my actions send the message that it is okay to believe in multiculturalism without changing my life. Bernice Johnson Reagon (1983) took it even farther when she talked about the importance of doing coalition work and working with folks who are culturally and politically different from yourself. She identified this as work that is very personal and very uncomfortable. She said, "I feel as if I'm gonna keel over any minute and die. That is often what it feel like if you're really doing coalition work. Most of the time you feel threatened to the core and if you don't, you're not really doing no coalescing" (p. 356). If that is true, how do we make that transformation?

Kiselica (in chapter 8) emphasizes the importance of peer supervision or consultation. This seems crucial, yet who do we rely on for guidance, support, and most importantly, challenge? How do we structure and maintain our own learning? Everything we know about systemic change says that creating structures and systems is necessary. How does that translate to our personal life? We need to build in time as well as rewards, both intrinsic and extrinsic, for engaging in the lifelong process of self-understanding and consciousness raising.

As much as this book addresses unchartered territory in bringing racism and prejudice to the forefront of multicultural training, there are also ways in which it falls short or gets stuck in some of the same pitfalls it hopes to eliminate. This third theme is one that requires we must always examine what we are doing and how we are doing it. Locke and Faubert raise the most critical question in chapter 3: Why do we keep writing about multicultural training by assuming the counselors, and possibly in this case the faculty and trainers, are White? Some of the language of the book asks us to increase counselors' sensitivity to culturally diverse people. Doesn't this language reinforce the notion that all of the counselors, students, and trainers are White? By talking about the role of self-disclosure in multicultural training without focusing on how it might affect individuals with similar and different backgrounds and life experiences, do we not minimize some of the complexity of the learning process? Some contributors do directly address the role of people of color, yet sometimes these discussions set those individuals and groups apart without suggesting how to integrate them into the process. How do we individualize the process so we can respond to each person's unique culture and life experience in meaningful and appropriate ways? Locke and Faubert (in chapter 3) as well as Tomlinson-Clarke and Ota Wang (in chapter 9) remind us that we are still working on finding the words that are complex enough to describe what we are trying to do. We are still struggling how to understand these issues and create a learning process that is optimal for all. That is what the work of Freire, as explored by Locke and Faubert, as well as the discussion of standpoint theory by Swigonski (in chapter 7) offer us.

The goals, tasks, and responsibilities we embrace will vary depending on our own racial and ethnic background, life experience, and worldview. Locke and Faubert emphasize the importance of authentic reflection on our lives to understand more fully how we have internalized racism and prejudice. That means that we as trainers and faculty may want and need to offer different experiences and challenges to different trainees and students. Swigonski emphasizes the importance of searching for multiple points of view and understanding the reality and context of all experiences and personal reflections. Our point of view is forever shaped by our life conditions, experiences, and opportunities and therefore inherently limited unless we continually examine our own perspective and attempt to value the worldviews of others. By learning to embrace multiple realities fully, we prepare ourselves to work more effectively with others.

Ramsey (in chapter 2) raised the fourth issue: the impact of dualistic thinking in multicultural training and how it affects all of us (counselors, trainees, trainers, and faculty). How do we move from simple conceptualizations of same versus different? D'Andrea and Daniels (in chapter 4) address the danger of zero sum or dualistic thinking. Dualism views the world in either-or terms in which dualities (right or wrong, black or white, good or bad) become commonplace. Dualism is often the dominant worldview in our society and our profession, and cultural analysis typically focuses on comparing and evaluating the merits of various worldviews, values, and cultural practices rather than on trying to understand them within their own context. Myers (1993) stated,

> While all worldviews are valid in the sense that how one sees the world is how one sees the world, we who have traveled the journey of these pages realize that the choice of conceptual system is ours. Power becomes the ability to define reality. How we define reality will determine our oppression, or will be the key to our liberation. (p. 93)

So how do we reconceptualize the problem of racism in the counseling profession and the process of addressing it? Ridley and Thompson (in chapter 1) focus on resistance as the door into creating change. We could assume resistance holds that power for understanding individuals and organizations. Swigonski (in chapter 7) suggests the importance of understanding context. Being contextual in our conceptualization of self, trainee, and even client is key. Such contextual thinking probably requires a paradigm shift that demands that we view the world differently. D'Andrea and Daniels (1995) suggested that we may need to shift many of the paradigms that have historically influenced our work and professional identity. Myers (1993) and others (e.g., hooks, 1994; Minnich, 1990) offered alternative conceptualizations to use in our work in multicultural counseling and training. Although their perspectives are very different, the common message is the same. How we shape reality affects how we view ourselves and others. This focus on worldview as central is powerful because it suggests that if we attend to how we, as trainers and teachers, and our students make meaning of multicultural issues, then maybe these meanings are the ideal point of intervention. For example, helping counselors and students understand their own personal experiences with racism, regardless of their racial and ethnic background, and their level of comfort with people who are different from themselves is an important area of discussion and intervention.

This leads to the fifth and final theme: the cognitive perspective taken by many contributors. Kiselica (in chapter 8) and Ridley and Thompson (in chapter 1) as well as Locke and Faubert (in chapter 3) suggest that trainers and faculty examine multicultural training from a cognitive viewpoint. Critical reflection and thinking, as offered by these contributors, may create a critical consciousness that allows us to make a leap toward viewing ourselves and others differently. The harder question, and maybe one not able to be fully answered by this book, is How do we instill critical thinking in ourselves and our students? How do we teach deconstruction skills that show us how to ask the questions that seem obvious? How do we deconstruct the cultural assumptions embedded in the therapy and training process? According to Katz (1985), the values of counseling, as historically and traditionally defined, are based on White, middle-class values. Deconstructing those underlying and often hidden values is vital to making counseling more accessible and relevant to some people of color and other individuals who may not subscribe to White middle-class values.

For example, it is often assumed that counseling can only occur in a private office and that effective counselors must be somewhat detached from their clients. However, that model is often unfamiliar to many people of color or individuals from cultural groups who are used to gaining support and assistance from family and friends. For some, talking with a stranger about personal or family difficulties often feels inappropriate, disloyal, and uncomfortable. Discovering these value differences between counselor and client, and trainer and trainee, can often lead to a deeper appreciation of the more subtle and invisible barriers and challenges to working with individuals who are culturally different.

This process of exploring cultural realities, uncovering truths, and expanding our self-knowledge is central to multicultural counseling and training. The core of that exploration must be an understanding of racism and other forms of oppression and its impact on us personally as well as on the counseling profession. As suggested by the many chapters in this book, there are as many ways to do that as there are individuals. Each of us must find our own way and engage in the process as fully as possible. As Audre Lorde (1984) once said,

> As they become known to and accepted by us, our feelings and the honest exploration of them become sanctuaries and spawning grounds for the most radical and daring of ideas. They become a safe house for that difference so necessary to change and the conceptualization of any meaningful action. (p. 37)

REFERENCES

D'Andrea, M., & Daniels, J. (1995). Promoting multiculturalism and organizational change in the counseling profession: A case study. In J. G. Ponterotto, J. M. Casas, L. A. Suzuki, & C. M. Alexander (Eds.), Handbook of multicultural counseling (pp. 17–33). Thousand Oaks, CA: Sage.

hooks, b. (1994). Teaching to transgress: Education as the practice of freedom. New York: Routledge.

Katz, J. H. (1985). The sociopolitical nature of counseling. The Counseling Psychologist, 20, 615–624.

Lee, C. C. (1998). Counselors as agents of social change. In C. C. Lee & G. R. Walz (Eds.), Social action: A mandate for counselors (pp. 3–14). Alexandria, VA: American Counseling Association.

Lorde, A. (1984). Sister outsider. Freedom, CA: Crossing Press.

Minnich, E. (1990). Transforming knowledge. Philadelphia, PA: Temple University Press.

Myers, L. J. (1993). Understanding an Afrocentric worldview: Introduction to an optimal psychology (2nd ed.). Dubuque, IA: Kendall/Hunt.

Reagon, B. J. (1983). Coalition politics: Turning the century. In B. Smith (Ed.), Home girls: A Black feminist anthology. New York: Kitchen Table: Women of Color Press.

Sue, D. W. (1995). Multicultural organizational development: Implications for the counseling profession. In J. G. Ponterotto, J. M. Casas, L. A. Suzuki, & C. M. Alexander (Eds.), Handbook of multicultural counseling (pp. 474–492). Thousand Oaks, CA: Sage.

12 | Confronting Prejudice: Converging Themes and Future Directions

Mark S. Kiselica

Several themes cut across two or more of the first nine chapters of this book. In this chapter, I discuss each of these themes and their implications for the future of confronting prejudice during multicultural education. Under each theme, I cite the chapter authors who expressed the theme, as well as other authors who have discussed the theme elsewhere in the professional literature on multicultural training.

THEME 1: MULTICULTURAL EDUCATION REQUIRES ORGANIZATIONAL SUPPORT

In the future, all attempts to teach cultural and diversity appreciation must be supported at the organizational level through a number of initiatives; otherwise, multicultural education may be viewed as mere window dressing and not a highly valued endeavor. First, educational institutions must mandate that diversity training is a priority (Ridley & Thompson, ch. 1). Second, a top-down commitment to multicultural training must include concerted efforts to recruit and retain faculty and students from traditionally devalued populations (Locke & Faubert, ch. 3). Achieving a diverse faculty should include the hiring of bilingual faculty who are perceived by students to be important agents for helping students develop multicultural competence (Constantine, Ladany, Inman, & Ponterotto, 1996). Third, procedures for evaluating and grading students opposed to multiculturalism must be developed (Steward, Morales, Bartell, Miller, & Weeks, 1998). Fourth, multicultural educators must be supported—if not protected—in the work they do through the development of formal, school-wide antiracist policies (D'Andrea & Daniels, ch. 4) and departmental policies and procedures for taking constructive action with counseling students whose rigidly held prejudices might do harm to potential clients (Kiselica, ch. 8). Creating this support may be as important as teaching is to the success of multicultural education because it communicates a systemic message that multicultural education is truly valued by the institution.

THEME 2: A CLIMATE OF TRUST MUST BE ESTABLISHED BEFORE PREJUDICES ARE CONFRONTED

Examining prejudice is difficult—and, for many students, impossible—in an atmosphere void of trust. Therefore, a climate of trust must be established before prejudices are confronted.

In order to accomplish this goal, Ridley and Thompson (ch. 1) suggest clarifying the learning objectives during the early stages of the course so that students know what to expect in terms of the experience they are about to undertake. Ramsey (ch. 2) recommends that educators establish ground rules with students, such as respecting others, permitting classmates to finish sentences before responding, avoiding personal put-downs of classmates, encouraging risk taking, accepting that everyone makes mistakes, and adopting a carefrontational rather than a confrontational approach to challenging. Ramsey (ch. 2), Locke and Faubert (ch. 3), and Kiselica (ch. 8) advocate that the instructor serve as a deeply engaged and caring role model for students throughout the training by actively engaging students in dialog and supporting them as they attempt to take risks. Ramsey (ch. 2) also advises having students participate in nonthreatening activities designed to foster group cohesiveness before more emotionally charged subjects are covered. All of these measures help students feel safe about exploring their own imperfections.

THEME 3: DISCOMFORT IS A NECESSARY BUT MANAGEABLE ASPECT OF MULTICULTURAL EDUCATION

Although efforts should be made to minimize the level of discomfort felt in the classroom, some degree of uneasiness is required in order for students to confront their biases and move toward more tolerant thinking and behavior. Recognizing this reality, the authors of the first nine chapters of this book describe their use of many consciousness-raising activities designed to create cognitive dissonance and foster empathic perspective taking, processes that inevitably cause trainees to experience growth-inducing psychic pain. Multicultural educators must accept the fact that following the recommendations provided in this book will spark intrapsychic conflict and tension in their multicultural education classes.

Employing the recommendations reviewed under theme 2 will not only establish an atmosphere of trust, but they will also help students manage their unsettling reactions throughout the training. Instructors can further manage potential problems in the classroom by not reacting defensively when students demonstrate resistance (Ridley & Thompson, ch. 1). Instead, instructors should understand the source and type of resistance that is being demonstrated (Ridley & Thompson, ch. 1), empathize with the feelings of the students, share their own experiences that are similar to those of the students (Kiselica, ch. 8; Swigonski, ch. 7), and recognize the contribution of racial identity issues to classroom tensions (Mobley with Cheatham, ch. 5). Teachers can also maintain a constructive learning environment by helping students channel their anger and other strong emotional reactions into appropriate, carefully planned courses of action (Swigonski, ch. 7). An implicit message of D'Andrea and Daniels (ch. 4) is that multicultural educators must be courageous in order to address these reactions effectively. Turning to colleagues for consultation and emotional support can help the instructor to address his or her own emotions that are stirred up by the training (Kiselica, ch. 8). All of these strategies will sustain an emotional climate that facilitates, rather than hinders, the professional growth of both the trainees and the counselor educator.

THEME 4: EDUCATIONAL STRATEGIES AND PROCESSES MUST BE ADJUSTED ACCORDING TO THE DIFFERENT DEVELOPMENTAL LEVELS OF STUDENTS

Students enrolled in multicultural education courses differ in terms of their psychological and multicultural development. A handful of students have a simplistic, hostile, and illogical racist disposition; others have a passionate commitment to eliminating racism; most students are somewhere in between these two extreme dispositions toward racism (D'Andrea & Daniels, ch. 4). Students also vary according to their racial identity development (Mobley with Cheatham, ch. 5), their level of critical consciousness (Locke & Faubert, ch. 3), and the degree to which they embrace multiculturalism (Steward et al., 1998). Chambers, Lewis, and Kerezsi (1995) argued that such differences influence how students experience the learning environment.

Multicultural educators must be good at recognizing where each student is in his or her psychological and multicultural development. As Locke and Faubert (ch. 3) suggest, the instructor may have to probe and work closely and actively with students in order to ascertain fully each student's level of development. Then the instructor must select classroom activities that stimulate the positive development of the student. Individual assignments tailored to the developmental level of particular students are necessary (D'Andrea & Daniels, ch. 4). Thus multicultural educators must be keen observers and assessors of their students' current development and flexible instructors who adjust their educational strategies and processes according to the different developmental levels of students. Furthermore, multicultural educators must be prepared to negotiate different opinions about multiculturalism among students throughout the training process (Steward et al., 1998).

THEME 5: THE RACIAL IDENTITY DEVELOPMENT OF THE INSTRUCTOR WILL INFLUENCE THE DYNAMICS AND OUTCOMES OF MULTICULTURAL TRAINING

Instructors also vary in terms of their racial backgrounds and racial identity development; these variations will influence the dynamics and outcomes of multicultural training. Mobley with Cheatham (ch. 5) describe the wide range of dynamics that can result when instructor and students are different racially or in different stages of their racial identity development. Kiselica (ch. 8) argues that instructors should be individuals who have advanced to high stages of racial identity development because they will be better able than instructors in the early stages of racial identity development to recognize and empathize with the fears and struggles of students who are in the early stages of racial identity development. Kiselica (ch. 8) adds that teachers in advanced stages will be better able to prepare students for the emotional and cognitive dilemmas and changes that are prompted by multicultural training. A similar suggestion was made by Rooney, Flores, and Mercier (1998).

These arguments are supported by recent findings suggesting that counselor supervisors who have a high racial consciousness appear to be able to form strong alliances with supervisees who are at lower levels of racial consciousness, perhaps due to the supervisors' ability to empathize with the issues of their supervisees (Ladany, Brittan-Powell, & Pannu, 1997). Supervisors with high racial consciousness are also perceived by supervisees with lower racial consciousness as having a positive influence on the supervisees' multicultural competence. By comparison, interactions between supervisors and supervisees in the low stages of racial identity development and between supervisors in low stages with supervisees in high stages do not appear to foster either strong supervisor-supervisee alliances or the multicultural competency of the supervisees (Ladany et al., 1997). Based on these considerations, it is recommended that department chairs assign teachers with high racial identity consciousness as instructors of multicultural education.

THEME 6: EXPERIENTIAL AND CLINICAL LEARNING ACTIVITIES ARE CENTRAL TO COMPREHENSIVE MULTICULTURAL EDUCATION

Racism, sexism, homophobia, ageism, ableism, and other forms of prejudice are not merely intellectual phenomena; they also are deeply felt experiences that occur during encounters between human beings (Sue & Sue, 1990). Therefore, comprehensive multicultural education must move beyond didactic forms of teaching and include experiential and clinical instruction in order to help students have a more complete understanding of prejudice, how it affects people affectively and influences their interactions with others, and how it can be eradicated. Innovative, experiential pedagogy must be employed in order to tap the lived experiences of students (Locke & Faubert, ch. 3) and to help trainees identify their sources of resistance (Ridley & Thompson, ch. 1), confront their own biases (D'Andrea & Daniels, ch. 4), and move toward increased self-awareness and diversity appreciation (Pedersen, ch. 6; Ramsey, ch. 2; Tomlinson-Clarke & Ota Wang, ch. 9). Small-group experiential exercises conducted in the classroom, personal journals written as homework assignments (Ramsey, ch. 2; Swigonski, ch. 7), and service projects completed in the community (D'Andrea & Daniels, ch. 4) are recommended as course requirements that can foster taking the perspectives of various oppressed groups and discovering individuals' positions of privilege in this world. All of these activities must be followed by skills training exercises designed to build competencies for working with the culturally different (Pedersen, ch. 6; Tomlinson-Clarke & Ota Wang, ch. 9) and supervised multicultural practica courses in which these competencies are applied with actual clients (Tomlinson-Clarke & Ota Wang, ch. 9). Thus a comprehensive multicultural education provides students with both a cognitive and affective understanding of prejudice, fosters student self-awareness and dedication to confronting biases, and arms students with skills to address intolerance in their professional endeavors.

THEME 7: MULTICULTURAL EDUCATION FOCUSED ON PROVIDING KNOWLEDGE ABOUT THE CULTURALLY DIFFERENT, EXAMINING CULTURAL BIASES, AND DEVELOPING CULTURALLY APPROPRIATE SKILLS APPEARS TO REDUCE PREJUDICE

The contributors to Part I of this book state either explicitly or implicitly that they believe multicultural education focused on providing knowledge about the culturally different, examining cultural biases, and developing multicultural skills reduces prejudice among trainees. This belief is consistent with the opinion of other authors who have recommended that multicultural training encompass the domains of knowledge, attitudes/beliefs, and skills and who contend that such training will reduce bias (Arredondo et al., 1996; Sue, Arredondo, & McDavis, 1992; Sue et al., 1982).

In light of this widespread opinion, we must ask ourselves a crucial question: Does an approach to multicultural education that encompasses the domains of knowledge, attitudes/beliefs, and skills really reduce prejudice? To address this question, this section overviews promising approaches to prejudice reduction, critiques empirical research examining the effects of multicultural education on prejudice among professionals in training, describes relevant research findings on the relationship between multicultural training and White racial identity development, presents conclusions about the efficacy of multicultural education for prejudice reduction, and provides suggestions for future research.

Promising Approaches to Prejudice Reduction

A large body of empirical research on prejudice reduction has been reported in the social psychology literature. In his comprehensive critique of this research, Jones (1997) concluded that there are six promising approaches to the amelioration of interpersonal and intergroup bias:

1. creating conditions in which culturally different individuals must work cooperatively, rather than competitively, to attain superordinate goals;
2. providing contexts that foster positive affect and interpersonal intimacy between culturally different people;
3. helping people have direct experience with what it is like to be stigmatized;
4. reducing the boundaries that exist between groups by challenging the tendency to treat individuals on the basis of their group membership (e.g., by making individual qualities salient; demonstrating multiple group membership);
5. expanding group boundaries to include a wider variety of others, that is, reducing between-group bias by increasing within-group diversity; and
6. adopting a transactional approach to intergroup relations (e.g., taking multiple group perspectives into account regarding decision making, requiring negotiated intergroup agreements, involving interdependent relationships).

Although these approaches were developed outside the domain of multicultural education, examining the extent to which these approaches are utilized in multicultural training can help us gauge the potential utility of multicultural education for reducing prejudice. Reading across the first nine chapters of this book, it is clear that the contributors apply these approaches throughout the multicultural educational process of providing knowledge about the culturally different, examining cultural biases, and developing multicultural skills. Several examples illustrate the application of these antiprejudice tactics by the chapter authors.

Some of the experiential exercises utilized by Ramsey (ch. 2) and the social action homework assignments prescribed by D'Andrea and Daniels (ch. 4) require students to work cooperatively on tasks whose aim is to achieve common goals.

Ramsey (ch. 2), Locke and Faubert (ch. 3), and Swigonski (ch. 7) have their students share stories from their personal journals as a way to promote interpersonal intimacy. To foster positive affective experiences among culturally different students during multicultural training, Ramsey (ch. 2) organizes a classroom meal consisting of different ethnic foods prepared by class members, and Kiselica (ch. 8) encourages students to reveal stories about the joys they have experienced in their cross-cultural encounters.

Ridley and Thompson (ch. 1), D'Andrea and Daniels (ch. 4), Swigonski (ch. 7), and Tomlinson-Clarke and Ota Wang (ch. 9) recommend employing didactic and experiential activities that help students to understand the perspectives of marginalized people.

Ramsey (ch. 2) challenges the tendency to view people in terms of their group membership by asking students to complete and discuss their Personal Cultural Perspective Profiles (Ramsey, 1994). This exercise teaches trainees that they may differ from each other on one cultural dimension (e.g., racial identity), but they may be similar on other cultural dimensions (e.g., sexual orientation and religious affiliation). Pedersen (ch. 6) attempts to dismantle between-group stereotypes by helping students discover the common ground expectations of people (e.g., concern for one's children) who come from different cultures.

Ridley and Thompson (ch. 1), Locke and Faubert (ch. 3), Mobley with Cheatham (ch. 5), and Tomlinson-Clarke and Ota Wang (ch. 9) acknowledge the importance of achieving within-group diversity. Representation of many different cultural groups among faculty and students not only adds to the rich array of perspectives that are shared in the classroom (Mobley with Cheatham, ch. 5; Tomlinson-Clarke & Ota Wang, ch. 9), but such diversity also conveys a message that educational institutions and programs are inclusionary (Locke & Faubert, ch. 3; Ridley & Thompson, ch. 1).

A transactional approach to intergroup relations is evident in the work of Ramsey (ch. 2), Locke and Faubert (ch. 3), Mobley with Cheatham (ch. 5), Kiselica (ch. 8), and Swigonski (ch. 7) whose educational strategies are designed to engender a shared sense of community among the culturally different people enrolled in a course.

Applying the collective recommendations of Part I authors, who weave effective antiprejudice tactics into the multicultural educational processes of providing knowledge about the culturally different, examining cultural biases, and developing multicultural skills, appears to have considerable promise to diminish bigotry among multicultural trainees. But is there any direct evidence that multicultural education incorporating the strategies described in this book does indeed reduce the biased thinking and behavior of professionals in training? With the exception of anecdotal data illustrating positive changes reported by counselors in training (e.g., see Locke & Faubert, ch. 3) and promising findings from several course evaluation studies cited in Tomlinson-Clarke and Ota Wang (ch. 9), the issue of evaluation is not addressed in Part I of this book. In this next section, I explore this issue by providing a synopsis of pertinent empirical research.

Critique of Empirical Research on Multicultural Education and Prejudice Reduction

Ridley, Mendoza, and Kanitz (1994) examined several studies evaluating the outcomes of multicultural training in a review of the research literature on multicultural training. Their findings indicated that much of the relevant research has been hampered by methodological problems, such as the use of subjective evaluation methods, which have questionable validity. None of the studies reviewed utilized formal measures of prejudice. Ridley et al. (1994) concluded, "Unfortunately, little systematic evaluation of the impact of training on students or their clients has been conducted" (p. 274).

In a more recent review of the research literature examining the effects of multicultural education on prejudice among professional trainees, Kiselica, Locke, and Maben (1999) identified several studies not reviewed by Ridley et al. (1994), including a case study that was reported in a series of articles (Kiselica, 1991, 1998, in press), four qualitative investigations (Anderson & Cranston-Gingras, 1991; Garcia, Wright, & Corey, 1991; Geasler, Croteau, Heineman, & Edlund, 1995; Heppner & O'Brien, 1994), and two quasi-experimental studies (Grottkau & Nicholai-Mays, 1989; Rudolph, 1989).

Each of these studies involved the evaluation of multicultural training (e.g., learning about one's own and different cultures) or diversity appreciation workshops (e.g., learning about the perspectives of gay, lesbian, and bisexual individuals). For the sake of simplicity, the review referred to both forms of training as multicultural education. In all studies, the trainees who had received multicultural training reported experiencing reductions in prejudice. In several of the studies (Anderson & Cranston-Gingras, 1991; Garcia et al., 1991; Geasler et al., 1995; Heppner & O'Brien, 1994; Kiselica, 1991, 1998, in press), no formal instruments for assessing prejudice were utilized; consequently, it is impossible to estimate the magnitude of the changes in prejudice reported by the participants of these studies. All studies were hampered by the absence of true experimental designs, which limited the ability of the investigators to make precise cause-effect inferences about the relationship between the training and prejudice reduction.

Thus each of the studies discussed in the reviews by Ridley et al. (1994) and Kiselica and Locke (1998) had methodological problems that limit our ability to conclude that multicultural education effects reductions in prejudice among professionals in training. However, the pattern of results reported in the studies suggests that professionals participating in multicultural education perceive themselves to experience a lessening of prejudice, although the extent of these decreases is somewhat unclear.

Synopsis of Research on Multicultural Training and White Racial Identity Development

According to several theorists of White racial identity development, positive White racial identity development involves movement from a racist (i.e., lower levels/ stages of White racial identity development) to a nonracist (i.e., higher levels/ stages) White identity (Hardiman, 1982; Helms, 1984, 1990; Ponterotto, 1988; Sabnani, Ponterotto, & Borodovsky, 1991). White racial identity development theorists also postulate that positive White racial identity development involves the intrapersonal emotional and cognitive changes that are characteristic of prejudice reduction (Hardiman, 1982; Helms, 1984, 1990; Ponterotto, 1988; Sabnani, et al., 1991).

Ottavi, Pope-Davis, and Dings (1994) reported empirical evidence indicating that multicultural training is positively correlated with higher levels of White racial identity development. Multicultural training also appears to effect movement from lower to higher levels of White racial identity development (Brown, Parham, & Yonker, 1996; Lawrence & Bunche, 1996; Neville et al., 1996; Parker, Moore, & Neimeyer, 1998). Although changes in prejudice were not measured in these studies, the consistent association between multicultural training and higher levels of White racial identity development, which are presumed to be linked to lowered levels of prejudice, support the conjecture that multicultural training reduces racism.

Conclusions About the Efficacy of Multicultural Education for Prejudice Reduction

Because most of the empirical research studies evaluating the efficacy of diversity appreciation and multicultural education are tarnished by several methodological problems, we are somewhat limited in our capacity to conclude that multicultural education reduces prejudice among professional trainees. Nevertheless, three strands of evidence suggest that multicultural education is a promising approach for combating intolerance. First, the multicultural education strategies for confronting prejudice that are suggested in this book are consistent with tactics that have been successful outside of the domains of multicultural training in reducing interpersonal and intergroup bias. Second, the best available research findings suggest that the recipients of multicultural training perceive themselves to confront and change their biases about the culturally different. Third, White students engaging in multicultural education tend to move toward higher levels of nonracist consciousness.

On the whole, the data indicate that multicultural education is based on sound principles and that multicultural trainees experience hopeful changes in their prejudicial thinking. Future investigators face the challenge of generating stronger support for the contention that multicultural education is the key mechanism of such changes.

Suggestions for Future Research

How can we enhance our understanding about the effectiveness of multicultural training in diminishing biased thinking? One of the consistent limitations of prior research has been the failure of investigators to conduct assessments of specific forms of prejudice utilizing objective assessment measures. Future researchers should evaluate the effectiveness of their multicultural education programs by diagnosing changes in prejudice with valid and reliable instruments that have developed for such purposes. Researchers are encouraged to consult Sandhu and Aspy (1997) for a list and critical review of such instruments.

Another limitation of past research is that investigators have relied on case studies, qualitative research, and quasi-experimental designs to evaluate the effectiveness of multicultural training, thereby limiting the cause-and-effect inferences that can be drawn from their findings. Some investigators have been forced to rely on these approaches to research because their work settings and circumstances have not permitted them randomly to select and assign students to different experimental groups. Nevertheless, it may be possible for other multicultural educators to take innovative steps that will enable them to conduct experimental evaluations of multicultural education. For example, all part-time students starting their graduate program in counseling at a particular institution could be randomly assigned to either a multicultural counseling course or some other course in counseling. After pretest-to-posttest changes in prejudice are assessed for both groups of students, the control students could then enroll in the multicultural course. Additional assessments of prejudice at the beginning and end of the course could be taken for control subjects. Such a design would allow all students involved in the study to accrue the benefits of multicultural education, control for threats to internal validity, and provide investigators with the opportunity to conduct both a between-group and within-group comparison of changes in prejudice. The findings from comparisons indicating both between- and within-group reductions in prejudice would increase our confidence in the utility of multicultural education. Therefore, future experimental research evaluating the effectiveness of multicultural training is recommended.

Future research should also include investigations that are designed to evaluate the relative contributions of different components of multicultural training to prejudice reduction. Most prior studies have examined training that has included didactic instruction, experiential exercises, and skills training. Although the contributors to this book argue in favor of the efficacy of all three components, in light of the extant research literature we do not know which component or combination of components is the critical mechanism for reducing prejudice.

Another area of uncertainty pertains to the effectiveness of single courses in reducing prejudice. Although most of the studies reviewed here found that the completion of a multicultural course or workshop may have reduced prejudice among trainees, Grottkau and Nicholai-Mays (1989) have suggested and Tomlinson-Clarke and Ota Wang (ch. 9) suggest that exposure to multicultural training across the curriculum over time, rather than in one course, may be necessary to reduce prejudice in some students significantly. Heppner and O'Brien (1994) added that additional training beyond one course is probably necessary in order to help students integrate changes in thinking with actual counseling skills. Future research should address these considerations by comparing the effects of short-term versus long-term multicultural education on prejudice reduction.

CONCLUSION

Thirty years ago few people were trained to explore their own personal biases or to understand the perspectives of the culturally different. Today, engaging in these activities is considered a professional obligation. This shift in expectations about developing cultural awareness and sensitivity is a sign that multiculturalism is here to stay. Consequently, we now can switch the focus of our efforts from justifying why multiculturalism is important to exploring how we can best help people eradicate the prejudices that separate them from their fellow human beings. As we devote more or our energies to this important endeavor, the recommendations offered in this chapter will help us to better understand what methods are most effective for releasing people from the shackles of their unhealthy intolerances.

REFERENCES

Anderson, D. J., & Cranston-Gingras, A. (1991). Sensitizing counselors and educators to multicultural issues: An interactive approach. *Journal of Counseling and Development, 70,* 91–98.

Arredondo, P., Toporek, R., Brown, S. P., Jones, J., Locke, D. C., Sanchez, J., & Stadler, H. (1996). Operationalizing of the multicultural counseling competencies. *Journal of Multicultural Counseling and Development, 24,* 42–78.

Brown, S. P., Parham, T. A., & Yonker, R. (1996). Influence of a cross-cultural training course on racial identity attitudes of White women and men: Preliminary perspectives. *Journal of Counseling and Development, 74,* 510–516.

Chambers, T., Lewis, J., & Kerezsi, P. (1995). African American faculty and White American students: Cross-cultural pedagogy in counselor preparation programs. *The Counseling Psychologist, 23,* 43–62.

Constantine, M. G., Ladany, N., Inman, A. G., & Ponterotto, J. G. (1996). Students' perceptions of multicultural training in counseling psychology programs. *Journal of Multicultural Counseling and Development, 24,* 241–253.

Garcia, M. H., Wright, J. W., & Corey, G. (1991). A multicultural perspective in an undergraduate human services program. *Journal of Counseling and Development, 70,* 86–90.

Geasler, M., Croteau, J. M., Heineman, C. J., & Edlund, C. J. (1995). A qualitative study of students' expressions of change after attending panel presentations by lesbian, gay, and bisexual speakers. *Journal of College Student Development, 36,* 483–492.

Grottkau, B. J., & Nicholai-Mays, S. (1989). An empirical analysis of a multicultural education paradigm for preservice teachers. *Educational Research Quarterly, 13,* 27–33.

Hardiman, R. (1982). *White identity development: A process-oriented model for describing the racial consciousness of White Americans.* Unpublished doctoral dissertation, University of Massachusetts, Amherst.

Helms, J. E. (1984). Toward a theoretical model of the effects of race on counseling: A Black and White model. *The Counseling Psychologist, 12,* 153–156.

Helms, J. E. (1990). Toward a model of White racial identity development. In J. E. Helms (Ed.), *Black and white racial identity: Theory, research, and practice* (pp. 49–66). New York: Greenwood Press.

Heppner, M. J., & O'Brien, K. M. (1994). Multicultural counselor training: Students' perceptions of helpful and hindering events. *Counselor Education and Supervision, 34,* 4–18.

Jones, J. M. (1997). *Prejudice and racism* (2nd ed.). New York: McGraw-Hill.

Kiselica, M. S. (1991). Reflections on a multicultural internship experience. *Journal of Counseling and Development, 70,* 126–130.

Kiselica, M. S. (1998). Preparing Anglos for the challenges and joys of multiculturalism. *The Counseling Psychologist, 26,* 5–21.

Kiselica, M. S. (in press). Confronting my own ethnocentrism and racism: A process of pain and growth. *Journal of Counseling and Development.*

Kiselica, M. S., Locke, D. C., & Maben, P. (1999). *Does diversity appreciation and multicultural education reduce prejudice among counselors in training?* Manuscript submitted for publication.

Ladany, N., Brittan-Powell, C. S., & Pannu, R. K. (1997). The influence of supervisory racial identity interaction and racial matching on the supervisory working alliance and supervisee multicultural competence. *Counselor Education and Supervision, 36,* 284–304.

Lawrence, S. M., & Bunche, T. (1996). Feeling and dealing: Teaching White students about racial privilege. *Scandinavian Audiology Supplement, 25,* 531–542.

Neville, H. A., Heppner, M. J., Louie, C. E., Thompson, C. E., Brooks, L., & Baker, C. E. (1996). The impact of multicultural training on White racial identity attitudes and therapy competencies. *Professional Psychology: Research and Practice, 27,* 83–89.

Ottavi, T. M., Pope-Davis, D. B., & Dings, J. G. (1994). Relationship between White racial identity attitudes and self-reported multicultural counseling competencies. *Journal of Counseling Psychology, 41,* 149–154.

Parker, W. M., Moore, M. A., & Neimeyer, G. J. (1998). Altering White racial identity and interracial comfort through multicultural training. *Journal of Counseling and Development, 76,* 302–310.

Ponterotto, J. G. (1988). Racial consciousness development among White counselor trainees: A stage model. *Journal of Multicultural Counseling and Development, 16,* 146–156.

Ramsey, M. (1994). Use of a personal cultural perspective profile (PCPP) in developing counsellor multicultural competence. *International Journal for the Advancement of Counselling, 17,* 283–290.

Ridley, C., Mendoza, D. W., & Kanitz, B. E. (1994). Multicultural training: Reexamination, operationalization, and integration. *The Counseling Psychologist, 22,* 227–289.

Rooney, S. C., Flores, L. Y., & Mercier, C. A. (1998). Making multicultural education effective for everyone. *The Counseling Psychologist, 26,* 22–32.

Rudolph, J. (1989). Effects of a workshop on mental health practitioners' attitudes toward homosexuality and counseling effectiveness. *Journal of Counseling and Development, 68,* 81–85.

Sabnani, H. B., Ponterotto, J. G., & Borodovsky, L. G. (1991). White racial identity development and cross-cultural counselor training: A stage model. *The Counseling Psychologist, 19,* 76–102.

Sandhu, D. S., & Aspy, C. B. (1997). *Counseling for prejudice prevention and reduction.* Alexandria, VA: American Counseling Association.

Steward, R. J., Morales, R. J., Bartell, P. A., Miller, M., Weeks, D. (1998). The multiculturally responsive versus the multiculturally reactive: A study of perceptions of counselor trainees. *Journal of Multicultural Counseling and Development, 26,* 13–27.

Sue, D. W., Arredondo, P., & McDavis, R. J. (1992). Multicultural counseling competencies and standards: A call to the profession. *Journal of Multicultural Counseling and Development, 20,* 644–688.

Sue, D. W., Bernier, J. E., Durran, A., Feinberg, L., Pedersen, P., Smith, E. J., & Vasquez-Nuttall, E. (1982). Position paper: Cross-cultural competencies. *The Counseling Psychologist, 10,* 45–52.

Sue, D. W., & Sue, D. (1990). *Counseling the culturally different: Theory and practice* (2nd ed.). New York: Wiley.

Index